THE MAP TO WHOLENESS

*Real-Life Stories of Crisis,
Change, and Reinvention*

SUZY ROSS, PhD

North Atlantic Books
Berkeley, California

Published by
North Atlantic Books
Berkeley, California

Cover art © gettyimages.com/hqrloveq
Cover design by Nicole Hayward
Book design by Cody Gates, Happenstance Type-O-Rama

Printed in Canada

The Map to Wholeness: Real-Life Stories of Crisis, Change, and Reinvention is sponsored and published by the Society for the Study of Native Arts and Sciences (dba North Atlantic Books), an educational nonprofit based in Berkeley, California, that collaborates with partners to develop cross-cultural perspectives, nurture holistic views of art, science, the humanities, and healing, and seed personal and global transformation by publishing work on the relationship of body, spirit, and nature.

North Atlantic Books' publications are available through most bookstores. For further information, visit our website at www.northatlanticbooks.com or call 800-733-3000.

DISCLAIMER: The following information is intended for general information purposes only. Any application of the material set forth in the following pages is at the reader's discretion and is his or her sole responsibility.

Library of Congress Cataloging-in-Publication Data

Names: Ross, Suzy (Susan L.), author.
Title: The map to wholeness : real-life stories of crisis, change, and
   reinvention / Suzy Ross, PhD.
Description: California : North Atlantic Books, [2019] | Includes
   bibliographical references and index.
Identifiers: LCCN 2019017338 (print) | LCCN 2019021627 (ebook) | ISBN
   9781623173838 (e-book) | ISBN 9781623173821 (pbk.)
Subjects: LCSH: Life change events. | Change (Psychology) | Self-realization.
Classification: LCC BF637.L53 (ebook) | LCC BF637.L53 R67 2019 (print) | DDC
   155.2/4—dc23
LC record available at https://lccn.loc.gov/2019017338

1 2 3 4 5 6 7 8 9 MARQUIS 26 25 24 23 22 21 20

This book includes recycled material and material from well-managed forests. North Atlantic Books is committed to the protection of our environment. We print on recycled paper whenever possible and partner with printers who strive to use environmentally responsible practices.

To Jane and Dave

A NOTE TO THE READER

The lives of Kenny and Radha are shared in this book. Each agreed to share their stories of transformation, opening their lives to you so that their struggles, pain, suffering and triumphs might be of some help, guidance, or even inspiration to you. It is for them, a gift they wish to give to others.

. Each was willing to divulge not only their victories and accomplishments but also their raw, private, and most humbling moments. My request to the reader is that you respond to the details of their stories with a gentle recognition that it is difficult to recount with perfection the details of one's life across a fifteen-year (and more) period. It is my hope that as recipients of their story, we offer them a bit of forgiveness should they have imperfections in their memory shared within this book. In an effort to protect privacy, many of the two interviewees' friends, family, and colleagues have been assigned pseudonyms.

Although I spent years interviewing, checking story details, and rechecking again, it is entirely within the realm of human error that they or I might have misunderstood or mistranslated a situation or person along the way or remembered the words spoken or timing of a circumstance incorrectly. In short, this is a note to let you know that Kenny, Radha, and I have worked altruistically towards the greater good, to recount in earnest, the details and experiences of their lives.

CONTENTS

PREFACE

In 1991, I had an epiphany while leading backpacking trips for teenagers in the Rocky Mountain wilderness. During one of those trips, I was with a group hiking along a mountain ridge at about 10,500 feet when I unexpectedly experienced what exists both beyond us and deeply within us. Drunk only on the grandeur of the majestic slopes that soared into panoramic vistas in all directions, I expanded into a different state of consciousness. I distinctly remember *becoming* all that I could see—and not see—and I was introduced to God itself. No longer limited by any form, I became immersed in the kind of love I had read about in the stories of people who had died and lived to tell about it. It's a love that would make the hardest of hearts weep. I felt the molecules of my body and all that exists in the entire universe as one. It was easy to understand how I could exist in many different locations simultaneously. I *became*—as opposed to *felt like*—a rock, tree bark, a cloud, stardust, and countless other things, named and unnamed. Although I have vague memories of feeling tears streaming down my face, I did not experience an emotion, nor could I see the landscape with my physical eyes or feel my body as "I" continued to walk. It was as though my body was on autopilot while I was very much outside of and distant from my body. I experienced the magnificence of our true nature.

A little while later, we were heading down from the heights of the ridge when I felt my spirit reenter my body. As this occurred, I saw dark clouds coming toward our group and forming around the mountain range, promising a good soaking. We had endured eight solid days of rain, and I was tired of being wet. Unhesitatingly, I knew—without knowing—that all I needed to do was to move the clouds (which were me) so they wouldn't rain on our group. This idea seemed perfectly normal at the time; it was as easy as moving my elbow. The clouds circled around us and did not rain on us. Instead, rainbows formed nearby as we continued our descent into the valley below. The response of the clouds brought me back to my normal senses. My knees nearly buckled as I felt and understood the immensity of what I was experiencing for the first time. With each step down the mountain I sank more deeply back into my body and became completely overtaken emotionally by the infinite love, knowledge, and power that exist inside and all around us at all times.

The experience left me with a visceral and cognitive memory of the vast consciousness, compassion, and interconnectedness of the universe, which continues to inform my daily life. Because of this event, I know rather than *believe* that we live in a benevolent cosmos in which nothing is separate, and each atom holds the knowledge of the whole.

For years, I said very little about what had happened to me, but in private I pored over books related to the topic and pondered expert perspectives on transformation and mystical experience. I discovered that what happened to me in 1991 is well described by scholars and spiritual leaders. I found the work of respected Canadian psychiatrist Richard Maurice Bucke particularly helpful. He was one of the first Westerners to study experiences similar to mine, and his writing gave me the language to make sense of what I had endured and validation that my experience was indeed real. I also found solace in the Indian teacher Krishnamurti's poetic description of his mystical experience by a pepper tree, where he "could feel the wind passing through the tree, and the little ant on the blade of grass I could feel. The birds, the dust, and the very noise were a part of me.... I was in everything, or rather everything was in me, inanimate and animate, the mountain, the worm, and all breathing things" (Lutyens 1997, 158).

In the weeks, months, and years after my out-of-body experience, I remained, in an everyday sense, relatively unchanged. I was the same Suzy I had always been—slightly nerdy, a bit awkward, professionally passionate, and energetic. After the awe of having endured the event subsided, I found myself stuck in familiar, limiting patterns of behavior and thinking. I lingered in the clutches of self-defeating beliefs: *I'm not good enough. Not very many people like me. I can't earn a higher salary because I lack the required abilities and I can't gain people's respect. I'm not smart, politically savvy, or quick enough.*

This is not to say I didn't perceive a slight improvement in my character or feel deeply moved at my core. But *feeling* transformed is not the same as *being* thoroughly altered. Nonhuman examples help illuminate the dramatic requirements of transformation, such as when a pleasant neighborhood becomes a pile of rubble after a tornado or a seed metamorphoses into an oak tree.

About a decade after my experience in the mountains, my insatiable curiosity led me to wonder: *what do I do now?* Something was missing from all I had read and heard. I remained preoccupied with the question of why I had experienced departure, initiation, and return—the three stages of the classic hero's journey—without being truly transformed. It wasn't until I decided to go to graduate school that this line of inquiry congealed into the most important question of my life: how do we integrate a transformative experience into daily life—if at all?

With my mind ignited, I set out to study this question formally, through a doctoral dissertation.

Founding Ideas

One way we can understand a life-changing event is by viewing it as an initiation. Initiation is a process that cultures use to accept new members into a group or to prepare members to change their social status. In a contemporary setting, we might label a life-changing event as somewhat initiatory if the experience involved going through the ritual of joining a religion, the hiring processes of a large corporation, or the social hurdles of joining a special-interest group. This type of initiation is led by leaders whom the group has chosen as knowledgeable and capable of guiding newcomers.

Ancient cultures also viewed spectacular acts of God, such as being struck by lightning three times and surviving, as initiatory. In this situation the divine endows the individual with new knowledge, experiences, and abilities, thereby initiating them into a higher social status that requires being more responsible to the whole. Initiation is human-led or divinely led transformation. For this reason, studying initiation became very important to me.

During my graduate studies many readings were helpful, but the work of mythologist Joseph Campbell was particularly beneficial because he offered a detailed, secular, cross-cultural account of how individuals transform into "heroes" or achieve their potential. Campbell studied initiation by analyzing traditional and legendary tales of the distant past. He chronicled stories told across countless cultures in which mythological characters rose to greatness, and he came to understand that a particular transformational pattern leads to becoming the hero of your own life's story. The pattern of the hero's journey appears not only in myth but in history, religious observances, and psychology. Film director George Lucas, inspired by Campbell's 1949 book *The Hero with a Thousand Faces*, brought the mythological story of the prototypical hero's journey (also known as the "monomyth") to the big screen through the character Luke Skywalker in the epic series *Star Wars*.

Among the hundreds of scholarly articles and books I pored over during my formal research, I found particularly illuminating guidance about transformation from anthropologists Arnold van Gennep and Victor Turner. Like Campbell, they outlined how elders in cultures around the world steward individuals through initiations, or rites of passage. They described the individual's transition from one status, such as teenager, to another, such as adult, as a three-step process:

1. *Separation.* The person recognizes their readiness to transform, or an elder identifies them as ready. The person so designated then solicits the support of others, prepares to become initiated, and either leaves home or goes into seclusion to enter into the unknown, where they will learn, grow, and receive a vision or new knowledge.

2. *The liminal period.* The initiate enters into a transitional, mystical time that involves challenges, insights, support from helpers, learning, and possibly dramatic events. This is when the initiate gains

new skills and may have a transformative experience that involves receiving wisdom, insight, or a vision.

3. *Reincorporation.* This is the journey home, when the initiate reenters their community and social norms. The initiate shares their stories and newfound knowledge and capacities (Campbell calls this the "boon"), and the community bears witness to and celebrates the initiates as a new being.

Campbell's analysis of initiation matches these phases, with distinct stages occurring within each of the three phases (making seventeen stages in total).

Even though these and other authors helped define a pathway of transformation, I was still frustrated, as were other scholars. Those who have critiqued Campbell's work question the degree to which the hero's journey depicts a woman's transformational journey. Campbell rebutted these arguments by explaining that although the hero's journey is often depicted as a man going far away on a noble quest, the monomyth is inclusive of a traditional feminine initiation where the woman is sequestered in isolation to embark upon an inward journey. Regardless, I wondered if my experience of transformation was reflected in his work, because something still felt lacking.

I also questioned whether the initiate had truly transformed into a new person just because they'd had a life-changing event, and if they did, how that occurred. The vague descriptions of initiates' post-transformation activities did not appear to address the many psychosocial and spiritual challenges of having returned "transformed." Was there more to the reincorporation phase that had not been accounted for in the literature? Ancient and traditional societies had demonstrated their ability to convert a budding leader into an elder or master, so I knew they understood how to help their young people transform. But how?

The Research

As mentioned, my research focused on the circumstances occurring after a life-changing event. I wanted to understand if it is possible to integrate a life-changing experience into daily life so that we are truly transformed by it, and if so, how that happens. I chose a research method called cooperative inquiry, which is a particularly holistic and non-Western way of investigating. Cooperative inquiry asks a group of people who have all had a similar experience (in this case, a transformative experience) to work together as co-researchers and to conduct self- and group analysis to understand a chosen aspect of the human condition. I give a detailed account of how I implemented the cooperative inquiry method (which can be complex and risky!) in my paper "Finding Our Way to the Precious Knowledge, Together: One Study's Use of Cooperative Inquiry." And my paper "The Making of Everyday Heroes: Women's Experiences of Transformation and Integration" describes the research that founds this book, including its methods, subjects (co-researchers), and results.

The goal of my study was to examine the process of transformation by putting our lives under the microscope of personal and group awareness. This approach asks participants to pay attention to their daily lives as much as humanly possible, as though ordinary events can provide information that will help answer the research question. We recorded and discussed emotions, thoughts, dialogues, synchronicities, and other experiences, even if they seemed to be only remotely related to the inquiry. Even our dreams became a source of information. Each person kept a journal and shared discoveries and quandaries during group meetings.

To deepen our insight into the discussion at hand, we sought to access our wealth of unconscious knowledge, body memories, cognitive memories, and curiosities through meditation, storytelling, art, music, metaphor, stream-of-consciousness exercises, walking outside in nature, visualization, movement, conceptual drawing, critical reflection, retreats, and ritual.

In all, the study group and I participated in thirteen months of research, followed by six months of analyzing the data we had gathered, and culminating in a weekend retreat intensive. Analysis required distilling reams of written and oral accounts down to their essences. I took our results and analyzed, coded, and refined the information they contained over and over again, repeatedly bringing it back to the group for review until it became apparent to the whole group that the answer was emerging and crystalizing.

On one hot, humid Sunday afternoon, sitting on the floor of a co-researcher's living room, I saw the information come together in a way that told me our task was nearly complete. The data revealed that it was indeed possible to integrate a transformative experience. Furthermore, a complete transformation—of which the transformative experience was just a part—had a distinct pathway consisting of thirteen predictable phases, nine of which had occurred where the models of Campbell, Van Gennep, and Turner ended. I saw the hidden side of transformation, and I knew in that moment my life would never again be the same.

The "Characters" in This Book

After the initial research was finished, I gave myself six months to play, rest, and recuperate. In fall 2008, I began writing the manuscript for this book. Intermittently, I also conducted both in-depth and casual interviews about transformative experiences with people I met or who were referred to me by colleagues. Most of their stories did not make it into this book, but I anticipate sharing them in future writings. In all, I interviewed people across a variety of ages, ethnicities, socioeconomic backgrounds, genders, and beliefs. Their accounts represent all types of transformation.

In presenting the Map to Wholeness in this book, I chose to focus on two individuals. I knew that the book's usefulness would hinge upon the quality and synergy of their stories and the degree to which I could eloquently and precisely portray their trials, surprises, magnificence, and power. In other words, I knew that no amount of great writing could make up for a mediocre choice of main characters. I wasn't looking for flashy anecdotes, but I needed accounts of transformation that were dramatic, interesting, and comprehensive enough to portray the intricate details of the journey to wholeness. When I met the first of the two individuals I chose and listened to her profoundly moving story, her capacity to love, learn, and grow motivated me to try to become a better person. I realized then that the chosen individual's character was at least as important as the details of his or her story.

I hope the two people in this book differ from one another enough that you might gain insight into your own experiences while reading about theirs. In each account, I relay powerful, delicate, vulnerable, and triumphant moments that are pulled, in accurate detail, from five years of in-depth interviews. I share their stories of transformation from beginning to end: wholeness. Along the way I point out seemingly mundane events and explain how they are clear indicators of transformation so you will know how to look for these same clues in your own life.

An Important Clarification

I was sitting in a quaint cottage on the north shore of Kauai revising a draft of this book when it occurred me that the reader might not believe that the events depicted in this book occurred in the sequence in which they are described. To explain why this matters, I need to share a bit about my interview process. First, I asked each person to review all of his or her major life experiences, highs and lows, from birth to the present day, in chronological order. This task is not necessarily easy; nor is it one that you do very often, if at all. For example, I might have documented that a woman sold her home in February 2010, felt estranged from her family from May 2010 to February 2012, and earned a promotion at work in July 2014. Then I would look over the timeline of her experiences and begin to decipher her movement on the Map.

It is awe-inspiring to witness the thirteen phases in the journey to wholeness emerge time and again through the life events of an individual: setting out into the unknown, experiencing a catalytic event, returning in shock to all that is known, experiencing relief and upheaval, harboring denial and grief ... phase after phase, like clockwork. The Map precisely illuminates and expresses the content of one's lived experience, revealing something invisible.

The point I'd like to make is that the interviewees did not somehow orchestrate their lives according to my thesis; besides, much of what happens in life is outside of our control anyway. During each interview, I diligently recorded the timing of each reported experience. Later, I cut, pasted, and rearranged the experiences into sequential order so I could begin to see the person's path toward wholeness. When the individual's experiences seemed to be out of order with the phases, I usually pulled my hair out and questioned the validity of my theory. Interestingly, each time this situation has occurred, I reinterviewed the person only to discover that the data was incorrectly reported or recorded, and the Map to Wholeness was once again validated. This is always stunning!

My Personal Experience with the Map

Ironically, a year and a half after my research was completed, I found myself in the throes of the most difficult transformation of my life. Therefore, I had the odd experience of living my own research, phase by phase. I have found myself saying, "Ahhh, yes, of course this is happening now," knowing full well why that type of event was happening at that particular time and what kind of experience I would soon encounter next.

As I continue to make my way through the most difficult parts of this process, I am grateful to know that my experiences are normal and, more importantly, that this arduous journey will lead to a satisfying outcome. I have seen the end result of transformation confirmed over and over again in the lives of many individuals. While the road is often long, and you might think it will never end, the process of transformation leads to wholeness.

ACKNOWLEDGMENTS

The soul of this book lies within the stories of two people—Kenny Dale and Radha Stern—who courageously opened their homes, lives, and very essences to me in the name of serving the greater good. Each of you are palpably awe-inspiring, profoundly driven toward personal excellence, deeply compassionate, and firmly dedicated to making a positive contribution in the lives of those around you by the ways in which you choose to live each day. May your suffering, learning, and triumphs be of great comfort, guidance, and encouragement to every reader.

The central message of this book—the figure-eight map and its thirteen phases—would not exist without the steadfast and sincere dedication of my co-researchers: Maggie Crowder, Monique Duphily, Kayla Forster, Maribel Gutierrez Villanueva, Beth Hardison, and Julie Swift. Each woman enthusiastically and sincerely committed many days—spanning more than a year—performing demanding work in hopes of learning, growing, and healing so they could produce information that might one day be of service to others. There are no words that express my feelings of gratitude for each co-researcher. Indeed, my entire being is stilled to reverence as I gently and lovingly hold as a steward the creation of our scientific labors.

When my first of many writing coaches read my writing and said with a blank stare and blunt tone, "You might not be teachable," I knew I needed to prepare for a long haul. I would like to especially thank my writing teacher Laura Davis for agreeing to take me on one to one. Without your willingness to teach me as an apprentice to your trade, I would not have been able to produce material worthy of being edited.

The Map to Wholeness

This book is graced with beautifully crafted transitions and clarity of word selection because of my longtime and beloved editor Brookes Nohlgren. I wanted more than anything to have an editor so gifted that our work would attract a publisher as fantastic as North Atlantic Books. Brookes, your brilliant skills, witty creativity, sensitive patience, and knowledge of the industry made my dream come true.

Finally, I want to thank you, Melissa Puckett, for your unwavering support, love, and companionship. You are always in my heart, inspiring me to be my "best me today."

INTRODUCTION

Mohandas Gandhi, known to his many followers as Mahatma ("great soul"), led India to independence from the United Kingdom in 1947. His father was prime minister of the state where they lived and had chosen Mohandas as the child who would succeed him. After dropping out of college, Mohandas decided to study to become a barrister in London, which incensed the elders of his social caste. Accordingly, he was declared an outsider. Once in England, the homesick Mohandas had trouble adjusting to the English lifestyle. During this emotionally distressing period, friends suggested he read the Bhagavad Gita, a sacred Hindu text—and his life was forever changed. The scripture's ancient teachings quickly became the central guide for his life and gave him a vision of how goals could be achieved through nonviolence.

Elizabeth Cady Stanton was a leading figure of the early women's rights movement in the United States. In 1826, when she was eleven years old, her older brother, Eleazar, died just before he was to graduate from college. He had been preceded in death by five of the other Cady children, leaving Elizabeth and her four sisters. When Elizabeth tried to console her grieving father, he told her, "Oh, my daughter, I wish you were a boy!" His insensitive remark reflected the limitations placed on women at the time. Determined to please her father, Elizabeth promised she would become all her brother would have been. In fact, she resolved to be the equal of any male.

When Gandhi read the Bhagavad Gita and Stanton heard her father's stinging statement about gender barriers, each had a life-changing experience. These events launched them into the transformation of a lifetime, although it's important to note that we undergo multiple transformations in the span of our existence. Gandhi and Stanton would move forward through the phases of transformation, ultimately attaining wholeness and changing the future of humanity.

When you have a life-changing experience, your normal, day-to-day life is interrupted, suspended, or even forgotten altogether. Your senses heighten, your awareness broadens, and you focus completely on the powerful occurrence unfolding in front of you—or within you. A life-changing event can create the impression that you have endured a fundamental shift and that you are no longer the same. Indeed, when you return to your daily responsibilities, you feel unsettled. But the truth is that you have just *started* to undergo a massive reorganization at your core that will take months, if not years, to complete.

Regardless of how long it has been since your most recent transformative event, subsequent chapters of this book will shed light upon your course. As you read, you will come to recognize that the highs and lows of your life form a pattern that leads toward your larger purpose. Using real-life accounts of people who have lived through the strains of birthing themselves anew (phase 10 on Map), I reveal actions you can take for a successful transformation and point out the junctures at which most people risk sabotaging their opportunities. I begin by defining transformation and explaining how to read the Map to Wholeness—the path to a state of fulfillment, stability, balance, joy, and peace.

Why Learn the Map to Wholeness?

As I walk you through stories of people who have transformed, you will recognize how prominent and seemingly unrelated periods in your own life are actually connected to form a pattern. This pattern, revealed through my research and detailed in the preface, is made up of thirteen specific, sequential phases. Pictorially, the pathway to becoming whole involves a process consisting of two distinct cycles that together form the shape of an upright infinity symbol, a figure eight. The first cycle is an upward-moving loop that culminates in a life-changing event, a crisis, or a peak. The second cycle is a descending integrative curve that culminates in letting go of old patterns and the emergence of a new identity, relationships, and abilities. The combination of both halves, the *entire infinity movement*, is what produces a complete transformation.

When you read the Map to Wholeness, you can determine which phase you are in now, what to expect next, and how far away your destination is. Knowing where you are in your transformation normalizes feelings that may seem strange or unexplained. It also relieves stress because you realize there is a reason for what you are going through. For example, if you are presently enduring one of the most difficult periods of your life, you are probably in the *Dismemberment* phase. If you feel restless about a nagging dream that it is riddled with impossibilities, you might be in the *Disorientation* phase. Or if you have recently emerged out of the darkest time of your life and are feeling a sense of relief, you can use the Map to discover that your current phase is called *Surrender and Healing* and that soon you will transition into a phase when you will realize your wishes—*Abundance and Creativity*.

Like signposts along a road that tell you where you are, how to navigate so you don't get lost, what to expect around the corner, and how far you have left to go, the Map to Wholeness illustrates a larger reason for your present circumstances. With uncanny precision, you can recognize why you are experiencing delight or sorrow, fortune or misfortune, and fulfillment or lack thereof. When studied closely, my research explains that our lives are far more predictable than we have known.

I hope the stories and ideas in the pages that follow will help you feel relieved, clearer, understood, and soothed. Because the journey is internal and often solitary, imagine that I am with you, holding a candle before you as you make your way, encouraging you when you feel you cannot go on, and offering you the intimate words of those who have gone before you as inspiration and guide.

Part I

Transformation and the Map to Wholeness

1

TRANSFORMATION

*I think that what we're seeking is an experience of
being alive, so that our life experiences on the purely
physical plane will have resonance within our innermost being and reality, so that we can actually feel the
rapture of being alive.*

—JOSEPH CAMPBELL

Your life circumstances, from your feelings to your relationships to your job satisfaction, can be made understandable in light of your transformation. "My transformation?" you might ask. Yes, your transformation! You are always in the process of transforming, regardless of your desire for change or how long ago your most recent life-changing event occurred. Transformation is inevitable; it is integral to life itself. Nothing ever simply stands still or remains frozen in time. You only need to reminisce for a short while to recall at least one experience that affected you so deeply you felt as though life—and you—would never be the same.

Transformation Is All around Us

We need only talk to neighbors, overhear conversations at a coffee shop, or chat with colleagues to be reminded that transformation is all around us. In our own social circle, there is always someone experiencing a major turn of events: sending a child off to college, returning from military duty, changing careers, becoming a grandparent. Every day, hundreds of thousands of women have a transformative experience through childbirth, students obtain long-sought degrees, and people end or begin relationships, go into the Peace Corps, study abroad, or retire.

The word *transformation* often connotes a positive experience: your best friend gets married, a coworker has an epiphany while mountain climbing, your aunt visits the land of her ancestors, your little brother completes a religious mission in Argentina. While positive events change lives, the truth is that life-changing experiences are not always pleasant, uplifting, or enjoyable. Sometimes, transformation involves a disappointment, trauma, or devastating occurrence, such as losing one's job, contracting a serious illness, being named in a lawsuit, surviving a major accident, or suffering the death of a loved one. Perhaps even more than positive events, negative circumstances throw your life into turmoil and turn your identity upside down, making you feel as if you may never regain your equilibrium.

Our shared notion of transformation assumes that you are transformed *because* you experienced a momentous event. For example, a close friend of mine was one of ten teachers in the United States chosen to participate in a ten-day *National Geographic* educational adventure cruise to the Arctic Circle. It was a once-in-a-lifetime opportunity. She witnessed the unadulterated stillness of the endless frozen horizon, polar bears so close she could hear their breathing as they hunted and played, and gargantuan crystal-blue glaciers. How could you *not* be changed forever by witnessing something so rare and spectacular?

Transformative experiences make an impression on the body, mind, and spirit that may cause you to think, *I will never be the same.* As with my friend who went to the Arctic, there is a way in which this statement is true; you are not the same. But does this feeling of not being the same mean you have transformed—become a new you? According to my careful research, the answer is no.

What Is Transformation?

What is transformation anyway? Is it simply big change? Or maybe fast change? Change and transformation are often linked, but they are definitely different. It is said that while all transformation is change, not all change is transformation. To use a metaphor, if change is what happens when you rearrange the furniture in a house, transformation is a full-scale remodel.

Change is linear, which means there is a cause and an effect, an action and a direct result. For example, when you *cause* the couch to move to the other side of the living room by picking it up and moving it, the *effect* is a different room configuration. The *action* of moving furniture might produce the *result* of a new look, feel, foot-traffic flow, or even room usage. Change implies that a part of a whole has been altered. In this case, a part of the house (the living room), has been changed. Transformation, on the other hand, signifies that all aspects of a whole have changed, producing something fundamentally different. Instead of a new living room, you have a new house.

The word *transform* consists of the prefix *trans-*, meaning "beyond," and the word *form*, referring to the shape of a thing. The form of an object derives from its underlying structure. The water in a swimming pool takes the configuration of its walls; a couch is contoured around its metal and wood frame; a giraffe develops around its skeleton, which includes an extremely long neck. The walls, metal, wood, and bones are the structures around which these entities take form.

When something transforms, both its form and its underlying structure alter fundamentally. The quintessential analogy of the caterpillar's metamorphosis into a butterfly is helpful to explain this idea. The caterpillar has a squishy, hotdog-shaped body with lots of stubby legs and two eyes on one end. A butterfly has a squishy, slightly shriveled, hotdog-shaped body; wafer-thin wings; six long legs; two eyes; and two long antennae. These two creatures look very different yet are still one and the same. The butterfly is a new version of the caterpillar, whose structure and shape have transformed.

What is it that shifts in human transformation? What is the human equivalent of the structure of a caterpillar? It's not as though people are walking around with new bones, comparable to the wings of a butterfly. In the case of humans, it is our identity that can be thought of as our structure. Your identity houses your values, beliefs, and ideas about who you are and how the world operates. Identity may be summarized in all the ways you can complete the statement "I am ...." For instance, you might complete the statement by naming a personality trait, such as "I am optimistic"; an aspect of biology, such as "I am tall"; or a role, such as "I am a mother."

The walls and roof of a house create a place to reside within, and they provide protection from the elements. Similarly, your identity gives you a place to be that is essentially "you." Having a sense of identity helps you feel secure, stable, and connected to your immediate purpose. However, transformation requires that you dismantle an outdated identity structure. This process can feel destabilizing, because your sense of self is being taken apart. When you undergo transformation, you alter the foundation of who you are.

How does transformation give you a new identity? Of the thirteen predictable phases of transformation, the one most popularly associated with transformation is the initial transformative experience, an event that takes you beyond yourself, outside the realm of what you thought was possible for you. When this event occurs, you access new possibilities for yourself. These possibilities arise from your latent wholeness—the person you were born to be but have not yet expressed. In other words, a life-changing experience exposes you to your true self, even if you are not consciously aware that this is happening.

Transformation is dynamic: fluid, variable, vital, and wide-ranging. You make choices each day, consciously or not, that invite novel experiences. These experiences take you out of your comfort zone and help you develop in ways you can't imagine. Transformation is never stagnant, even though you may, at times, feel immobile. Rather, you are constantly moving forward, either quickly or slowly. Transformation invites you inward; at the same time, it expands you outward, toward your potential. To live is to transform, so you are always experiencing one of the phases on the path to wholeness.

As you transform, you grow holistically in all areas of your life. For example, the challenges you face increase your personal power. What you learn broadens your consciousness and improves your ability to make healthy decisions. The healing you undergo increases your compassion and your ability to love and be loved.

The Role of the Unconscious Mind

Transformation involves the unconscious because that is where transformation begins. Although transformation may seem to be thrust upon us by external events, *we always initiate transformation*. We are almost never aware of this fact, however. A desire for change triggers the transformation process, but in most instances, this desire is unconscious. We will explore the unconscious origin of transformation in the chapter on the Seed phase. Because the unconscious mind plays such a critical role in transformation, I will explain a bit about how it works here.

The unconscious is the part of the mind that functions when you act without intention—which, for most of us, is often. When you operate from the unconscious mind, you respond automatically, without reflection. Therefore, when you are doing something you have done many times before and are doing it "without thinking," you can be assured that the unconscious mind is taking care of your perceiving and decision making. You use the conscious mind, on the other hand, when you act intentionally.

Together, the conscious and the unconscious make up the whole mind. The metaphor of an iceberg is often used to characterize the relationship between the two parts of the mind. The conscious mind is the part of the iceberg above water; the unconscious mind is the part below. The exposed part of the iceberg can be seen, like the conscious mind can be accessed. The submerged part of the iceberg cannot be seen, like the unconscious mind cannot be accessed. About seven-eighths of an iceberg's mass is underwater. Likewise, the unconscious mind is much greater in its capacity and power than the conscious mind.

The unconscious is a vast storehouse of information that includes memories, thoughts, information, and feelings associated with your past experiences, coupled with beliefs inherited from your family system. The unconscious mind is often judged harshly because it tends to be irratio-nal, uninviting, and childish. It contains desires and emotions (fear, anger, and sadness) that our conscious minds find unacceptable. We instinctively avoid uncovering our unconscious thoughts and feelings. Defense mech-anisms such as denial help shield us from these hidden aspects of our-selves. The unconscious is often referred to as the "shadow" because it represents our dark side and is hard to see.

You might wonder whether there is anything good about the uncon-scious. The answer is yes. Because the unconscious stores a ton of infor-mation, it saves us an enormous amount of time and energy by keeping us from having to think through everything we do during the day. In addition, the unconscious plays a central role in our ability to be creative and innovative. The unconscious mind can combine seemingly unrelated pieces of information to form an insight—an awareness that illuminates or helps solve a problem.

Most of our decisions are informed by both our conscious and uncon-scious minds. When making a decision, we consult the known aspects of ourselves, our conscious thoughts and feelings. We also unknowingly take direction from the unconscious mind. In other words, despite good inten-tions, you will make decisions influenced by your repressed desires and emotions. As a result, you may find yourself unhappy, unhealthy, or suf-fering from bad luck. Usually, we need the perspective of an outsider—a friend, loved one, religious or spiritual leader, or therapist—to help us identify why we have encountered such troubles. The bottom line is that the unconscious mind has more control over us than most of us realize.

The decision to change your life plays a key role in initiating transfor-mation; therefore, understanding the role of the unconscious in decision making is important. We will address the choice for change in more detail in the chapter on the Seed phase.

Three Types of Transformation

Joseph Campbell is best known as a mythologist. He studied ancient stories that teach the nature and origin of the universe and serve as guides for our purpose and values as humans. These myths often involve superhuman characters who undergo challenges and triumphs in the reconciliation of major forces, such as good and evil. In *The Hero with a Thousand Faces*, Campbell concluded that people transform as a result of three major causes: trauma, unexpected powerful experiences, and consciously intended journeys.

Transformation through Trauma

The first type of transformation occurs because of a crisis, such as a terrible accident, the death of someone close to you, a serious medical diagnosis, or a robbery. No one wants to have a traumatic experience. Yet trauma can lead to deep personal transformation: An incest survivor discovers her personal power. A mother becomes an advocate for crime victims after the abduction of her child. A war veteran becomes a peace activist. A man hit by lightning discovers a previously unexplored passion for music. As traumas are faced and healed, people change in ways that might not have been possible if the terrible events had not occurred.

I interviewed a woman, Ruth, who experienced an unusual transformation through trauma. She was raised in post-Depression Brooklyn by her widowed mother and her grandmother. They were very poor, and they had no other relatives and very little social interaction. When Ruth's mother was elderly, she told Ruth, "I almost aborted you."

"I was the unwanted child," Ruth explained, "and my sister was prized. My mother loved my sister; she provided care for me. I was clothed and fed, and that was about it." Ruth endured a childhood that left her feeling fundamentally alone and lonely, unwanted and ostracized in her own home.

Seventy years later, Ruth's daughter set up a social media profile for
Ruth so she could continue some research she had begun into her gene-
alogy and connect socially with family and friends. Thank goodness
she did; it was through social media that Ruth's life changed abrupt-
ly—a story she shared with me.

> About four days into investigating my genealogy, a cousin named Eran instant-
> messaged me on Facebook. He is of my children's generation, on my mother's
> side. He had been searching for me, I guess, for several months. It was hard to
> find me because of name translations and name changes.

> After a month of electronic interchanges with Eran, we agreed to talk on the
> phone on Palm Sunday. He told me some shocking news: "Your father did not
> die in the war. Do you want me to continue?"

> I was calm. "Yes."

> "He lived until 1997 and was 87 years old. Do you want me to continue?"

> "Yes."

> "You have a huge family, including two sisters. Should I continue?"

> I couldn't speak.

> I was in utter shock, exhilarated, delighted, and looking forward to talking to
> my mother. I planned to tell her on Easter Sunday what I had found out about
> my father. I viewed the timing of the news, coinciding with Easter, as a sign
> of a new life with my mother. I wanted to believe that this new information
> would give my mother and me a chance for a new beginning. As I got ready for
> the phone call with my mother, I felt like I was emerging from a dark tunnel
> that I didn't realize I had been in—and I could see the light.

> She promptly crushed me by being rigid, stoic, and unyielding in admitting
> anything. It was horrible. It was really sad. I was angry.

> When Eran and I finally met in person, he went over everything little by
> little, piece by piece: he showed me my father's voter registration card and pic-
> tures.... My father had come back from the war. No one seemed to know what
> happened, why he'd left, or what my mother did at the time.

It finally began to sink in: I had lived within my mother's lie for so many years. I didn't know anything about my father. The foundation of my identity shattered. Somewhere deep inside, I might actually have a family and people who I could love and who could love me. It was a very painful and confusing time. I was still in darkness. I cried a lot. And yet, hope burned inside me that I might have a new beginning.

Ruth's life-changing event—the discovery of the truth about her father— was extremely exciting yet essentially traumatic. She relived the loss of her father, experiencing profound despair upon learning that although he had been alive for most of her life, she had never gotten a chance to know him.

EXAMPLES OF TRAUMATIC TRANSFORMATIVE EXPERIENCES

According to my research, the following personal traumas have the potential to lead to transformation, though they do not guarantee transformation. This list is not complete; it gives only a sampling of the many types of traumatic transformative experiences. Pondering the items in the list might help you identify some of the major events in your life.

- Abuse
- Active-duty military service
- War (as a survivor or rescuer)
- Natural disaster (as a survivor or rescuer)
- Car accident
- Crime
- Abduction
- Death (or other loss) of a child, spouse, parent, or sibling
- Loss of a significant amount of money (for example, through an investment, scam, or lawsuit)
- Significant or sudden illness or injury of self or a family member
- Secondary (observed) trauma, as experienced by health-care workers and others

- Marital infidelity or abrupt ending of a significant relationship
- Loss of a job or career
- Emigrating to another country

If you don't see an example from your own life on this list, you are likely very fortunate. If you are trying to determine whether a challenge you have endured belongs in this category, keep in mind that countless types of profoundly painful experiences don't result in transformation. A major falling out with your sister, for example, might be devastating but not life-changing. There is a distinction between a crisis that is deeply distressing and one that changes the course of your life. Only when a terrible experience alters your existence can it produce transformation. The types of transformation covered in the next two sections are triggered not by traumas but by positive or uplifting experiences.

Transformation through Surprise

Two types of surprises can lead to transformation. The first type is something totally unanticipated, such as getting an unforeseen promotion that will alter your life or receiving an e-mail from a brother you haven't seen in forty years. This kind of transformative experience occurs suddenly or unexpectedly. It happens when you are engaged in an activity that is ordinary to you, so you are not expecting an occurrence that is unusual, let alone life-altering.

The second type of surprise that can lead to transformation is something that happens while you are engaged in an activity that is out of the norm for you and that you expect to be awe-inspiring or emotionally powerful. Examples of this kind of transformative experience are visiting your ancestral homeland for the first time; traveling to a sacred place, such as the Holy Land; going into the Peace Corps; swimming with whales in the South Pacific; having plastic surgery; or donating an organ. At the outset of a significant, one-time-only, or novel experience, you anticipate that it may be intense. You may prepare yourself for the possible power of the event by reminding yourself that it will be difficult and that it might not turn out the way you planned. You may even speculate that the experience has the potential to change your life, but you are not actually seeking transformation.

In an example of the second type of surprising transformative event, Orvol and Jamie, a middle-aged couple, went to the Big Island of Hawaii for some rest and relaxation. While there, they spent considerable time engaging in rejuvenating activities. One day while they were snorkeling, a pod of dolphins approached them. Orvol described what happened:

> When the dolphins came over to us, we were so excited. It was almost as if they wanted to play with us. They jumped around and under us and squeaked to one another. When the dolphins began to swim off, we felt like they were saying, "Follow us"—so we did. When we snorkeled off after them, we began hearing a whale singing. Jamie and I immediately looked at each other, wondering where the whale was. Just then, the dolphins swam off, and we were left floating there.

> Then Jamie poked my arm and frantically pointed down. Directly below us was a huge, magnificent whale. We couldn't believe it—we were directly above her! It was as though the dolphins had taken us to her! We floated there in awe, listening to the mesmerizing, magical sounds of this unbelievable creature. Simultaneously, we both felt drawn to be near her, took a breath, and dove down to get closer. As we went down, we realized she was rising up toward us. We both stared in disbelief as the whale rose until she was literally beside us. Suspended in the blue waters, Jamie and I both had an experience that changed our lives—we looked directly into the eye of this whale. It was only a hand's distance from our own eyes. It was huge and black and deep.

> For weeks and weeks after our return from Hawaii, Jamie and I just couldn't shake the mystical feeling. We felt as though we had looked into the eyes of God. A year and a half later, I closed my healing business and she closed her clinical psychology caseload, and we moved to Hawaii.

Jamie and Orvol had planned a rejuvenating vacation. They expected to go from stressed to relaxed, disconnected from each other to connected, exhausted to revived. They figured that snorkeling would expose them to wonderful marine life, uplifting them in joy, curiosity, and appreciation. What they couldn't know was that they would be graced with such a unique and extraordinary experience.

EXAMPLES OF SURPRISING TRANSFORMATIVE EXPERIENCES

Following are examples of unexpected experiences (the first type of surprising transformative experience) and anticipated experiences with unexpected effects (the second type). Experiencing the listed occurrences may be life-changing, but not necessarily.

- Reconciling with or becoming estranged from a family member
- Getting married or divorced (in not understanding the full degree of the aftereffects)
- Becoming pregnant or giving birth
- Meeting a long-lost lover, friend, group of friends, or family member
- First or last child leaving home
- Marriage of a child
- Birth of a grandchild
- Remodeling your home
- Moving
- Starting a new form of leisure, recreation, or lifestyle
- Purchasing a very costly item (for example, a luxury car, boat, house, or second home)
- Engaging in an unusual, infrequent, or novel activity that has a strong impact (for example, running a marathon, manta ray snorkeling at night, helping your best friend give birth, or witnessing an indigenous people's ceremony)
- Retiring
- Getting fired or laid off (as long as it is not traumatic to you)
- Being promoted

- Going back to college after years of being in the workforce
- Changing careers
- Going on a religious mission, volunteering, or giving to others for a significant period
- Traveling, especially to a place that is extremely different from your daily environment
- Having an epiphany about your life, which can happen anywhere or anytime (but often during deep relaxation or travel)
- Seeing a particularly beautiful view or being in a stunning or spectacular place in nature
- Effective psychotherapy
- Spending time alone, possibly in nature
- Realizing a new identity for yourself (for example, coming out as gay, bisexual, or transgender)
- Dramatic change in your body (for example, significant weight loss or gain, surgery, or cosmetic surgery)
- Giving to another person in a way that involves great sacrifice (for example, donating an organ, being a surrogate mother or foster parent, or taking care of an elderly parent or medically compromised spouse)

Both types of surprising transformative experiences change your trajectory, offering you the chance to start over or venture into new possibilities. My impression is that people transform through surprise and through trauma more frequently than the third way, through intention.

Transformation through Intention

The third type of transformation is purposely chosen; that is, you consciously seek an experience that will lead to transformation. From the outset, you begin soul-searching, planning, and taking action to induce an experience that will radically affect you. Your primary motivation is to transform. This motivation differs from that for transformation through surprise, in which your primary ambition is to travel, escape, socialize, bond, or the like.

The motivation to transform may arise because you have been listening to the call of your heart, mind, or body for deep change—and that call is now a scream. Or you may have come to realize that your life, as it is currently configured, is no longer satisfying or fulfilling. You want more, and you set out to find it. When we pursue transformation intentionally, we listen closely to our aspirations. We then begin looking outside ourselves for a scenario that will offer the challenge, adventure, or stillness we need, or that calls for the skill, spirit, or passion we want to develop.

We can create the conditions that make a transformative experience more likely to occur. However, even those who are fortunate enough to have the guidance of a wise master and the support of an interconnected community know that mystical experience cannot be induced on demand.

Andrea, a retired therapist and the author of a memoir titled *Daughter of a Nazi*, shared one of the most striking intentional transformative experiences I have heard. Disillusioned by the religion of her birth, she set out on a three-month journey to find a belief system that would help her feel closer to God. Andrea was an adventurer of the soul who got lucky.

When I was twenty-seven years old, I read Autobiography of a Yogi by Paramahansa Yogananda. It felt like a download. I knew it already, even though I was raised Christian. I was getting ready to have a normal life—on the waiting list for a clinical psychology program. But Rudy, my boyfriend, was just begging me to go to India. I had money and a boyfriend guide. I was really scared to do it, but then I just decided, "Being scared is not acceptable. You are going."

We hitchhiked six thousand miles across Europe and the Middle East. In 1972, we arrived in Pondicherry after a three-month pilgrimage. I was twenty-nine years old. The guru at the ashram, called "the Mother," was ninety-two years old. She was having darshan, an opportunity to sit before her for a few seconds. I heard the lines were long, and I was not looking forward to the day. I didn't think much of it.

We were leaving the hostel where we were staying and the owner asked, "What are you doing today?"

"We are going to see the Mother."

His eyes got huge. "But you don't have flowers. She loves flowers!" He ran into his living quarters and grabbed a big flower. "At least bring this to her."

I sat in the heat all day. Countless hours of smells and fatigue and waiting. My flower, the only flower I had, was wilted by the hours of blazing heat. Its head was facing downward, and it looked completely pathetic. I was finally feeling the benevolence of the hour, but it didn't matter; my flower was drooping, and there was nothing I could do. I looked around to see if I could ditch it somehow; it wasn't much of a gift now.

Finally, it was my turn. Everyone told me, "Don't look into her eyes." But I wanted to look, because I had heard that gazing into the eyes of a guru is how you can receive his or her knowledge, love, and wisdom. I kneeled in devout reverence. I bowed my head, looked toward the ground, and prayed that I was worthy.

The flower was just beneath my face, and then the most unbelievable thing happened. It was like I was on acid or something. The flower started moving upward, toward the Mother, until it was entirely upright. I was completely unable to speak. I looked up and into her eyes in disbelief. I had totally forgotten that I was in front of her at this point. It was all about the flower, so I didn't remember not to look into her eyes. I just looked.

Everything went black, and I was in a vast, stark universe. Far, far in the distance, I felt her. It was as though she was a hundred thousand galaxies away from me. We were rushing instantaneously at tens of thousands of miles per hour toward one another into a crashing embrace. Like long-lost sisters, we were ecstatic to see one another: "We are finally together!" Speaking through energy, she said to me, "I have been waiting one thousand years to see you." We were lost in a timeless, dancing embrace, and I could feel the relief at being rejoined after separation. We could have been in that gaze for hours or mere minutes; I could not tell the difference.

I felt people touching my shoulders and pulling me. "Come on, come on," they were saying. Slowly, I felt the tear of another reality forcing me. "I am sorry, ma'am, you need to move." My awareness was going back and forth between this place that was forever and this line where people were pulling my body away from her.

Our eyes would not unlock. I didn't want to let go. Someone tore my body away, and our eyes unlocked. I was now sobbing. I wept for days. Even in the mess hall, I would sit over my cold food, staring into nothing, and cry. "Don't mind me," I would say. "I can't stop crying."

Andrea's transcendental experience left her in an altered state for weeks. It was so powerful that she couldn't bear to leave the presence of the Mother. She secured a menial job at the ashram and moved into a small cottage on the property. Her boyfriend soon left. Years later, Andrea got married and raised two children at the ashram. She lived there for nearly thirty years, serving and supporting the community.

There are many factors, known and unknown, behind the mystery of a life-changing event. If you set out with the primary purpose of changing your life and being changed by the circumstances you design, you will realize—in hindsight—that you can, indeed, affect whether or not transformation occurs. But because life is uncertain, if you want to transform, the best you can do is to learn as much as you can about yourself and the transformation process, form a plan, and set out on your journey.

EXAMPLES OF INTENTIONAL TRANSFORMATIVE EXPERIENCES

Scenarios that have the propensity to produce a transformation include those in the following list. A few items are repeated from the list for surprising transformative experiences. Whether an event is surprising or intentional depends on the circumstances.

- Giving birth to a baby under unique circumstances (for example, when you are older than forty, in the farmhouse where your entire lineage was birthed, in water, or overseas)
- Intended pregnancy or adoption

- International travel

- Diaspora travel (visiting a traditional homeland)

- Volunteering for the Peace Corps (or something similar)

- Living in another country for an extended period or frequently

- Studying abroad

- Religious or spiritual pilgrimage or mission

- Traditional initiation or rite of passage

- Getting married

- Ending a relationship

- Moving to a new city, state, or country

- Quitting a career or job

- Retiring

- Elective surgery

- Giving to another person in a way that involves great sacrifice (for example, donating an organ, being a surrogate mother or foster parent, or taking care of an elderly parent or a medically compromised spouse)

For centuries, people have sought out peak experiences—uplifting, dramatic, or invigorating encounters. Our ancestors ventured into the rugged wilderness in the hope that connecting deeply with nature would transform their inner world. The quest for a vision, for spiritual guidance and purpose, reflects an age-old yearning for the body to be enraptured, the mind to be boggled, and the soul to be enlivened.

The Unknown
Transformative Experience

When I speak to groups about the Map to Wholeness, some people can't identify their most recent life-changing experience. Even though transformative events can be obvious, as in the example of Andrea, who watched a wilted flower revive before her eyes and then ecstatically united with a guru, many catalytic experiences are less dramatic and can even be elusive. Many people assume that transformation is linked to a peak experience. This cliché reinforces a partial truth that transformation requires a magical, mystical, or extraordinary event. In actuality, transformative experiences can occur during circumstances that seem ordinary, such as changes in relationships, careers, or housing.

To assist individuals in recognizing their latest transformative event (phase 3 on the Map to Wholeness), I help them pinpoint their most recent Dismemberment phase (phase 8). Then I work backward, asking, "What happened in your life about one and a half to two years prior to that?" I have received responses such as, "I went to Africa," "I moved in with my mother to help her while she was dying," and "I started college." As soon as we both hear the words, the magnitude of the event becomes much more obvious: "Of course it was life-changing to care for your mother as she prepared to die." I can almost see the shift in the individual's perception as he or she reframes the memory as a life-changing event rather than an ordinary occurrence or something that he or she had to do.

How are we supposed to know a life-changing event when we experience it? Unless we encounter a moment that is completely striking, most of us do not have the training to recognize that a given experience is going to change our reality. If you are trying to determine whether a particular event in your life was life-changing, contemplate two questions:

- To what degree was the experience *novel* or a *departure from your routine?* An example of such an out-of-the-ordinary experience might be living away from your spouse for the first time in thirty-five years.

- To what degree do you *minimize the magnitude* of the experience because it was within the range of what is considered ordinary— that is, what an "ordinary" person would do in the same situation? An example of a seemingly ordinary experience that is actually life-changing might be moving out of state to take care of your son as he goes through chemotherapy.

Regarding the question of how novel the experience was, transformative experiences are more likely to occur when you are engaged in activities that are far outside your daily norm but not outside your belief system. For example, an interviewee named Johan left his relatively predictable life and moved to the other side of the state to live with his mother as she was dying. He had to integrate himself into his mother's routine and learn her needs and idiosyncrasies, as well as locate the city's amenities and navigate unfamiliar highways. Everything in his life was new. Johan was immersed in novelty and underwent a major readjustment in his routine, which is key to a transformative experience. If you have a car accident while driving to work, the fact that you didn't arrive at work safely and on time indicates that the incident was a deviation from routine.

The second question, about minimizing the magnitude of a seemingly ordinary experience, is a tricky one. This is the reason why so many people misinterpret a transformative experience as an ordinary one. Johan helped his mother because he was in a position to do so. He wanted to give her the kind of love and support he felt she deserved. He felt that he could not have acted any differently. In Johan's mind, he was only doing what an ordinary person would do in his circumstances. He did not view his actions as extraordinary, and transformation tends to be associated with extraordinary actions. If you believe what you are doing is conventional, it becomes very difficult to perceive it as transformative.

Transformative experiences can get lost in the volume and momentum of your life's demands and responsibilities: picking up the kids, finishing a work project, setting up the neighborhood garage sale, hustling to the hardware store before it closes so you can fix a leaky valve—all in one afternoon. If you are not used to viewing your life through the lens of transformation (and you haven't learned about the Map to Wholeness), it is quite easy to miss the meaning of your experiences in the larger picture of your life.

Transformation does not happen in an instant. Consider the example of a caterpillar's metamorphosis into a butterfly. The life cycle of a monarch butterfly is six to eight weeks; the insect spends up to a quarter of that time, about ten days, transforming inside the chrysalis. Similarly, human transformation takes place over a relatively significant period and occurs so slowly that we may not realize it is happening. Indeed, when viewed through the lens of daily life, deep changes are difficult to notice—unless, of course, you know what to look for. In the next chapter, I will walk you through the thirteen phases of transformation and explain the figure-eight shape of the Map to Wholeness.

2

THE MAP TO WHOLENESS

The journey of ascent is that of shedding and separation
leading to the simplicity of singlehood,
the journey of descent is that of integration and union
leading to the richness of wholeness.

—A. H. ALMAAS

Transformation is an ongoing process that tends to appear ordinary when in fact something extraordinary is taking place. How do you know which phase of transformation you are experiencing? The Map to Wholeness can help you figure it out. Knowing where you are in the journey to wholeness can bring you clarity, relief, and inspiration: clarity to make conscious decisions, relief that what you are experiencing is normal, and inspiration to continue moving toward a healthier life.

The Cycles of Transformation

Transformation involves two cycles: transformative and integrative. The Map to Wholeness depicts these two cycles together in the shape of an upright infinity symbol or figure eight. A simplified version of the Map is shown here. The top loop represents the transformative cycle, which includes the life-changing event at the apex of the upper loop; the bottom loop represents the integrative cycle, which involves assimilation of the life-changing event into daily life. Both halves of the figure eight, the entire infinity movement, delineate a complete transformation resulting in a new you and an entirely different life.

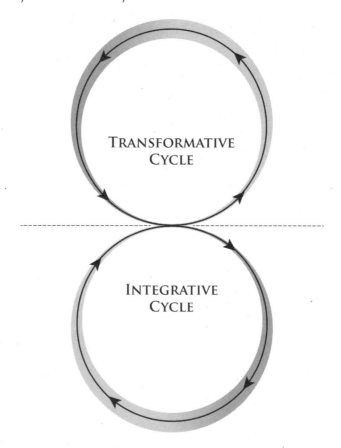

The Cycles of Transformation

The Transformative Cycle

The transformative loop of the Map to Wholeness comprises the first four phases of transformation. It culminates in a transformative event, which can be either a *peak experience* or a *traumatic experience*. During the transformative event, something larger than your current self—perhaps your soul or your potential—is accessed. In this state, you move beyond the boundaries of yourself and into something larger than you are.

Having a *peak experience,* a positive life-changing event, is similar to reaching the summit of a mountain, where you glimpse a new self and a new life. You expand into your "higher self" and conceive a new identity. This episode can involve feeling light, having an epiphany, or experiencing total stillness or peace within. These moments often have a mystical quality; time may appear to slow down, speed up, or even stop. You may feel high on life because of your newfound proximity to or union with energy that feels as if it exists beyond you. During this heightened experience, you may feel grand, vibrant, clear, or free because you are more wholly yourself. In a real sense, you have become impregnated with a new you.

A *traumatic experience* involves a sudden shock to the body or mind. It's like an explosion that splinters your current self into a thousand pieces. This fragmentation allows your psyche to manage the unimaginable. It creates space for your soul or spirit, or for the divine or something larger than yourself, to come into your life in a way not previously possible. Transformation through trauma is a harrowing experience, which—like it or not—offers an opportunity to change yourself and your life.

The Integrative Cycle

The integrative loop of the Map to Wholeness includes phases 5–13 of transformation, which represent the hidden part of transformation. This cycle can be thought of as hidden because much of what happens during it is unseen by others and occurs deep within your interior. Regardless of whether your life-changing event occurred at work, in a hospital, on a sports field, or while visiting a distant country, the lower half of the figure eight begins when you literally return home, whatever "home" is to you at the time. At the place you call home, you begin integrating your life-changing experience by relaxing into the comfort and relief of all that is familiar to you.

During the integrative cycle, you digest your peak or traumatic experience, but more importantly, you release old and outdated aspects of yourself and your life to make room for your new, healthier self. Releasing old patterns is not easy. These aspects of yourself hold feelings that you have rejected or avoided, such as anger and fear. The deepest, innermost part of this process entails emotional surrender and the birth of a new self. The process can be daunting, but if you commit to personal growth, you will soon begin the upward curve of integration, where your life will sprout with new relationships and fantastic opportunities.

When you have a transformative experience, you feel transformed; when you integrate a transformative experience, you become a transformed person.

The Thirteen Phases of Transformation

The Map to Wholeness charts thirteen phases that everyone goes through in the process of transforming, from the inception of a life-changing idea (Seed) to the full realization of a new identity (Integration). Following is a brief overview of these phases, which we will explore in depth in this book.

Phase 1: Seed

Transformation begins in the darkness of your unconscious with the notion of something you can become. The possibility of a new you emerges as a spark of life and awakens you to a new possibility for your life that inspires you to take action toward something enlivening.

Phase 2: Departure

An opportunity arises that gives you the chance to act on your desire to remake yourself. Knowingly or not, you begin to take steps toward your life-changing event. This phase involves making choices that move you closer to a different life. You might place a phone call, make a down payment, sign your name, say "I do," or write an email. This action spurs something that is latent inside you into the unknown.

Phase 3: Transformative Experience (Peak or Trauma)

You experience a life-changing event—a moment of expanding in the case of a peak experience or being shattered if you encounter trauma—in which you move into realms of the unimaginable and unspeakable. You go beyond typical human experience and touch realities you have not known.

Phase 4: Return

The supernatural nature of your peak or trauma is immediately overwhelming and captivating. As you Return toward home or as everyday life draws ever closer, the shock and mystique of the life-changing event slowly wear thin.

Phase 5: Displacement—Relief and Upheaval

You return home or to work and face the world. You are initially relieved to be surrounded by all that is familiar, even though you are acutely aware that you are not the same.

Phase 6: Denial and Grief

Relief wears away, and you are left with the bleak awareness that you have had a life-changing experience and are profoundly different, yet the rest of your world has remained the same. Rather than being wherever you are, you long to return to the past, either the peak of a positive event or life before your trauma.

Phase 7: Disorientation

Questions such as "Can I really have the life I want?" stir within you, as you find yourself increasingly confused or unsettled. You want to change your life for the better, but doing so seems impossible.

Phase 8: Dismemberment

You have an experience in which all control is taken away from you. You enter into darkness, sometimes called a dark night of the soul.

Phase 9: Surrender and Healing

You experience a moment of surrender that perfectly forces you to break free of an outdated, dysfunctional pattern, leading to a period of nourishment, support, and guidance.

Phase 10: Birth

The new you, conceived during your peak or trauma, enters into the world in a series of three moments; you timidly and yet boldly step into a larger realm and leave your former life behind. You step into a situation that asks you to show others who you have become.

Phase 11: Abundance and Creativity

Your long-held wishes become a reality with seemingly little effort. Help, support, and resources arrive through synchronous events. You can barely keep up with the joy and the work that opportunities bring.

Phase 12: Power

You are the master of your area of expertise; people know you for this and seek out your gifts. You are pleased with what you have accomplished and grateful that your creation is flourishing. Daily life settles down because you are not so inundated with opportunities, you have support systems in place, and you feel great inner stability, satisfaction, and strength.

Phase 13: Integration

You achieve an unmistakable sense of peace and fulfillment that comes not from what you created or did but from who you have become. You are intact, whole, and complete. You feel no yearning or sense of lack.

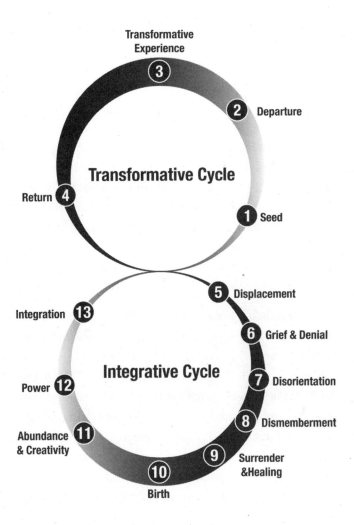

The Thirteen Phases of a Complete Transformation

Reading the Map to Wholeness

When I teach a group of people about the Map to Wholeness, I often encounter those who, despite learning about each phase of transformation, need help determining their current location on the Map. I ask them to describe a bit about what is going on in their life and what it feels like to be in their circumstances. Within a minute or two, I hear the characteristics of a particular phase. When I tell them the name of the phase and explain a little about why it fits the state of affairs in their life, they often sigh or gasp, or their eyes light up, with clarity and confirmation.

Understanding the phases is certainly the most important part of navigating the Map. But in order to accurately interpret your life situation, you need to know a bit more. When learning to read a road map, for instance, you discovered that highways, expressways, and residential roads were all depicted differently, and you were able to determine which type of road was most desirable based on your needs at the moment. Similarly, our research discovered details about the Map to Wholeness that will help you better apply it to your life:

- *Each phase of the transformation process has distinct milestones, is progressive, and is not revisited.* Each phase has qualities and landmarks that pertain to all people as they go through it. For example, an aspect of the Surrender and Healing phase is that you will let go of relationships that no longer match the new you. These recognizable characteristics are predictable and can therefore help you to determine your location and track your progress. As time elapses, the qualities of each phase will increase in intensity, and you will develop the skills that each phase demands. After you complete a phase, it is common to experience lingering aspects of recent previous phases, but you will not repeat an earlier phase.

- *Phase circumstances are unique to you.* Because the journey is yours, the pace at which you move through each phase, what you experience, and how you experience it will be unique to you and your personal journey. Even though everyone has changes in relationships during the Surrender and Healing phase, what changes is exclusive to you. You might, for instance, adopt a child, while another person might begin going to church and gain a new friendship circle, and someone else might end his or her marriage. Everyone has a life-changing experience during phase 3, but yours is one of a kind.

- *The phases overlap, and some have definite transitions.* Because transformation is organic, the phases tend to blend from one into the next. During the shift between phases, you may notice aspects of both phases, and once you have fully moved to a later phase, you may still experience lingering hallmark aspects of earlier phases. As a transition to the next phase draws nearer, you will often get a taste of what is to come. A few phases, such as Dismemberment, Surrender and Healing, and Birth, have recognizable catalytic events signifying the entry point.

- *The magnitude of your transformative experience in phase 3 affects the size of the figure eight.* A massive life-changing experience (according to your standards, not anyone else's), such as surviving the death of your child in an accident, going to Nepal and seeing a mountain spirit materialize before you, serving in active combat, or volunteering for disaster relief, means each phase along the Map to Wholeness will display an analogous emotional depth, intensity, and duration. When you have a life-changing experiences of great magnitude, you can expect that the entire figure eight will take at least a decade and often more. In contrast, if you have a significant experience that affects you deeply but is not life-changing (according to you), such as delivering a commencement speech or having your house robbed, you will still enter into a figure-eight journey, but each phase will be relatively brief and will trigger subtler versions of each phase.

- *The figure eight is both holonic and fractal.* The word *holon* stems from the Greek words *holos* ("whole") and *on* ("part"). A holon is both a whole in itself and simultaneously a part of a larger whole. Our body is holonic because it is composed of atoms that make up molecules that combine as cells, which are organized to become organs, and so on. The cell is a whole, as is an organ. When put together, they become a system of wholes.

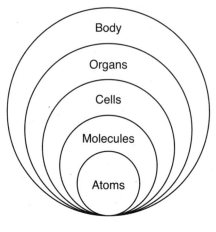

Our body is holonic

The Map to Wholeness is a holon because it is a whole process in itself, a complete transformation, but it is also embedded within a larger figure eight. In other words, the transformation journey you are in right now is also embedded within a larger figure eight that extends across most of your lifespan.

The Map to Wholeness is also fractal, a related term meaning that these larger and smaller "wholes" are not only embedded within each other; they are also replicas of each other. The image of the fern shows how the pattern of the entire branch is replicated in smaller configurations as "leaves" along the spine of the branch, and the pattern is replicated again along the spine of each "leaf."

When applied to the Map to Wholeness, this idea of holons and fractals coincides with the idea that at any given moment you are experiencing several figure-eight journeys simultaneously. To illustrate this, let's say you are laid off from your job, and you recognize this as a major life-changing event (phase 3). Two years later, you are further along in your journey across the Map and are in phase 6 when a rattlesnake bites you as you are hiking. You are rushed to the hospital and recover. This ordeal causes you to feel as though you are in phase 3 again, even though you clearly have not completed the Map to Wholeness that pertains to being laid off.

Fractals as shown in a leaf

If this information leaves you wondering how to determine where you are on the Map to Wholeness or which figure eight to pay attention to, you are not alone. As a remedy, I find it most helpful to track the figure eight that contains your most significant life-changing experience that you have not yet integrated, meaning that you have not completed all thirteen phases. Fortunately, doing this is what comes naturally. If we go back to the example of the person who was laid off from his job, we can learn that despite having smaller yet significant life events such as a snakebite, his present circumstances will overwhelmingly reflect the characteristics of phase 6. He can interpret this event of being bitten by the snake as both a part of his process in phase 6 and also a mini-transformative event (phase 3 of a different and much smaller cycle).

The idea of a holon helps us to understand that it is possible to concurrently experience a larger figure eight (related to being laid off) while also experiencing a smaller figure eight (pertaining to getting bitten by the snake). The larger cycle of transformation will last many years, and its phases will be more emotionally and physically intense. The smaller figure eight will be significantly shorter in duration and far less emotionally demanding than the larger transformation.

Holonic framework of transformation

When we take a closer look at the Map to Wholeness, we can see another characteristic of holons: the interrelatedness of every phase. The phases are nested within each other, which means that you carry the lessons of each phase forward into the next, and these lessons help you to make informed choices in your present circumstances. Just as phases build upon one another, each figure eight will build upon the one preceding it.

Part II

The Thirteen Phases
of Transformation

3

PHASE 1: SEED

Great innovations never come from above; they come invariably from below, as the trees don't grow from the sky downward, but upward from the earth.

—CARL GUSTAV JUNG

Far beneath the surface of your awareness is a new you that, like a seed, is just waiting to burst forth, grow roots, and sprout. This seed is the new, transformed you—but in a dormant form. It is your potential, what you have always wanted to become and, more accurately, who you know yourself to be in your clearest and most loving moments. Keep in mind that you will undergo multiple transformations in your life, and each one brings you closer to the true self you were born to be.

You can get a peek at the seed within you when a situation makes you think, "This is me." "This" may refer to an activity that makes you feel most like yourself, such as climbing a mountain, making a holiday meal for your family, singing in the shower, volunteering to support people affected by a particular disease, or praying with your religious or spiritual community. You may get a sense of your latent potential when gazing proudly at your beautiful home, giggling with your children in the park, lingering in the embrace of your beloved, socializing with friends, watching waves lap the shore of a pristine lake, or relishing a job well done. When you feel your essence, you have glimpsed your wholeness.

The difference between *glimpsing* wholeness and *living* wholeness is the difference between the first phase of transformation, called Seed, and the final phase, called Integration. The way to achieve wholeness—the end result of transformation—is to embrace your experiences as they arrive, learn about yourself, receive support from those who appreciate you, and let go of what no longer serves you. This process may sound trite as I've condensed it here, but it successfully produces transformation.

Consider the seed of a flowering plant. Two factors are necessary for it to start its journey to blossoming. First, it must possess a natural propensity to grow. Second, the conditions that support growth, such as soil, sunlight, and moisture, must be present. A person's passage toward wholeness begins just as a seed's does. The Seed phase occurs when an inner readiness to change encounters favorable circumstances. This readiness is the desire to be happier, which is the spark for transformation. Joseph Campbell said the hero's journey begins with a call to adventure. Similarly, you enter the Map to Wholeness when you hear the call to become new.

You Might Be in the Dark

The degree to which you can recognize the Seed phase while it is occurring depends on the type of life-changing event you are about to experience. If you are headed toward a trauma, such as being laid off from your job, or a surprise, such as witnessing an unexpectedly powerful traditional ritual performed by Māori people while you are vacationing in New Zealand, you will probably be unaware that you are in the Seed phase. For this reason, most people are able to identify this phase only in retrospect.

To identify your most recent Seed phase, look back to the period prior to your most recent life-changing event. You will probably notice a time frame lasting several months or perhaps longer when you felt restless or discontented about your job, your home life, or the health of your body, mind, heart, or spirit. If the unease intensified, you may have felt a desire for change. If this desire grew strong enough, you may have started to look for opportunities or pursued a prospect you had always aspired to.

If you set out to transform yourself, you enter the Seed phase fully conscious of what is happening. You are aware of the feelings of discontent that sparked the process. You know you are ready for a big change, similar to being ready to have a child. The recognition of your desire and the suitability of your life circumstances for facilitating change cause you to be in a state of willingness, openness, and enthusiasm to transform. You may even be alert for just the right experience to move you into an altered state, beyond your own boundaries.

For instance, a student of mine used to see a flyer in the student lounge advertising my study-abroad course in Costa Rica. She would stare at the flyer day after day. This invitation to an experience that would expand her worldview tugged at her heart and weighed on her mind. After many conversations with peers and mentors who encouraged her and gave her emotional support, she decided to answer the call. Her Seed phase had begun in her unconscious, where all that manifests in our lives begins. As the yearning to realize her potential grew, her awareness of the need for change emerged, and that need was met by her choice to act. A choice to change indicates the culmination of the Seed phase.

Whether your transformation happens through trauma, surprise, or intention, the Seed phase involves a growing need for change. This need always arises from the unconscious and indicates that you are ready to become a new version of yourself—one that is closer to your true self. Transforming through surprise, and especially through intention, feels much better than transforming through trauma, which is harrowing by definition. The more self-aware among us may receive hints from the unconscious that we are ready to transform; in response, we will seek out a transformative experience. The rest of us, unaware of our need for change, will experience transformation through surprise or trauma. Both the conscious and unconscious mind participate in making our decisions, including the decision to transform. As a seed germinates in the darkness of the earth, transformation begins in the darkness of the unconscious with the spark of desire to remake yourself.

To help you understand the phases of the Map to Wholeness, I will present the real-life stories of two people: Kenny and Radha. Beginning here with the Seed phase, we will follow these individuals through their transformational journeys.

Kenny

Kenny Johnson was born in rural Star City, Arkansas, in 1948. The oldest of seven children, Kenny never knew his biological father, and he was raised by his mother and stepfather. In Kenny's childhood, food was scarce, parental supervision was nonexistent, and conditions were ripe for trouble. He was a Boy Scout and a member of the school marching band, but he was also in the "hoodlum club." At about age six, Kenny began pilfering coins from his mother's and grandmother's purses. He quickly progressed to stealing from stores, supermarkets, and even a commercial truck that delivered potato chips. Because Kenny couldn't afford clothes or the equipment needed to participate in positive recreational activities, a life of crime became increasingly appealing to him. He felt entitled to what he needed but lacked the means or moral education to obtain it legally. In his circumstances, he could not perceive constructive alternatives.

Kenny learned the skills of the streets well, and before long, he was a professional criminal. He was arrested thirty-seven times and spent a total of thirty-one years behind bars, with little time between stints of incarceration. Each time he was released, he would work an honest job for a while until his attraction to the money, autonomy, and power of stealing overwhelmed him, and he reverted to his original career.

In 1966, Kenny became a father while living with a girlfriend in Kansas City, Missouri. The relationship ended six months after the child's birth. Because of his criminal lifestyle and time in prison, Kenny did not get to know his daughter until she was a grown woman.

Although Kenny gained great satisfaction from his livelihood as a criminal, his years in prison caused him to spiral deeper and deeper into despair. When he felt demoralized, he would turn to spirituality. He read spiritual texts, did yoga, meditated, and discussed spiritual philosophies with his fellow inmates. Engaging in spiritual activity was the only thing that ever helped him.

The context for Kenny's Seed phase arose in 1992, about a year after he had finished serving ten years in prison. Like many times before, he intended to stop stealing and remain clean. He had a good-paying job— until he slipped back into criminal behavior.

It started with stealing a newspaper so I could take it to work and read it, like a real businessman. My buddy Jerome said, "Why are you doing that? It's stealing!" It never occurred to me that I was stealing or that I was a criminal. It just wasn't part of my thinking.

Then I started doing other things … sneaky things, like stealing jewelry and selling it. I thought I was still "the Hustle"—the best at what I did. I didn't realize the technology, the tricks, had changed. I didn't understand that hustling was really over for me. It took quite a while of paying attention to the kids around me to awaken to the hard realization: "Man, you're a dinosaur."

This awareness made me seriously depressed. I didn't know how else I would make money. Regular jobs just couldn't hold my interest and didn't offer the freedom and control I needed. What else was I going to do with my life? In desperation, I thought I had one last street hustle up my sleeve: cashing checks. So I started stealing checks, forging signatures on them, and cashing them. I wanted to believe I still had the scheme going. There was no reason for me to do it. I already had a job and was doing fine with that income. But as time went on, I was making so much money stealing and forging checks that I quit my job.

A year later, in February 1993, I was a full-blown criminal again, with three major charges against me that could send me to prison for a very long time. I'd been digging a hole to hell without even knowing it.

I was also beating up my girlfriend.

I was messed up!

Something had to change. Kenny was desperate to get out of crime and alleviate his depression.

> It finally came down to a night when I had to decide to turn myself in or continue stealing. With three pending charges, prison was inevitable; the question was where. If I continued on the street, I was likely to get caught up with the feds—federal prison. Turning myself in now meant that I would have state charges. I knew I could survive in state prison. It was six in one hand, half a dozen in the other.

With few options, Kenny knew it was time to extricate himself from a lifestyle that could only destroy him. He called his parole officer:

> "Listen, I am coming in. I want to turn myself in."

> My parole officer said, "I have been watching you and wondering when you would come in. Good decision. Come on in." He had been keeping tabs on me. He knew I was going down a slippery slope.

> I went in the next day. They locked me up and sent me to Springfield, Missouri, which was what I wanted. My family was there.

> When I turned myself in, I was lost.

> I was depressed enough to commit suicide.

Kenny's decision to turn himself in resulted from the conscious recognition that he was at a major crossroads, requiring a critical choice: to transform or to lead an empty existence.

> I started hanging out with meditators and the yoga people, doing all the things I had done before … reading spiritual books, too. But it didn't seem to help. Overall, I was depressed, sad, and feeling like a loser. All I knew was that I wanted out. I just wanted to be home, with my family, and not go back again. I had all the same thoughts and feelings of doubt and frustration that I experienced the other times I had been in prison—but this time was different.

> I was about forty-five years old, and I wasn't about to die a dejected loser.

Kenny didn't want to hustle anymore. He had felt hopeless like this too many times before. He came to terms with the fact that he needed something bigger than himself, a higher power or God, to help him make a drastic change. Staring yet again at the stark walls of a prison cell, he resigned himself to trying spirituality again. Yet he wasn't very optimistic. Years earlier, in federal prison, he had dedicated himself to spirituality only to gain nothing.

> I knew that something great had to happen to me in order to transform—something drastic to change my mindset from the type of guy I was when I came in, so I could become another guy. Something had to happen there, a major awakening, in order for me to let go of the old ways of doing business. So I could become something new.
>
> To become a new creation, something had to die.

In his miserable and weary state, Kenny was reaching for a different reality. But he had no idea what that was.

> It was an internal drive but not clearly defined. How can you have a vision for your life to be unlimited without knowing that such a thing is possible? How can you clearly define what you really need? I didn't know what I wanted. How can you know what you want if you haven't experienced it? How could I know that I had an ideal?

As Kenny describes, it is keenly difficult to fathom a life other than the one you know. But you can, like Kenny, open yourself up to the unimaginable and decide you want it. His receptivity and sincere seeking constituted his readiness for change, his desire to be happier. This spark, which is essential to the Seed phase, was met by the right conditions: Kenny had the support and camaraderie of spiritual friends, in a quiet and contained environment that was buffered from the outside world and its demands. In a real sense, the circumstances could not have been more perfect for the beginning of Kenny's transformational journey.

Kenny embarked on transformation through intention. His actions suggested that he wanted to transform via spiritual means. With the motive of becoming a healthier person, he identified an experience he believed could transform him, and he committed himself to pursuing it. This combination of factors is characteristic of the Seed phase for people who are transforming through intention.

Radha

Radha Stern was born in San Francisco, California, in 1954 to parents who were intellectual and eccentric. Her mother enjoyed hosting creative dinner parties and having rigorous philosophical conversations. Her father was a self-absorbed visual artist, historian, and fringe-movement leader who lectured at Harvard. Both had been married three times, with ten children between them, two together: Radha and her brother Adam. When Radha was two months old, her mother left her father.

As a child, Radha enjoyed spending time with her mother's trailblazing friends and came to be known as someone who had an old soul. She was shy and a "pretty good kid." Culturally, Radha is Jewish, but her mother taught her and her siblings about many different religions and told them to choose the one that worked for them. As a child who spent time walking across the wide-open spaces of a nearby wild game preserve and lying next to its babbling waterfall, Radha came to believe she could experience something holy—a divine force—wherever she happened to be.

Radha was married by seventeen and pregnant with her first child, Christina, at eighteen. At the same time, her mother became extremely ill and then died three days after her second child, Christopher, was born in May 1974. The death of Radha's mother left her feeling very bleak and alone, and she received very little emotional support from her husband. She had Christopher when she was nineteen; she separated from her husband when she was twenty; and they got divorced when she was twenty-one.

Life as a single mother with two children was daunting. With barely enough money to buy baby formula and pay the electric bill, Radha was forced to work several jobs. These humble, arduous, bittersweet years cultivated Radha's inner strength, resilience, and inspirational outlook. This time in her life would later motivate her to give back to people in need.

Radha's transformation began in her early forties, when her children were independent young adults. She had spent twelve years working her way up to a top administrative position in the food industry. As a woman in a male-dominated field, she worked long days and weeks to prove her worth and produce excellence. Increasingly, her job required frequent travel, and the cumulative effect of her hectic schedule made her work less and less appealing to her.

> Christina was still living at home but didn't want a whole lot to do with me. She was doing quite well in business school and was in high demand as a babysitter. I worked long hours and traveled a lot for my job and found that I needed help around the house, so my best friend, Bettina, and my childhood friend Mark were living with me.

> Christopher wasn't living at home. He was trying to find himself, running around with his buddies—trying to see the world and figure out what he wanted to do.

> I was dating Gary. We spent every weekend together, alternating between our two houses.

> I was tired of travel; it was really hard. I wanted to do something more meaningful and make an impact on the world. Selling food was meaningful on one level, but I had been doing it for a long time. I needed a change. I wanted an opportunity for growth.

Radha felt chronically underappreciated, and her job had become unfulfilling and repetitive; it had reached its natural conclusion. Her yearning for change was the spark needed to trigger her transformation. Her life was stable, her children grown, and her relationship enjoyable and fulfilling. These conditions were supportive of her desire for change, and she set out on a voyage toward wholeness. Unbeknownst to Radha, however, she was headed toward a trauma—the biggest one of her life.

❋ ❋ ❋

Radha wanted a more fulfilling life and Kenny sought fundamental personal change. When their circumstances became conducive to transformation, their journeys on the Map to Wholeness began. These individuals then moved into the next phase, Departure, by taking action to become their new selves.

4

PHASE 2: DEPARTURE

We must be willing to get rid of the life we've planned,
so as to have the life that is waiting for us.

—JOSEPH CAMPBELL

The Departure phase of transformation begins the moment you make a move, knowingly or not, toward a different life. Making a decision, such as "I am going to find a new job," is the culmination of the Seed phase; actually submitting a job application would signify the beginning of the Departure phase. When you move from thinking to doing, when the need for change becomes so overwhelming that you must take action, you depart from your former self into the unknown.

If you recall the months leading up to your most recent life-changing event, you may notice how your desire propelled you into action. For example, you always wanted to go to Italy (Seed), so you finally purchased a plane ticket (Departure). You were dating the love of your life (Seed), and you finally popped the question (Departure). You wanted to lose weight (Seed), so you joined a weight-reduction program (Departure). In other words, Departure starts with a deed that launches your journey: you sign up for a retreat, start looking for a house to buy, tell your boss you want to retire, and so on.

Departure is movement across a threshold, and once you cross the threshold, you can't go back. Your movement sets the transformational journey in motion. For example, if your Departure phase starts with making a refundable payment to participate in a marathon, you can still get your money back, but you can't reverse the intention that has been set in motion. Putting your money down is a statement of commitment to yourself and everyone else. It's like throwing a rock over a cliff: you can't get the rock back. You are invested, literally. Once you start the process, you are changing your life.

The form of the commitment may not always be money, of course; it might be your spoken or written word. If you pledge your involvement by saying yes or shaking hands, you're in, even if the venture doesn't go well or last very long. In the same way, you let others know you are obligated when you sign your name on the dotted line or click "submit" on an online form. When you make a promise, you activate wholeness. What spurred you to action may or may not play a future role in your journey, but your action served the important purpose of setting you on the path.

Anthropologists Victor Turner and Arnold van Gennep contributed invaluable information to our understanding of transformation through intention. They dedicated their lives to understanding how traditional societies facilitated rites of passage, initiations, pilgrimages, and ceremonies that helped people transform into adults, parents, leaders with specific roles and skills, and elders.

As mentioned in the preface, Turner and van Gennep delineated the three major phases of the initiation process: separation, the liminal period, and incorporation. In separation, much as in the Departure phase in the Map to Wholeness, the initiate ventures into the unknown in order to grow, develop skills, discover information that will contribute to the community, and become the person he or she is destined to be. The individual purposefully leaves his or her loved ones because of an inner calling or an appointment by an elder. In traditional societies, initiation entails a responsibility to the whole.

Turner and van Gennep carefully chose the word *separation* because it helped convey the key ingredient needed to trigger a life-changing experience: disconnection. Transformation requires that you leave people, places, and your old life behind—figuratively, energetically, and in many cases, literally. This doesn't mean that in the Departure phase of transformation you must travel across the country, fly across the ocean, sell all your possessions, or leave forever. But it does mean you must say yes to something very new, which means saying goodbye to something familiar so you can step over the symbolic threshold into a psychological and possibly physical place you have never been.

Kenny: Turning to Spirituality

Kenny wanted a life without crime. He was jolted out of his bleak outlook and into the Departure phase when he heard about Gangaji, an enlightened teacher who had come to the prison to help inmates meditate and find peace within. Hearing about Gangaji gave Kenny a feeling of hope. A live teacher could deliver what books could not. Despite being locked up, he wanted to break free of his bondage of crime and escapism. He acted on his impulse to learn more.

> My friends told me that a spiritual teacher named Gangaji had recently finished a series of regular visits to the prison over the past several months.
>
> So I started watching videos of her teaching. There was something about her that made me say, "Wow, I would like to see her." I didn't understand what she was talking about, but I knew I liked her. I enjoyed hearing her voice even though the things she was saying were totally foreign. I had no reference point for what she was teaching. I would hear her say, "Don't resist, and let go," but that didn't mean anything to us in prison. We had no idea how to do that. We had not let go of our way of seeing life and had not yet embraced her way of seeing life. We hadn't experienced the oneness she was talking about.
>
> I started meditating. Exposure to her teachings made the hunger inside of me grow, but I still wasn't sure how to feed it. Of course, I was tired of prison. But desire to change wasn't enough; there was a part of me that had to be awakened.

It wasn't until *April 1994*, about half a year later, when she decided to do another series of meditation sessions in the prison, that I actually saw her.

Venturing into new territory is both exciting and scary. Most of us, like Kenny, walk forward unknowingly, making guesses at each turn. Kenny's next notable experience occurred as a result of one of Gangaji's visits. As a follower of Hindu traditions, Gangaji offered *satsangs* followed by meditations. A satsang is a gathering for the purpose of cultivating spiritual learning, practices, community, and awakening. It is often led by a religious teacher or guru who may give a teaching, read from spiritual texts, lead a meditation, or answer questions.

About eight years before that time, Kenny had spent a year praying devotedly for a spiritual teacher to come to Gangaji's. With this memory of his prayers in the back of his mind, he attended her next prison satsang with his closest friends. One sincere seeker was John.

When Gangaji finally returned, John and I and all of us sat in on one of her satsangs, not knowing what they were. About ten or twelve of us had already been going to Buddhist meetings.

That day, after John came out of the satsang, he was speaking differently. He was talking about love and peace. He was talking about how much he loved Gangaji. We knew right then something had happened, because he was usually a cranky, mean guy.

So my friends and I that did spiritual practices started watching him. We assumed John was in love with Gangaji and really didn't realize that he was in love with what was beyond Gangaji. We were looking at it like he was in love with the woman, not realizing that it was her essence—the spirit—that he was in love with. Over the days and weeks, we saw a big difference. I thought, "Wow, man, he has really shifted. This is major."

It was perplexing to try to understand what happened. At some point, the source of the change we saw in John became irrelevant to us. Whomever—whatever—he was in love with, whatever he had, we wanted some; we wanted to experience it. We knew that whatever had a hold of him was far more precious and valuable than the shit we were experiencing in prison.

We knew that John had experienced something because he was able to say things and share his insight with us. Even though we hadn't had a similar experience, we could appreciate what he had to say. We didn't understand a lot of it, but we knew our brother had shifted, and we were going to support him and listen to him.

That was when the desire came and the cravings came. I still didn't know what the craving was for exactly. I had an inkling, but how can you know the Source until you know it?

Desire is a key ingredient of the Seed phase, but it is not uncommon for desire to continue or even grow during Departure. We experience the impulse of life through the sensation of desire. If you are fortunate, you notice your desire during the Seed or Departure phases. This is especially the case if you are like Kenny and Radha who were motivated to change.

Departure happens when you take action toward happiness, and Kenny had begun his pursuit. At phase 2 on the map, he leaped into possibilities and became committed to exploring a new way of life, going to both Buddhist meetings and Gangaji's satsangs and meditations. As an added bonus, he had a community of friends who wanted to talk about their experiences, learning, growth, and even feelings. Not everyone is fortunate enough to depart on the journey surrounded by fellow seekers. Kenny was now on a one-way path toward his destiny.

During the stimulating phase of Departure, you leave what is comfortable and familiar to save yourself from the perils of outdated patterns of behaving, thinking, and believing. At this place on the Map to Wholeness, you need only pay attention, seize opportunities when they come along, go beyond your fears toward a healthier life, and enjoy the ride.

Radha: "You Should Hire Me"

Radha was ready for change. She had a wonderful man in her life, but her children were grown and her successful career was unfulfilling. She was restless and eager to be invigorated. Her feelings and life conditions prompted her to keep vigilant watch for the right opportunity.

A person I know very well had a family charitable trust. The trust helped women and children with critical needs and funded basic stability services. Over the course of several months, my friend had been confiding in me that the work was overwhelming. As he talked, I thought, "I would certainly be good at this." It took me a while to get up the courage to offer my services. One day when we were hiking, I just said, "You should hire me. I'd be good at it."

This approach came from my sales training: You just put it out there, because the worst they can say is no. I continued: "I will need a car and a computer." He said, "Okay."

That September, I started working for the trust, which was founded to provide funds to support food banks, low-income housing, emergency medical services, crisis counseling—anything that would help families to stabilize, to fill the huge hole left when life falls apart. I always say, "You can't think about housing if you are hungry," meaning that food is the most basic necessity when comparing the two.

It was a really quick ramp-up. I was on a big learning curve. I had to learn how to give money away, literally. I had to find the people and organizations that were doing good works so I could tell them about the trust, and then I had to develop a system to give the money away fairly.

Learning something new felt like being a kid in a candy store, and I did it quickly. There was very little information out there that could help me figure out how to do what I needed to do. I sent away for a brochure to an organization, thinking it was going to give me sage advice. It turned out to be just a investment pitch: "If you invest your money with our charitable trust, then …" I remember calling the government organization that gives out the 501(c)(3) nonprofit ID numbers and asking for help: "Can you give me a list of all the nonprofits in the area?"

"We couldn't possibly do that," was the response. "There are too many." How was I going to give away money if I didn't know who needed it? It was another dead end.

I called the Support Center, an organization that provides support to nonprofits, and I said, "I want to learn how to give money away." They thought I was a quack. But I met with a guy there and ended up becoming best friends with him. He helped me immeasurably, and we figured it out. It took a lot of going by my gut, and I have a pretty strong one.

I began to establish myself pretty strongly and was feeling fantastic.

Radha's new adventure had begun. She entered into an exhilarating whirlwind of learning. For many, the Departure phase is filled with excitement and anticipation about the future, coupled with trepidation. Everything is new and uncertain. In this type of Departure, you are venturing out into the grand possibilities of the unknown.

✳ ✳ ✳

Departure involves leaving the world you once knew, knowingly or not, to achieve your destiny. You step into the unknown with excited apprehension. No one can predict what will happen next: it may be tragedy, or it may be exquisite beauty. Either way, you will soon experience a life-changing event—the next phase in the journey of transformation. If this event is traumatic, keep in mind that, in the end, you will become an entirely different person who can appreciate the purpose of the journey's pain.

5

PHASE 3: TRANSFORMATIVE EXPERIENCE

Creation and destruction become one in the act of love,
and during a fraction of a second man has a glimpse of
a more perfect state of being.

—OCTAVIO PAZ

Whether it is a euphoric peak experience or a traumatic crisis, every adult has had at least one life-changing event. Pondering this notion may awaken memories of one of your own transformative experiences—the time when you reunited with your estranged sister after twenty years, moved to Florida, survived an earthquake, or scuba-dived at the largest coral reef in the world. Whether the event that forever changed your life happened yesterday or many years ago, your memories of it and feelings about it are likely to be vivid.

Some transformative experiences only take a few moments to occur. Others unfold over the course of days, weeks, or even months, such as those involving international travel, military service, extended stays away from home, or legal trials. These longer transformative experiences don't hit you like a bolt of lightning; they alter you like a steady rain eroding a hillside.

The transformative experience is all-consuming: you are captivated as you gaze across the Great Wall of China, time stands still as you receive a lifetime achievement award, your focus intensifies as you listen to the doctor explain your husband's cancer diagnosis, your heart swells as you realize the dream of walking across your ancestor's farmland. The thoughts and feelings that typically occupy your attention and require your energy, having to do with obligations, relationships, and grievances, are swept away by the immediate experience.

The transformative event is, by definition, indescribable. You enter into a different time and space, detached from everyday reality. You become immersed in an extrasensory experience that informs your body, mind, heart, and spirit. Because of the altered state transformative experiences induce, they are often described as "mystical." Professor, psychiatrist, and scholar Arthur Deikman explains that a mystical experience occurs when your "senses and faculties of thought feel suspended" (Deikman 1966, 328).

Mystical experiences happen when we stop striving or fighting and become passively receptive to the mystery of life, its possibilities, and what is unimaginable about it, in the way a scuba diver takes in the magnificent colors and creatures of the vast undersea world. Mystical experiences are captivating even when they are traumatic, in the way traffic accidents can be riveting for passersby.

Theologian and philosopher William James is arguably one of the most influential contributors to our understanding of the qualities of the mystical experience. In his book *The Varieties of Religious Experience*, James finely examined and elaborately categorized the transcendent, identifying four main characteristics of mystical experiences (James 1902, 371–72):

1. They defy expression and are ineffable.

2. They "are states of insight … illuminations, revelations full of significance and importance" that "carry with them a curious sense of authority for after-time."

3. They are transient and unsustainable.

4. They require passive receptivity.

These characteristics help us understand how to identify a life-changing experience and show us what we can expect from it. Transformative experiences are so deeply moving that words fail to capture what transpired; they transfer wisdom; they are momentary; and they demand that you are alert and open, in the way you might be when gazing across a beautiful vista or watching a wild animal in the woods.

James's second characteristic of a mystical experience, illumination, is the centerpiece of a transformative experience. This third and pivotal phase on the Map to Wholeness occurs during what Turner calls the liminal period, or time between, in traditional rites of passage. During this period, the initiate experiences an epiphany, receives knowledge, or has a vision. Turner describes the liminal time as occurring after separation but before returning to one's home, when the initiate is neither here nor there, betwixt and between. During the liminal period, the initiate exists in an ambiguous and altered state, detached from social roles, obligations, and status.

The altered state that is emblematic of liminality may allow us to receive and perceive something much larger than we can normally grasp. In these delicate experiences, we have direct access to the vast unknowable, whether we call it the unconscious, higher self, soul, or God. Turner characterizes this state as one of "pure potentiality" where "the past is momentarily negated, suspended ... and the future has not yet begun" (Turner 1982, 44). Turner's idea of pure potentiality holds vital information for unlocking the mysteries of transformation, as I will explain.

When most people describe a life-changing event or when most experts talk about transformation, they identify the life-changing event itself as constituting the transformation. In other words, having the life-changing experience means that transformation has occurred. However, transformation is a process, not an event. When we use the words transformative experience to describe this phase, we acknowledge the event's power to activate our potential to transform. This type of experience has the tendency to eventually produce a transformed person—but there are no guarantees. Some people have life-changing events without transforming as a result. Aspects of the transformation process are difficult to undergo and can even be excruciating. There are points where, understandably, many people opt out of transformation. This is discussed in detail later in chapter 21.

As you continue to read, keep in mind the difference between a transformative experience and transformation. Again, I use transformative experience to refer to the life-changing event of phase 3 and transformation to refer to the entire thirteen-phase process.

Kenny's Transformative Experience: September 1994

The teacher Gangaji, her satsangs and meditations, and her teachings were no doubt an answer to Kenny's prayers. The few encounters he had with her were enough to touch him to the core. Truth be told, she was aesthetically beautiful, but despite his love for the ladies, it was not her beauty that was captivating him. In her presence, he encountered fleeting sensations of hope. He had sampled enough of her presence to realize how fortunate he had been to meet her, and he became increasingly eager to experience more. But she had completed her round of prison visitations, with no guarantees of return. In order to manage his feelings and to continue his progress, he resorted to writing letters to Gangaji as a sort of lifeline.

> By the time she came back to the prison for a another round of visits in September 1994, I was extremely ready to experience something other than "Kenny."

At this point Kenny had spent many years engaging in spiritual practice of one type or another, but this time he was like a devoted servant, a first-string player on a championship football team, or a veteran air traffic controller: he was unwavering and present. One day in September 1994, after several weeks of attending Gangaji's services, Kenny stepped into the chapel—and into the rest of his life.

There were about ten of us that day. It was customary to do a ten-minute meditation and then a talk. I was sitting to Gangaji's left on a cushion; she was on a chair. I was about three feet away from her.

We meditated for about twenty minutes. It was deep, and I felt such peace. When we came out of the meditation, Gangaji looked over at me and said, "Kenny, I have been thinking about you."

Before she could say anything else, I blurted out, "Gangaji, Gangaji, Gangaji, it is my understanding we have to die before we can see God's grace." I had no idea where that came from.

She said, "Kenny, God's grace is here now."

What she said didn't make sense to me.

She continued: "You think you are a black man, a convict; but you are neither of these things, Kenny."

I still didn't understand her. But something inside of me was rearranging itself.

After I experienced the truth or whatever that was, my mind rested; it became silent. Two friends of mine nodded, confirming that something was happening or had happened. Gangaji bent her head over toward me, and I bent my head toward her, as if I somehow knew what to do. Then she took her small mallet, the one she used to hit the meditation bowl, and tapped it three times lightly on top of my bald head.

It was like a confirmation or a ritual or a ceremony that I believed had to happen between guru and student. I had been reading about those things, and I must have figured that she would have to touch me in some way—so she touched me with the mallet.

I just relaxed and became silent.

Kenny was consumed by the tingling, magical, mystical experience. He succumbed to the magnitude of the beauty he had been waiting to behold for years, or perhaps for his entire life. His story continues:

> I had one hustle left when I met Gangaji, and when she walked out that day … it was gone. She took the hustler Kenny and left me with consciousness.

> That was the beginning of my life.

> I felt an awakening. I developed a wisdom, an insight. I thought, "Ah, this is what freedom is," and "Ah, this is why I was so hungry and so desperate," and "Ah, this is what I wanted all along."

> After several weeks, Gangaji stopped coming. There was no need to return. It was as though she had accomplished what she had set out to do.

For weeks, Kenny sought only solitude and silence. That was all he wanted—in fact, it was what he needed.

> I was a microfiche operator researching mechanical parts for federal prisons. If someone needed screws in one prison, I would check to see if I could find a prison that had that part. I could move five thousand bolts from Austin, Texas, or get three thousand feet of springs from Wisconsin.

> After that day with Gangaji, I would go into the dark microfiche room, but I did not turn on the light. The other inmates knew to leave me alone. They would not bug me. I would go in there, shut the door, and just sit there and be totally empty—witnessing, watching. All day.

Kenny had believed with his entire being that a mystical experience would save him. Then he sought out transformation; and then it happened. Kenny was basking in the afterglow of a major transcendental experience. He was uninterested in eating, talking, or engaging with others in any way. He wanted only silence and stillness so he could dwell in the experience of the new reality he had stepped into. He was wistfully detached from—yet intricately connected to—everything and everyone around him. There was no more seeking or yearning.

Something about being in Gangaji's physical presence, hearing her teachings, and meditating with her helped Kenny access a different realm of reality, self-understanding, love, and beauty. Kenny had spent a lifetime torn between extremes of being distressed and depressed and being on the run, being in full control and being completely out of control. In this sublime passage, he was one of the fortunate few in circumstances as extreme as his who, for whatever reason, had the opportunity to be exposed to something so great that closing down would never again be an option.

Radha's Transformative Experience: March 21, 1996

Radha was feeling strong. She was gaining momentum in her new job. She was applying all she had learned in her years of management—only now, there was no one with more status, power, ranking, or money standing in her way. She enjoyed spending time with her beloved partner, Gary, and their future seemed sweet and alive. It was during this time that Radha received horrifying news.

My son was murdered by his thirty-four-year-old college roommate in the kitchen of their school housing apartment, and my life was altered in one second. That transformation was completely against my will. It happened the moment I heard the news. Most people probably wouldn't talk about it that way, but that's what it was—an against-your-will transformation.

My life changed forever on that one day in March 1996. Before Christopher died, I was no stranger to grief. I had lost my mother, all four grandparents, two brothers, a sister, and dear friends. But this was very different. You don't ever practice for this kind of shock. There is nothing like losing your child.

One day my life was completely normal. I was making lunch for my brother Abram, who was visiting from New Jersey, and my best friend, Bettina, when the doorbell rang. I answered it, with my apron on, to an officer from the sheriff's department. He informed me that another officer needed to speak with me and I should call a number he handed me.

With the sheriff's officer looking over my shoulder, I phoned, and on the other end someone answered, "Coroner's office." I could barely speak. The voice informed me, that my son was dead, that he had been shot four times by his roommate during an argument about dishes.

Christopher was twenty-one years old. He had been studying heating and air conditioning at trade school. He had always been the kind of person who brought home all the kids no one else would talk to on the first day of school. He had brown hair and startling green eyes.

I had just seen Christopher a few days earlier. When he came to visit, I had stocked him up with enough food for the coming week. After we did his laundry together, he gave me a huge hug. "I love you, Mom," he said as he left, his green eyes sparkling. He was my only son.

Now Christopher was dead. My body rocked back and forth as I repeated, "Someone killed him." In those first fifteen minutes, I lost every liquid a body can lose.

The emotional impact was so much more physical than anything I had ever imagined. I felt like I had been run over by an eighteen-wheeler, but without visible bruises or breaks. You don't have any broken bones, but everything is broken. And the violence of Christopher's death made it more difficult.

I remember thinking that Christopher's chapter with our family was over. We wouldn't watch him graduate or get married, and I wouldn't be a grandmother to his children. Our photo albums would not be filled with him.

Then an earthquake of reality struck: I realized I had to share this shocking information. I needed to tell my family and friends. Abram, Bettina, and I started making phone calls. There were so many to make—to my brothers, sisters, father, ex-husband and his family, and so many friends.

After the calls, we waited together until my daughter, Christina, arrived home from college for a visit we'd already planned. I had decided that Gary would be the one to tell her. Her school was an hour away, and it seemed safer to get her home first. When she arrived, she got out of the car happily, because she was excited about seeing her uncle Abram.

But as soon as she saw my face, she knew something was very wrong.

"Christopher has been shot," Gary told her.

"What hospital is he in?" she asked.

It never occurred to me that she might assume Christopher was alive. When Gary told her Christopher had died immediately, she collapsed. We had to carry her into the house. Seeing my child in so much pain was the worst of my suffering to that point. As a parent, I wanted to kiss Christina, put a Band-Aid on her, and have everything be better. But I was in so much pain myself that it was hard for me to do anything. And this time, I knew nothing would help.

Though Radha is a woman of great strength and insight, she still thought, "How will I ever survive this?"

That evening, as I lay in bed alone, Christopher visited. He came from the corner of the room, like an angel. I could see his face and his body down to his waist. He reached out his hand to me, hovering above, and said, "I am fine, Mom." Then he sparkled away like a magic mist.

I wasn't surprised to see him. When I first learned of Christopher's death, I had a vision of him falling into my mother's arms. In the vision, my mother was with her best friend, Shirley. My mother had passed when I was young, and Shirley had passed recently. That night, I felt so grateful. Christopher's visit gave me a feeling of peace, and I was able to sleep.

The next morning, I awoke to waves of grief that rolled into me, body and soul, and engulfed me. They wouldn't let me come up for air. My skin was salty from my tears. My reality was so shaken that I felt unconnected. Before this happened to me, I wasn't aware how physical shock was. I always thought it was mental. I had to go outside to feel the cold, to sense where my body ended.

In this state of heartbreak and haze, I couldn't help but wonder if I could ever get over this unbelievable loss. As an overachiever, I felt pressure to figure out how I would rise above it. The woman I considered to be my mother in the absence of having my biological mother's support offered me the first bit of reprieve when she suggested, "Radha, you know that you don't have to get over this, ever." That was comforting ... and still is, to this day. I was relieved that people did not expect me to "get over" the death of my son. How can I ever get over him, if he is part of me?

Radha's life as she knew it had shattered into an irreparable wreckage. Powerless before her raw agony, Radha did what she does best: she met the moment with her full presence, and let go.

✳ ✳ ✳

Whether a transformative experience is freely chosen or forced upon you, whether it is traumatic or sublime, life as you know it has forever changed. Whether you have an uplifting life-changing event, as Kenny did, or a traumatic one, as Radha did, you have turned a major corner in the process of becoming whole. It may feel like the struggle has just begun, but if you pay attention to your feelings and examine your experiences, you can enter into the next phase, called Return, and head back toward the people and places you left behind.

6

PHASE 4: RETURN

Once you have flown, you will walk the earth with
your eyes turned skyward; for there you have been,
there you long to return.

—LEONARDO DA VINCI

Many life-changing events are short in duration, occurring over a span of just minutes: you witness a total solar eclipse while standing on the beach at the equator, gaze with veneration across the icy expanse of Mount Everest, or stand breathless at the altar with your new spouse ... and then the event is over. The Return phase begins after the transformative experience has finished and you are left standing, sitting, walking, or lying down where it happened: on a boat, in a stadium, in an empty conference room, on your living-room couch, on a muddy canyon floor, in a city-hall stairwell, in an airport terminal. You are likely to be in shock: "Did that really just happen?" Your world has changed forever, and you are in a state of suspended belief.

This phase is called Return because it constitutes your journey back—to your home or to your routine—after a transformative experience. The venture is often filled with ambiguity. You may notice conflicting feelings of wanting to return to your normal life and being apprehensive about having to explain what has happened to you.

If you have to wait a while before you arrive home or get back to your routine, you may sink deeper into the struggle of reconciling the life-changing event with your beliefs. The transformative experience may have put your understanding of yourself and of reality in question, because it exposed you to something outside the realm of what you thought was possible. You are in a disorienting dilemma; your ideas about how the world is supposed to work have been shaken. For example, if you went to Thailand and were deeply affected by its loving, simple, and abundant people, you may sense an inner heaviness fueled by inquiries such as, "Have I spent my whole life in deprivation?" and "How can I be surrounded by that much love every day, not just on vacation?"

The Return phase constitutes everything that happens between the time of the life-changing event and the day you go back to work or fully reenter your routine. During this phase, your customary activities are interrupted, significantly altered, or suspended altogether due to the event. For example, if your transformative experience was having your house burn down, the Return phase constitutes the period right after this horrendous misfortune, when you might take time off to grieve, make phone calls, rummage through the rubble, find a place to live, and handle insurance matters. You are dealing with the immediate and direct effects of the life-changing event on you and your life.

If your transformative experience is a positive one, as in the Thailand example, you can recognize that you have entered the Return phase as you start dreading the idea of going home, even if you can't do so for some time. If you had a transformative experience in the process of giving birth to your firstborn, the Return phase might begin halfway through your maternity leave when you catch yourself daydreaming about how to avoid returning to work. Such feelings of resistance illustrate the internal aspect of Return: the passage back to your core. The transformative experience expanded or shattered you outward, whereas the Return phase contracts you toward your center. The inward movement of Return is the beginning of your journey deeper and deeper into your interior, which will last for many phases.

During the Return phase, you remain in the subtly or intensely altered state of the transformative experience. You are no longer who you were, yet not who you will become. You may feel as though you are in a daze because you are still in the clutches of the life-changing event.

As you come closer to the end of this phase, you may have positive thoughts about going home or reentering your normal routine. The promise of familiarity can be comforting—surprisingly so if you don't have a happy home life, dislike your job, or both. If you endured a traumatic transformative experience, you may be eager to get back to life as usual, although you may not feel normal on the inside. The desire to share what happened to you with people who know you is common in this phase, even though you probably surmise that others will not understand you or the story of your life-changing event.

Kenny: Stuck on the Mountaintop

Kenny stayed in solitude and silence for nearly a year after his transformative event—twelve months of being uninterested in whatever was going on around him and being transfixed by what was going on inside of him. Mystical experience is profoundly altering and captivating, and the Return phase functions to help us to grapple with the immensity of integrating an experience we cannot comprehend.

> All my old friends fell away. I quit walking the yard with them. I was less interested in the external world and more interested in the internal world. Being in the silence was all I wanted.

> The inner world was more fascinating to me. I wasn't trying to figure anything out; I was simply meditating. Prison is a perfect place to have a spiritual awakening because all you have to do is follow orders and be quiet.

When the altered state wears away, we reenter the mundane world. Attempts to get the feeling back are futile, and you must admit that you have rejoined normal living. When this happens, you have completed the Return phase of transformation.

> The inmates started noticing me. They would say, "How come you are so peaceful?" and "Seems like you are at one with everything." I started to teach them about meditation and how to do it. I became available to help them. I talked, listened, helped them write letters to their girlfriends. After my experience of awakening, it seemed like I was more of a counselor, an advisor. It went on like this until I got paroled.

Gangaji had already helped set Kenny's heart, mind, and soul free; now his years of being physically imprisoned had given way to a new possibility. As the time for Kenny's release drew closer, he struggled with intense anticipation as he began his transition from the Return phase into the next phase, Displacement. He wanted desperately to be near his emancipator and teacher.

> I wanted to be closer to Gangaji. The feeling was so strong. I was scheduled to be released and go home. But the authorities from Iowa put a detainer on me, and I had to go to Iowa state prison for sixteen months. It was a messy moment. I had thought I was going home. I got depressed for a week or two.

Kenny transferred to Iowa to finish out his time. Something surprising happened there.

> It was really great in Iowa. I was really conscious of this quiet spaciousness. I was grateful to it.

> I was able to share my experience with the guys. It was like a honeymoon, you know—my meditation, my spiritual experience with Gangaji. These guys were so hungry. I was just having a great time.

> I was grateful, happy, and relieved. My stories gave them a way to occupy their time and gave them hope. There were very few guys who would talk the way I was talking. It was about transmitting awakening through conversation.

Kenny loved to be a teacher and guide. In Iowa, he may have been the happiest he had ever been. He was sharing something helpful, and he was finally doing something that felt right. But then, like many who have endured long-term incarceration, he anticipated his release with anxiety.

> The biggest depression happened when I realized I was going home. I was miserable. I was sad. I was scared as the day drew nearer. "This is terrifying," I thought.

> I had never felt freedom like this before. I was stepping into an unknown place, and I just didn't know what to expect. I became anxious and afraid, not knowing how I was going to survive out there.

Kenny had an unusually long Return phase. Being in jail buffered him from "reality"—an important bookend for this phase. He was free from the responsibilities of taking care of himself, maintaining a job, paying bills, and nurturing a family or relationship. Because he was confined behind bars, he could still tap into his mystical experience with Gangaji. If you have a life-changing event while on vacation, studying abroad, helping others on a religious mission, volunteering in the Peace Corps, or serving in the military, and you have not yet returned home, you have not completed the Return phase.

It is seductive to remain near the people and places associated with a positive life-changing event, because you want the experience to go on forever. For this reason, among others, Kenny had such an enjoyable experience in prison in Iowa. Even though he wasn't in Colorado, he was still in prison, an environment that enclosed his every move. In the familiarity and safety of prison walls and the social norms of incarceration, he could relive the magnificence of his transformative event.

Radha: Can This Possibly Be a Joke?

For the first three months after Christopher's death, Radha was in shock. The door to the life she had known was forever closed. This period was devastating, full of wrenching emotions and the practical steps that must be taken after a sudden death. She had to pick up Christopher's things from school, make funeral arrangements, and face people who had not yet heard the news.

> The first thing that really hit me strongly was that the situation was final. That was very hard, because children are supposed to take care of you when you grow old. A child's death is so out of the order of things.

> The violence of Christopher's death was very difficult for me. I found myself wishing that he had died in a car accident, from an illness, or due to something I could really comprehend. I don't understand murder or violence even to this day. I know it happens, but I don't understand how a person can get so mad they take a life.

> While I was not suicidal, I did feel like I had died. I said to myself, "I have so much to live for, my daughter and my family." It was a real conscious decision. I had seen people stop being there for others around them in similar situations. I felt I had a responsibility to be the best of who I was for my family and others. I said to myself that I was never going to abandon my family.

> I felt like I was living in a jar, separated from the rest of the world. I was an absolutely muddled, shocked, destroyed human being. Waves of grief, like huge, white horses galloping on the beach, trampled over me. It was constant, never farther away than my hand; it was just right there. We had Kleenex on every possible surface. There were so many tears. It was so, so, so hard.

Shock is the dominant experience of the Return phase for transformation through trauma, and it affected Radha on every level. Her physical distress acted as a buffer, protecting her from emotions she was not yet ready to feel. Whenever people enter the transformative cycle through trauma, the experience is so unexpected and incomprehensible that the psyche cannot absorb it. The posttransformative experience as described in the scholarly literature involves a pervasive, intense, immediate sensation of separation between you and all other humans, just as Radha describes with uncanny clarity. At times, she couldn't believe her son was really dead. She said, "April Fools' Day was shortly after Christopher's death, and I remember thinking, 'Can this possibly be a joke?'" even though she knew full well the horrifying facts told her otherwise. Disbelief like this follows a traumatic experience. Something inside shatters, and reality seems illusory.

> I was in a haze. Nothing seemed real, and everything was dulled. Even though I functioned fairly well, for a long time after Christopher's death my thinking was slow. I had this feeling of having a cover over me, like a shroud of sadness and shock. I would think, "I birthed somebody and then somebody else made a decision to take him away by violence." That horrifies me still.

Radha sought help and support immediately, which is commendable, because trauma can be immobilizing. She knew she could not survive this crisis on her own. In less than a month, she and Christina joined a support group for people grieving a death.

> Christina and I were the only ones in the Compassionate Friends group who were grieving death due to murder. We still are, and it's been twenty-three years. The group was a comforting place—even though it was really hard for me to go—because I didn't feel alone. People who were further along on the path were there to help me. I met some really nice folks, and I remember thinking at the time, "This is a lousy way to meet people."

Being with others who had survived the loss of a loved one took one kind of courage; walking out the front door to face the rest of the world took another kind of courage. Daily life was punctuated by moments that might previously have been ordinary but were now excruciating: seeing an advertisement that provoked a memory of Christopher, driving past his high school, or listening to the women at the beauty salon get all worked up over something insignificant. Triggers were everywhere, and going out in the world was easier said than done.

Most people do not want to talk to anyone during Return, as illustrated by Kenny's self-created isolation in the microfiche room and Radha's desire to stay at home.

When I went out in public for the first time, I just wanted to scream, "I am in so much pain—don't you know? Do you know how much pain I am in?" And of course, people don't know. It would take a really intuitive person to figure that out.

When your world is blown up, you notice more. I became hypersensitive to everything. I was so proud to go to the grocery store the first time after Christopher's death. I know the staff and the owner there. A tourist stopped me and asked, "Would you show me how to get to Muir Beach?" I watched him reach down into his deep bag, and internally, I freaked out. Inside I screamed, My God, what if he has a gun? I made my way through the conversation. I couldn't believe I was even having such a thought. Afterward, I promised myself, "I never want this to happen again—to be judgmental. I don't want to prejudice my future actions because my son was murdered with a gun."

For a while, I narrowed my circle of friends. It was just easier. People do not know what to say or do in these circumstances. Now when I am asked, "What should I say?" I tell people, "Say hello. The words will come."

When Christopher was murdered, people would ask, "How are you?" and I'd answer, "Fine." Despite my grief over losing Christopher, I often felt I had to take care of other people. The situation was too awful for them to think about. So, when someone wanted to know how I really felt, it was a relief that I didn't have to take care of them. I could respond fully. "This is really a nightmare. I miss Christopher, and it's unimaginable that he's not coming back."

Most people were afraid to mention Christopher, for fear of upsetting me. But if I wanted to talk, he was what I really wanted to talk about. Telling those stories brought Christopher back into the room.

Radha was consumed by the grief of losing her son and the knowledge that his final moments were so terrifying and gruesome. As she was comforted and supported by those who had experienced the type of pain she was enduring, she slowly began to feel the ground beneath her feet.

❋ ❋ ❋

As the Return phase comes to an end, there are few certainties. You are out of danger or bliss. You have left the environment that was extremely stressful or heavenly. You sense that you have irreversibly turned a corner. You move toward the next phase, Displacement, in which you will reenter the existence you had before your life-changing experience.

7

PHASE 5: DISPLACEMENT— RELIEF AND UPHEAVAL

Home is the place you grow up wanting to leave, and grow old wanting to get back to.

—JOHN ED PEARCE

If your return home after a transformative experience is literal, the Displacement phase commences when you arrive at your front door, turn the handle, and go inside. For example, you may be returning from volunteering at the cleanup for a natural disaster, undergoing cosmetic surgery in Argentina, or working your first day in a new career.

If your return is more symbolic, Displacement begins after the people in your life know about your life-changing event, the business matters related to it have been addressed, and you face life again. You must also feel reasonably certain that you are going to be physically okay. For example, if you and your partner have a disastrous argument and you need to move out, Displacement begins when you have secured at least a semi-permanent place to live.

Displacement is a clear demarcation between the upward aspect of the figure eight that involves transformative experience and the downward processes of integration. The initial impact of the transformative event is over, and in this brief period of time, you have a moment to catch your breath, gather your wits about you, talk with your closest friends, and maybe rest.

Displacement is one of the shorter phases on the Map to Wholeness. Don't be surprised if the whole thing lasts about two weeks. Displacement literally means that you are out of place. You are not really "here" (because you are still focused on the past), and you are no longer "there" (because your transformative experience is over). Even though I used similar language to describe the liminal state, there is an important distinction. The liminal state is essentially a mystical experience, whereas Displacement is hard reality.

Relief

There are two major aspects of Displacement: relief and upheaval. Relief can be described as a honeymoon of sorts. You are elated to have returned to the comforts of home. You can sleep in your own bed and eat your favorite foods. Familiar sights, sounds, and smells help your body, mind, and spirit relax. When you are in this state, your annoying neighbor or your children's messy bathroom might amuse you or even be oddly soothing.

If you cannot return to your former home, relief begins with attempts to make a home for yourself by surrounding yourself with objects, music, foods, or a routine that helps you feel comfort or familiarity. For those who are already living at home when the Return phase ends, the relief comes when you attempt to reinstate some sense of normality, try doing chores, address a long-time obligation that has been shelved, or reach out to a close friend or community.

If you are undergoing transformation through trauma, relief means you are safe. You may sense some shock if, during the previous phase, you were not sure you would be able to return home. Disclosing your story tends to offer release even as it also engenders intense feelings of vulnerability.

To summarize, in the context of the Displacement phase, relief can take the form of delight at coming home, the feeling of being in a comfortable and familiar environment, a sense of physical safety, and the psychological freedom of sharing what happened to you.

Upheaval

The second aspect of Displacement is upheaval, a disruption that ranges in intensity from inconvenient and unpleasant to deeply distressing. Upheaval in this phase is an incident that happens seemingly out of the blue that tends to affect survival. It may relate to money or to your home, body, job, or primary relationship. Upheaval can happen at any time during Displacement and is proportionate to the magnitude of your life-changing event: the bigger your life-changing event, the more noticeable the upheaval.

A minor upheaval might be getting new job responsibilities, receiving an unexpected bill that forces you to dip into your savings, or having a virus wipe out your hard drive. At the other end of the spectrum, a major upheaval can be an awful event. For instance, upon returning to the United States from one of my study-abroad courses, many of my students called family members from the airport while walking in the terminal and waiting for their luggage. One student learned that his grandfather had died, another was told that her sister had been assaulted by a family member, and a third found out that her landlord had sold her apartment and was giving her one month to move out. We hadn't even left the airport, and many students had already experienced upheaval.

In a more recent example, my partner returned home after living elsewhere for three months following a bone marrow transplant. Within the first two weeks, one day while she was alone in the house, she had a painful drug reaction that was so severe she thought she was going to die.

If you are lucky, however, you may have an upheaval that triggers *positive* stress. Some students from the same study-abroad course experienced major turns of good fortune, including getting a new job, receiving a promotion, and securing a new place to live. There doesn't seem to be a pattern explaining why a person experiences a positive upheaval versus a negative one; just hope that the next time you are in this phase, it is gentle on you.

Kenny: The Honeymoon Is Over

Kenny walked out of prison a free man for the first time in more than a decade. Equipped with the knowledge he had accessed during his peak experience, he returned to his family ready to live according to his new reality. Unfortunately, freedom required more than not being behind bars.

> I moved to Kansas to be near my mother, daughter, nieces, and nephews. Everything was smooth. It was like a honeymoon in a sense. Being out, being with my family, being just normal ... I was meeting people and going places.

> But that wore off. They didn't really know what to make of me. I wasn't stealing or robbing like I normally did, so they were curious to know what happened to me. In the past I would come home for a day or two and then I would leave again, get out on the streets, and start robbing. I was going to church and everything. They didn't understand; especially my mother. Unlike normal, I was hanging out with the grandkids and looking for a job.

> And I was okay. I knew I didn't want to do those things, my old ways. They would say, "What's going on? What happened to you?" I tried to explain my spiritual experience, what was inside of me, about meditation. But it didn't go over too well. They didn't understand. They really didn't. I quit trying to explain after a while.

Like a cold glass of water on a blistering hot day, being reunited with family, friends, and familiar places quenched Kenny's thirst to be home. He had been away for a very long time, and the reunion was joyful. But reconnecting with his daughter caused upheaval.

When I got out of prison I stayed with my daughter, her husband, and their kids. I didn't know my daughter as a woman until I got out of prison and moved into her house. Immediately, she knew something had happened. I wasn't in the streets, wasn't with my hustling buddies. She was curious and interested and said to my mother, "He's hanging around the house. What's going on?"

She was very affectionate with me. I wasn't raised with affection, so I thought it was abnormal for her to adore me all the time. When she wasn't affectionate, she was pissed at me and tried to run my life, even to the extent of not wanting me to have any women friends. It was really embarrassing. My daughter and I squared off in opposite corners.

It came to a head about a month after I was paroled. I was out with a woman, and I came home about 2 a.m.—and there she was, standing at the door like a mother. She said, "You have been with another woman!"

"Yes, so, what is wrong?"

She cursed me out. I was up all night. The next day, I moved in with my mother. But her controlling behavior kept getting worse when I had a girlfriend. I couldn't be around that energy. I was confused.

Kenny's daughter had been deprived of her father's presence for most of her life because he had spent so much time behind bars. Now that he was a free man, she was eager to finally get the attention and affection she did not receive from him for all those years, so it was understandable that she wanted him all to herself. In her mind, the care he was giving to other women rightfully belonged to her, and she was angry about not receiving it.

Kenny was stunned and bewildered. He hadn't expected his daughter to act in such a controlling way. Even though he didn't really want to move in with his mother, he was grateful to have another housing option because he couldn't take the turmoil caused by his daughter's demands and emotional reactivity.

Even though Kenny was accustomed to navigating life in prison, coming home always gave him great reprieve from the stressors of survival. Because of his transformative experience, his return home this time was not only filled with liberation; it brought unexpected problems with his daughter.

Radha: Getting My Feeling Back

About three months after Christopher's death, Radha noticed a distinct shift in her body, thoughts, and feelings. Her initial shock had formed a padding that protected her from intense pain. This padding was so dense that when it came off, she couldn't help but note the change.

> I experienced a real demarcation. It happened one day when I was at home. I felt a lifting of the shock. It was obvious to me. I felt when the cloud lifted. I thought it would feel like the heaviness was being lifted off my shoulders, but it actually came off my whole being. It gently floated away in one moment. It was almost as if it went up into the clouds.

> I was really grateful that the shock lifted. This was an important moment. I was getting my emotions back; I was healing and feeling the sensations in my body. I was becoming a full-feeling person again. I imagine it would be like if you had bad eyes and all of a sudden got glasses. Things are a little bit sharper and brighter; you can navigate a little easier.

I would like to take a moment to differentiate among the kinds of shock that occur on the journey to wholeness. The shock that happens during the Return phase, after a traumatic life-changing experience, occurs in your body, as Radha describes. It has dual qualities because shock can be debilitating but also life-preserving. It acts as a powerful buffer, allowing you to deal with the body's perceived threat and to take action that requires great mental, physical, or emotional strength. The body goes into survival mode. When Radha was informed of Christopher's death, her body was overtaken by shock, because the news was too big and disturbing to assimilate.

In contrast, the shock that occurs during Displacement and the following phases is psychological. It does not originate in your body. When the grip of physical shock releases, your body moves out of a state of survival and into ordinary living. Shock that occurs during Displacement happens when you reenter a familiar environment and it is difficult to believe that you have returned.

When Radha's physical shock lifted, she transitioned into Displacement and regained the "home" of her body, demonstrating that after a transformative event, you might not be returning to a *physical* home. In fact, Radha had been at home almost exclusively since she answered the door to the sheriff's officer.

After Radha returned to her body, she was "really grateful" that her shock had lifted. That's an expression of relief—one of the two main characteristics of Displacement—which arises from the joy you experience when you return home. Accordingly, Radha was happy to be home in her body again. Note that Radha's physical shock disappeared when or because she started to *feel* again.

Her example illustrates that you cannot return home to your body and be able to feel a range of emotions if you are in a state of physical shock. Radha had been able to feel anger and sadness, but she had lost access to a host of emotions that are normally available to us. Think of people who have endured childhood or domestic abuse, military combat, or life on the streets. Their spirits probably left their bodies during their traumatic experiences, inducing a state of shock that protected them from feeling the full horror of their situations.

Radha's experience of upheaval—the other main characteristic of this phase—was unlike any other I've heard described. Upheaval is typically an experience that takes you by surprise, but in Radha's case it was a planned experience amid turmoil. Many months prior to Christopher's death, Radha and Gary had made plans and booked flights to travel to Europe. It just so happened that the date of their planned travel was only two months after his death. Radha had this to say about what transpired:

When tragedy strikes, you crave normal. Normal for us was two big trips a year. I was conflicted about going because of the legal side of things but decided it was best to go ahead with plans. A lawyer friend told me, "Don't let this man take any more from you. Don't not go on vacation. Live." Others I trust told me to do normal things, so we decided to go.

During the last part of the trip we were supposed to visit a longtime friend and colleague from my previous career. We had a big joyous reunion planned. I had to call and tell him, "We are still coming, but Christopher has been killed." It was the first time that I was going to be around people who didn't know me very well. They understood that I would not be social in the ways I normally would be and that I might take a nap or something like that if I needed to take care of myself.

We went abroad for a month. First, we went to England and did some hiking, and then we went on a long boat trip before visiting my friend in France.

Radha's upheaval consisted of being forced (by virtue of having already made plans and bought plane tickets) to go on vacation so soon after losing her son. The profound juxtaposition between her loss and embarking upon what is supposed to be a joyous activity—international travel and visiting with a friend along the way—made the act of leaving an odd if not dreadful experience. The fact that an experience that was supposed to be filled with fun, playfulness, joy, and anticipation was shrouded in a context of profound pain and suffering was a great upheaval.

Nine months after Christopher's death, Radha and her family had to face their first holiday season without him. Even though Radha's family is Jewish, they had always celebrated both Christmas and Hanukkah because Christopher and Christina loved both holidays. It seemed as if it would be impossible to go through those weeks without him. At the same time, the holiday season inspired in Radha a deep appreciation for all the support she had received from others since her son's death.

Not long after Christopher died, Radha "made a conscious decision to live with this tragedy in the most graceful way possible." In dedication to this vow, Radha decided to write her first holiday letter ever. "I felt people had been so kind to support and love us through such tragedy that I needed to let them know what was going on in our lives," she said. The first two paragraphs of the letter speak volumes about Radha's spirit and consciousness despite feeling displaced in her own life.

Dearest friends and family,

My first wish is to thank you all for being there for us in what has been a very difficult year. The loss of Christopher has changed our lives forever. I also feel that the love of my friends and family during this hard time has changed my life forever in a very wonderful way. It is a difficult way to find out what a loved person you are. I have never written a holiday letter before. I wanted to write each one of you to catch up on what has been happening in our lives.

First ... all the good news. We are all healthy and happy (working on happier!). We have many pleasant moments mixed with some sad, but we are very positive about life. It seems like grief is three steps ahead, one back.

For Radha, writing the letter was an attempt to do something normal. It was a communication to all those she loved that said, "I am okay. I survived. I love you." It was an attempt to assure herself, and everyone else, "I am still capable me."

During this phase, Radha came home to herself. Having successfully reentered her life, she was eager to move forward. But moving forward doesn't necessarily mean moving toward brighter days. The organic process of transformation requires facing new challenges.

※ ※ ※

The transition between this phase and the next occurs when you have dealt with the destabilization of your basic needs and the period of harmony associated with your return ends. You will now experience what it is like to be you after your life-changing experience. Unfortunately, doing so is laden with grief and denial.

8

PHASE 6:
GRIEF AND DENIAL

I shall be left with the inconsolable memory of the treasure
I went into the forest to find.

—T. S. ELIOT

Once the upheaval of Displacement and honeymoon of your return is over, the Grief and Denial phase begins. You must begin dealing with the fact that your life has been deeply affected. Whether your life-changing event was inspiring or painful, you endured a situation that was not ordinary. The indelible experience continues to cast a shadow across your existence.

The Grief and Denial phase has a distinct psychological basis. The transformative experience, whether positive or negative, created a sense of loss; in essence, you left behind part of your old self in your journey toward your new self. You now long to return to the ecstasy of your peak experience or to your life before the traumatic event. Grief—keen mental suffering or sharp sorrow—arises as a natural response to your losses and to your inability to recapture what is gone. Denial—refusal to embrace your current situation—kicks in as a way to manage the grief. It is emotionally overwhelming to completely accept that you experienced a life-changing event, so you would rather pretend your life is different from what it is. The journey to embrace your experience is the process of integration, and the state of full Integration in the thirteenth phase is where you are headed.

Longing

In the Grief and Denial phase, you are gripped by an inescapable longing to return to something, someplace, or someone in another time and space. If your transformative experience happened locally and was positive, you will probably visit the spot where it happened or spend a great deal of time with an individual who was with you. For example, if your life-changing event involved seeing a whale while kayaking, you are likely to go kayaking again in hopes of repeating your luck.

If your life-changing experience happened far from home, trying to recreate and relive it can be more challenging. You may do things you did during the transformative event, such as listening to certain music, eating specific foods, engaging in similiar activities, wearing the same clothes, or carrying the same objects. You may also participate in routines that help take you back to that experience. For example, you may spend time outdoors like you did when you were "there," or make coffee just like "they" did.

If you had a peak experience in a group setting, you may want to host a reunion in order to share stories, photos, and a sense of camaraderie and community. If you were alone in your transformative event, you may seek the support of those around you, hang a large picture at home or at work representing the experience, or share relevant photos with friends and family.

Grief and Loss

After a transformative event, something is gone that you can never experience again. If your transformative event was positive, you are likely to be grieving the loss of beauty, love, connection, health, joy, grace, or ease.

If you survived a painful event, you may be mourning the loss of people, places, possessions, or a lifestyle. The difference between the grief during the Return phase and the grief you experience in the Grief and Denial phase is that the former is an initial reaction to loss ("I lost my job!"), whereas the latter is what you feel when the meaning and implications of this loss sink in more deeply ("I am so sad that I lost my job. Am I going to find another one?").

Ironically, it doesn't matter whether you experienced a peak event or a crisis: when your life changes irrevocably, the outdated self that is being reconstructed into a new you is gone, which is the deepest of losses. The transformative experience exposes you to a new reality about what is possible, which you must now incorporate into your understanding of your world and yourself. Think of a curtain rising in a theatrical production to reveal an entirely new scene. The world you were accustomed to no longer exists, and the angst that comes from not being able to go back in time to reenter that world contributes to your grief.

You may look fine on the outside, but when you lose a part of yourself, it is normal to feel somber and dazed. You may also feel devitalized, like a sack of potatoes. The memory of your life-changing experience is still vivid and emotional. Life seems surreal. Most people attempt to mitigate these painful feelings with tried-and-true coping techniques such as prayer, volunteering, work, support groups, physical exercise, hobbies, or recreation. Activities such as these mean the difference between suffering and getting by.

If you are particularly sensitive or emotional, the sadness may permeate your existence, affecting your ability to concentrate, communicate, eat, sleep, work, and engage with others. Sorrow tends to come in unexpected waves that can be all-consuming. During this period, you may vacillate between wanting to be alone and wanting to be with others who can relate to your transformative experience. Most importantly, keep in mind that what you are experiencing is normal. Transformation is as natural a process as the sun's rising and setting. If you are very sad, look ahead on the Map to Wholeness and remember that you are going somewhere—and the place where you are going is brilliant.

Denial

Denial offers you escape from your intense, enveloping grief. In fact, the fundamental theme of this phase is a rejection that says either "I refuse to believe the experience is over" (in the case of a peak transformative event) or "I cannot believe this happened to me" (in the case of a traumatic transformative event).

Experiencing grief can feel like having a natural disaster going on inside of you. Denying your grief by throwing yourself into your job, children, or community can be very therapeutic. You may make rapid, drastic adjustments to regain a temporary sense of balance, as if you are a boat whose sail has dipped dangerously close to the water's surface. Some people quit their job, sell old possessions, adopt a dog, or change their relationship status.

If you had a traumatic transformative experience—for example, you lost your wife to cancer—the episode is still too fresh and difficult to incorporate into your reality. Denial in this case means that a part of you believes the event never happened. Rejecting the truth temporarily protects you from painful sensations, memories, and feelings. It is remarkably comforting to imagine life the way it used to be as much as possible.

If your crisis involved sudden and abrupt news—as happened with one person I interviewed who told of receiving a phone call informing her that her mother had committed suicide—it is not uncommon to carry on as if nothing has happened. An ocean of grief may lie beneath the surface, but denial helps you keep your bearings as you process the overwhelming event. It is sometimes best to let the pain hide deep within you until you can deal with it at some time in the future.

Kenny: It's Okay to Be Sad

Kenny was a free man, but he was still imprisoned by his old thoughts and behaviors, and by a network of people who could see him only as he once was. His past was a challenge to his efforts to remain free from a life of crime. Fortunately, he landed a job with a hotel chain, with the help of a pen pal he had met through Gangaji.

> I had been out of prison for four months. At work, I was hanging out with people who were hustlers. My boss, who had been my pen pal, saw this and was concerned. I knew I was fine, though. I had no choice; I had to hang out with somebody, and my coworkers were around me. I was growing, and I was very aware, very clear. I wouldn't get caught up in the game.

> My boss knew I hadn't seen Gangaji since prison, which had been several years. "You better go see Gangaji," he said.

> So he bought me a ticket. Looking back, I am grateful that he did. I may not have seen her on my own, because I didn't have the skills, the way of thinking that said seeing her was even an option. I just thought, "I have to survive." I never learned to think about helping myself by going to retreats, intensives, or anything like that before.

> But my boss did. He would go online to see what was going on, where Gangaji was, and check out the opportunities available to see her. I didn't even know to do that. I was doing what I knew: existing.

Even though a life-changing event alters your internal world, you return to the external world with the same skill set and limitations you had before. For example, Kenny's remark "I wouldn't get caught up in the game" was not necessarily a function of wishful thinking or even determination to have a better life. This type of comment is a natural response to feeling transformed on the inside. Kenny was genuinely certain he could overcome the odds, when in fact he was not yet transformed. A life-changing experience instills a feeling of transformation that is so compelling, you become certain that you are different and that important people around you can see this about you. The problem is that because you have not completed all thirteen phases, your abilities to act and think are still just as they were before the life-changing event. Kenny revealed this fact when he said, "I was doing what I knew: existing."

New realms of possibility had opened up to Kenny, but living out new truths would be his journey for years to come. He still had not developed the basic skill of knowing he needed help, let alone knowing what kind of help he needed and how to obtain it. Fortunately, his boss's help came at the right time. Kenny needed to know there were types of people besides hustlers—spiritual people—with whom he could be friends and spend time.

I flew out to Boulder, Colorado, for a weekend intensive. My friend Suta picked me up from the airport, and we met another guy. She drove us to the meditation hall. All sorts of people were there. It was the first time I had been in the satsang with them. Then Gangaji came in.

It was nice being out and being free, meeting people, being recognized. It was overwhelming, in a good way. And there were so many people—wow.

I had a great time and hung out with the others. I met a lot of folks who had heard about me through Gangaji's writings and who wanted to meet me. Over the years, she would write about the letters I wrote her once a week from prison.

I gave a talk and an interview. People wanted to shake my hand, hug me, talk to me, and ask me questions.

I was happy. It was probably one of the happiest moments of my life. I was really able to connect. It was like a homecoming or something—like meeting my real family.

If you had a positive life-changing event, as Kenny did, the source of emotional strife during this phase is your unquenched desire to be near the people, animals, places, sounds, smells, and even foods associated with your transformative experience. You will desperately want to "go back." If you cannot take the opportunity to satisfy some of this desire by engaging in activities such as looking at pictures or talking with those affiliated with the event, your movement through this phase will be much more difficult. Not only is it is deeply soothing to spend time around people who appreciate your transformative experience; you can also begin to accept and assimilate what happened to you and who you are becoming.

This is why, upon returning to his hotel job, Kenny could not stand the discomfort of being away from Gangaji and his newly adopted spiritual community. He felt this discomfort so strongly, it was as though his very survival required connecting with them.

After I got back from the retreat, it became clear: I wanted to be closer to the sangha, the community. So I asked my parole officer, and he said yes, that I could move. I started to save money.

With few possessions and no one holding him back, Kenny hastily moved to Colorado. Upon arriving, he eagerly got involved in meditations and events. But moving closer to his spiritual community was not a cure-all.

I got really depressed. My depression was about realizing that living straight was way more terrifying than surviving on the streets. I had never really tried living a clean life before. My depression was pure fear. I understood how things worked in prison. I knew how to survive. I even knew how to save myself if someone wanted to kill me. I had confidence that there was some way out.

But out here, in regular life, how are you going to make a living when the only thing you've ever done is hustle?

The slump into sadness during this phase is inevitable. If you are not accustomed to experiencing grief, it is easy to be confused by these feelings. Kenny's interpretation of the grief as being fear was a way of coping. Even though he was genuinely afraid of not knowing how to survive without crime, it was easier to focus on fear than sadness.

Everyone in the community told Gangaji I was depressed. She and I talked, and she said, "Kenny, I see that you are depressed. It's okay to be sad. It's okay to be depressed." She just acknowledged my sadness, and it went away. Ever since then, I can acknowledge it. When I am sad, I let myself be sad, and when I am depressed, I am depressed—and it's okay.

This inner shift gave Kenny momentum, and he landed a job waiting tables. He began hanging out with friends from his spiritual community again, met a girlfriend, and started to make a life for himself. Just as life was beginning to settle, a big change came upon him: Gangaji and her foundation decided to move their headquarters to the East Coast.

Even though Kenny was developing a sense of stability, he was still extremely vulnerable. Fortunately, he had a network of people who looked out for him, as well as many who were eager to meet him and to be inspired by his story. At this time a small group of Gangaji followers invited Kenny to speak at a retreat in Pasadena, California, which was a welcome diversion from the news about Gangaji's relocation.

> When I arrived at the retreat in Pasadena, many had already heard about me. They sponsored me to do teachings, satsangs in their homes. I really enjoyed it, and they did, too. Word got out, and some people in the Berkeley area decided to start organizing small gatherings, too, so I went up there to join in. When I went back to Boulder, I was on a satsang high.

> People were falling in love with me. "He is talking nondual," they would say. "He is coming from a different angle." "He is a preacher." "Wow!"

> When I came back in April 1999, I came back as a teacher.

With the Gangaji Foundation's move, Kenny felt few ties to Colorado, and after his visit out west, he felt California was calling. Many people in California encouraged him to move there. In particular, a woman named Inga who was part of the spiritual community in San Francisco was cheering him on. She told him, "Come out to California! You can live with me. I have a massage practice, and you can do satsangs." Kenny needed to survive, and doing so meant being near his spiritual community. He got clearance from his parole officer to transfer to a different geographical jurisdiction. A month later, he moved.

There are many ways to perceive Kenny's motivations and actions. Even though Kenny had some positive experiences during this phase, the underlying tone was one of Grief and Denial. Naturally, Kenny did not want the elation of his divine awakening to be over. On the surface, Kenny's need to be close to his community was an attempt to get the feeling back by telling his story and being around others who had a similar yearning to transcend ordinary states. Reliving the experience is an important way to cope with the natural reaction to having to face mundane reality after a transformative experience.

On a level beneath Kenny's awareness, his relocations were also motivated by his need to survive. Because he had spent most of his adult life in prison, he was still at risk of returning to crime. Like the prison walls that had preceded this period in his life, he now needed the structure of regular satsangs and the built-in support crew that came with the gatherings. It was simple: he would go wherever they would go.

There is yet another, deeper perspective of denial that is worth mentioning. Kenny assumed that because he'd had a spiritual awakening, he was destined to be an up-and-coming guru. Thus, of course he needed to be wherever the community was located. The logic behind this reasoning is that transformative experiences result in a *feeling* and *belief* that you have transformed, when in fact you have not. When this happens you deny your incapacities—specifically the fact that you don't yet have the capacity to be the self you accessed during the life-changing experience.

Radha: Working for Justice

As Radha succinctly put it, "There was no denial. Christopher was dead, and I knew it." Denial doesn't necessarily mean that you don't believe something has happened. More often, it is a subtle sense of disbelief that surfaces when you least expect it: when you awaken in the middle of the night, turn down a certain street, or look into someone's eyes. With her intense shock in the past, Radha experienced denial in connection with her lingering sadness: "I can't believe he is gone." "How did this really happen?" "What happened to my life?"

During the first two years after Christopher's death, Radha and her family and friends awaited the trial of his killer, Mark Taylor. Meanwhile, Mark's family had posted his bail. Knowing that Mark was walking around free added to Radha's feelings of unfairness, because no amount of money could allow her son to walk the earth again. This angst is one way in which Radha's normal feelings of denial manifested. To her it seemed infathomable not only that he had died but that he had been taken through unspeakable violence.

> For two years, the trial felt like a huge job looming on the horizon. It was unbelievable to be a grieving human being and also to have to deal with the waiting. The trial was on and off, on and off, on and off. We would hear, "The trial has been pushed up a month," and then, "It's delayed again." The unknown sucks.

Even though the repeated postponements were enormously exasperating, the wait did Radha some good. It gave her time to continue to work through the awful reality that Christopher had died in the way that he had. Grasping to comprehend this truth, inside she cried out for some sense of justice or remorse: "What is Mark's mother going through? Does she think about me? Does she think about Christopher?" This period served as a buffer of sorts, allowing Radha's grief to trickle through her rather than engulf her. Grief of this magnitude can be digested only so quickly, and the seemingly interminable waiting gave her the space and time needed for this phase of her process.

While the trial date was in limbo, Radha needed to do something to deal with the vastness of her grief, so she began volunteering for a group now called Gifford's Law Center. It provided a way to take action when so much in her life was out of her control.

> I did whatever I felt I needed to do to slowly make it, and working for prevention seemed to be the right fit. Had a gun not been involved, Christopher would not have been dead. I had always believed in gun control, but I'd never done more about it than vote. After Christopher was killed, I thought, "Something should be done about this. If I can save one other parent from going through the trauma that we have been through as a family, it will be enough." So I threw myself into gun-control work in an effort to be of service. I worked tirelessly for six years.

Engaging in activities that allow them to be an active part of a remedy for what harmed them has been an effective way for survivors of trauma to cope.

About two and a half years after Christopher was murdered, Radha's wait ended. Mark Taylor was about to face justice. Radha's friends, family, and extended network were poised as a solid front of unwavering support, which she absolutely needed. "I knew this would be the biggest job of my life: to defend my son, who is not here."

Finally, we had the trial—a five-week, slow-motion nightmare. The trial just happened to take place during the worst mass-transit strike in the history of this area, which made our days that much more grueling.

Because it was a crime, I was thrown into another new world—a legal mess that I had to be present for on behalf of my son. A trial is everything you don't want to know about a murder. There is no emotion in it; it is all factual, and that's hard when you are a hurting and grieving person. At least we had the perpetrator, but it was unnerving because we didn't know what the sentence would be. I was afraid that some technical problem would happen and he would get off. Manslaughter would not have been okay with me, because it was murder. Manslaughter is not a deliberate act. There was no question about it: Christopher's death was not an accident.

After the trial, Radha had to wait again; it took six long weeks of more waiting to learn Mark's fate. In the end, he was convicted of second-degree murder and sentenced to nineteen years to life.

Given the laws that were in place at the time, I was satisfied. The sentence made me feel wonderful about the jury and the trial system, even though you can never be satisfied with anything that has to do with the taking of a life. When it was over, I remember taking a deep breath and saying, "Okay, that big, huge thing is over. Now here we go, starting on life again."

Radha had survived the biggest ordeal of her life: her son's heinous murder and his killer's trial. Once justice was served, Radha could finally begin to move on—exactly what happens when you transition from Grief and Denial to the next phase, Disorientation. The drama of Radha's life-changing event was over, and she had to face her life in the reality of

Christopher's permanent absence. Due to the magnitude of the trauma she endured, she would find more questions than answers.

✳ ✳ ✳

Whether a life-changing event is positive or negative, the aftermath always involves suffering, because we experience the absence of something we once had. However, grief can be overwhelming, so our psyche offers us relief through denial, even for those among us who are adept at personal growth. It is perfectly healthy during this phase to shield yourself by pretending your loss doesn't exist, as long as you allow yourself to dip into periods of sadness or engage in a pursuit that allows you to digest your grief over time. If you can tolerate uncomfortable feelings when they arise, you can help yourself see more clearly in the next phase, Disorientation.

9

PHASE 7: DISORIENTATION

I haven't a clue as to how my story will end. But that's all right. When you set out on a journey and night covers the road, you don't conclude the road has vanished.

—NANCY WILLARD

Denial eventually becomes impractical. You realize that if you continue to keep aspects of your existence on hold or unacknowledged, there will be significant consequences. You must face your life—and more importantly, yourself. You can no longer pretend that your situation could be different. As denial gives way to sober reality, you question yourself and your circumstances: "What happened to me?" "Who am I?" "What do I do now?" "Why me?" "Why do I have to be stuck here?" "Why now?" This loss of perception of personal identity is called disorientation.

In an effort to gain stability and clarity, you may initiate actions to take control over your health and well-being, such as cooking at home instead of going out to restaurants, exercising more and being on your computer less, maximizing time with supportive friends and minimizing time with draining ones. As you begin to implement such changes, your progress is likely to be irregular. "Relapses" toward less positive ways are counterbalanced by instances in which you meet your new goals. You experience an inner tug-of-war between the less healthy self you were *before* your transformative event and the healthier self you are *becoming*.

In the Disorientation phase, you fully enter your life, which triggers an internal pushback. You may look the same as you've always looked and do the same activities you've always done, but on the inside, you feel like a different person. It's important to remember that on the Map to Wholeness, *feeling* like a different person and *being* a different person are not the same thing. Feeling as if you have transformed when you haven't is the core reason for disorientation. In this condition, it is easy to become frustrated with what seems to be wrong with your external world: your salary or employer, traffic, the economy, the government. But your lack of harmony with your surroundings actually stems from the incongruity between the old you and the new you.

Exacerbating your frustration, the routines, behaviors, and activities of people around you have remained the same. In other words, the world has not changed just because *you* have. One woman I interviewed whose son was murdered while working abroad said, "I just wanted to scream at strangers in the grocery store, 'Don't you know how much pain I am in?'" Interestingly, Radha spoke nearly the same words shortly after her son's death. But you need not experience the trauma of murder in order to feel this way.

The contrast between your inner and outer worlds may leave you feeling as though you no longer fit in with your coworkers, circle of friends, household, town, state, country, or all of the above. The transformative experience itself plays a role in this angst. For instance, if your life-changing event took place in a community in the Netherlands where people spent the day talking, eating, socializing, and being outdoors, you might become preoccupied with the differences between that culture and yours. You might lament, "Why do we spend so much time in front of screens?" If your transformative experience involved the loss of a loved one, you might complain, "Why is it the norm to work so hard that we don't have time to spend with family and friends and to play?" Life-changing events elevate an associated belief or value to the highest level of importance. During Disorientation, you desire to incorporate such values into your life, but this process necessitates adjustments that may be difficult.

When I meet people who are in this phase, I can see that they have what they need to get by, as well as friends and perhaps a romantic partner. They are content but not thoroughly fulfilled. Due to various circumstances, they have had to settle for less than they want. Once we get past their surface troubles, the core of their dissatisfaction becomes clear: Their life does not reflect their true desire. They say things like, "I want to quit my job and become a schoolteacher." "I want to have a simpler life and move to Arizona." "I want a career that allows me to be more creative." "I want to find a wife and settle down."

Knowing what you want is fantastic—if you believe that achieving it is possible. But when you are in the Disorientation phase, a canyon seems to lie between you and what you desire. For example, the job that would bring you joy is lower-paying than your current job, and you would have to sell half of your possessions and move out of your comfortable home in order to take it. Barriers such as money, location, gender, age, socio-economic status, and education may make it difficult to have what you want, even if you are passionate and ingenious about attaining it. In these circumstances, you may feel stuck in mediocrity or even depressed.

During Disorientation, it is important to resist the urge to deny your feelings so you can move forward by giving yourself permission to feel all of your emotions and by accepting each one as valid and important. Trust that you can reach your dream on the other side of the canyon by following the meandering path to wholeness.

Kenny: No Angel

Kenny needed a place to call home. Even though he loved his family, they didn't understand him; more importantly, they didn't share his spiritual

beliefs or lifestyle. Like all of us, he needed to be surrounded by supportive people who appreciated his true essence. In his attempt to continue
to survive outside of prison, he packed his bags and headed to California.

> I had $200 in my pocket and a 1988 Volvo. Inga and I weren't together
> romantically when I moved in with her, but within a few months, we were
> married. She became everything to me.

Somewhere along the way Kenny adopted a formula for how to survive
after prison: get married, settle down, and make a life for yourself. He
simply did what he thought he was supposed to do. It didn't help that
because of spending so much of his life behind bars, he had probably
missed out on some mentorship around impulsivity. It is also quite possible that his mode was to seek safety by coupling with a woman. So,
although this could appear to be an impulsive move indicative of the
Grief and Denial phase, his action was motivated by survival.

> Meanwhile, I had speaking engagements and satsangs booked out for at least
> seven to eight months. I was a teacher. People would see me in a group or hear
> about me. "That's Kenny!" they would say. "That's the guy!"

Kenny's awakening was made public and he was now seeing the practical results of his transformative experience. It seemed as though he was
rising to a position of personal power and finally getting to do what he
loved. Despite his increasing visibility as a teacher, however, his personal
life began to slip out of control.

> Here I am, the teacher, and people are loving me, and I return home to a wife
> who is throwing shoes at me.

> She was becoming jealous of the women. I was seeing so many people; they
> would come over to the house and call me, and I would hang out with them. I
> was oblivious to what I was doing. I thought I was just talking, not flirting. I
> didn't realize that women were becoming attracted to me, and I didn't think I
> was doing anything wrong.

> Every day I left work happy, but by the time I was partway home, I was dreading
> getting there because I was wondering, "Is she going to be in a good mood?" I

*sent fear ahead of me, and she picked up on my projected fear. I'd get home, and
she'd say things that created fear and rage—and then the night would be shot.*

Disorientation centers on the struggle between your old identity and
the one you are moving toward, between who you *were* and who you
will *become*. It also highlights the dissonance between what you *have* and
what you *want*. You might ask, "How do I live the life I know I should
be living?" Kenny was confident that, based on his spiritual experience,
he was completely trustworthy and well-intentioned with women. He
expected himself to behave this way. His old self, however, may have
related to women in a manner that was unconsciously sexualizing, and
this former identity still influenced his behavior. The discord between
his two selves created a vicious cycle in which Inga felt threatened and
Kenny was defensive.

Another reason Disorientation occurs is that at this point on the Map
to Wholeness, you wrestle with understanding your true identity. Serendipitously, Kenny received full funding to attend a men's retreat in Florida
on the topic of identity—the precise focus of conflict in the Disorientation phase. Eli Jaxon-Bear, Gangaji's husband, was the teacher at the
retreat. He helped participants learn about others and themselves using
the Enneagram, a spiritually based personality system. The retreat was
pivotal for Kenny.

*I was learning all about the Enneagram. Eli explained to me that there was
a reason for all the stuff going on with Inga. I learned that I am an "eight"
personality type according to the Enneagram. He explained that, as an eight,
I think I am the boss; I think I am entitled to things. He also explained how I
cause suffering. I said, "What?"*

*About three-quarters of the way through the week, I had a major breaking
point. I will never forget it. We were taking a break, and I was leaning on a
railing at the edge of the ocean. I looked at Eli walking on the beach, and I got
so angry at him. I got so enraged because he took the illusion of myself away.*

*Before that experience with him, I didn't even know I had a shadow—my
unconscious fear, anger, and desire. All of a sudden, I was no longer a unique*

spiritual person. I did not want to know there were millions of us eights moving around, acting the same way I did, like I was a machine plugged into some unconscious way of being. I had to face the fact that I was just like the other millions of eights. He took away this illusion I had of myself. It was like I had been living a lie. "Oh my God," I thought. "I am doing things out of my unconscious, my shadow—it's like I do things in a trance, based on old stories and an outdated belief system."

Kenny found himself in the dizzying tornado of emotions that the Disorientation phase can bring. He realized that his entitled attitude and old behaviors were at odds with his burgeoning identity as a spiritual teacher.

This realization about the power my shadow has over my behavior was the beginning of the destruction of my marriage with Inga. I hated that I was so vulnerable to my own unconsciousness, that at any moment I could find myself in the middle of doing something that "wasn't me." It was a major turning point. That was when the anger came up, the rage came up, and I became violent. It was a major letdown.

I was in a constant state of fear. "Oh, man, what is going to happen now?" It felt like I suddenly had little knowledge of what was going on inside of me, and I was putting all the pressure on her to make me happy. She was beating on me, and I was beating on her.

Gangaji told me to do anger-management classes, so I did. I learned a lot, and I quit beating up on women to solve my problems.

But it was too late. Inga wrote a long letter to Gangaji, and Gangaji sent me a letter telling me to move out of the house and get a divorce.

I was the cause of the problems, because I became violent—and if I kept being violent, I would end up in jail.

At some point during Disorientation, you wake up to your life's circumstances—to the reality you have been denying. The strong hold that the transformative experience had over you dissipates significantly as the demands of daily living increase. Like Kenny, you simply cannot spend as much energy pretending to be someone or somewhere you are not. You must face your life and yourself.

The mundane tasks of living that you have delayed require attention now. During Disorientation, you begin to take inventory of the details and take action. This action was forced upon Kenny when his violent behavior became public and he destroyed his marriage. Like Kenny, you probably want to change your life for the better, to become healthier. You may create a mental or physical list of improvements you wish to make related to your routine: eat more fresh foods, exercise regularly, call loved ones, drink less, get outside more, leave work on time, play with the kids, and so on.

These improvements also probably include eliminating a habit or two that have become so old, worn out, and annoying that you are sick of them. Kenny's need to improve his anger management, self-insight, and communication skills was no longer something he could dismiss or avoid. Whether the habits you really want to change are merely annoying or dangerously destructive, these patterns of behavior are incongruent with who you are becoming, which is the real reason these particular habits bug you now. Even though you intend to do it, the cliché about breaking habits is true: it's not easy.

Kenny was obviously not an angel or an enlightened man. Yet before Gangaji's letter, which was informed by Inga's report of his atrocious behavior, he had been unable or unwilling to see it. He was busted, but this time, not by law enforcement.

Kenny's Disorientation phase provided a rude awakening. It smashed his image of himself. He could not deny that he still had a long way to go to live in alignment with the knowledge he had accessed during his spiritual awakening. This fall from grace gave him renewed motivation, and even a sense of relief.

He could start over.

Radha: "Making My Life about Me"

At first, having the trial behind her felt tremendously liberating for Radha. As she put it, "There was a sense of optimism in a dark time. I didn't have to wait for anything else. I didn't have a big trial looming over me. I had no responsibilities, no big cause to tend to."

Radha knew that the absence of a major focus could be both a blessing and a curse. Now that the intensity, suspense, and sleeplessness of the trial were over, she had more free time and far fewer distractions from daily life. She was confronted with a question typical of the Disorientation phase: "What do I do now?"

Radha finally had the opportunity to pay attention to the changes that had occurred deep inside her. She had to face the loss of her son.

> This was when the real grieving began. I could begin soulful grieving, the heart work, instead of jumping through the hoops of the legal process. Not that I hadn't done anything in regard to my grief, but you don't get to the heart work, processing the real grief, until the big job of the trial is over.
>
> Grief is a foreign language. No one gets to practice for this. I remember thinking, "Will I ever smile again?" "Will I ever be happy again?" "Will I ever have an orgasm again? Can I be that happy?" The answers are yes, of course. But I didn't know that at the time. It's a really deep sink. I was lower than I had ever been—ever, ever, ever.
>
> Another strange thing was that people would say to me, "You look so beautiful." Grief doesn't make you ugly. People seem to think you have to look awful when you are sad.

Loss leads to grief, and as we discussed earlier, feelings of grief are integral to transformation. This makes loss or the absence of something you yearn to have or become an important catalyst for the most important ingredient of transformation: grief. And because grief is so integral to transformation, it cannot be isolated to a single phase. Radha's account illustrates that grief is not limited to the Grief and Denial phase. If you heed your inner world closely, you may notice that grief is with you throughout most of the transformation process. Its quality, however, changes along the way. Grief may arise from the loss of innocence or a change that causes tremendous upheaval. It may stem from regret over not making certain changes because you didn't have the courage. Grief also changes in intensity. As you move down the figure eight from the height of the transformative experience in phase 3, you may perceive that grief becomes heavier and heavier until you reach phase 9, Birth.

Radha experienced grief during the Grief and Denial phase, but the grief she felt during Disorientation was worse. For some, the grief of Dismemberment, the next phase, is even worse. Since Radha's grief was more than she could handle on most days, she became creative in finding ways to manage it.

> I knew it was important not to ignore the grief. A big part of my grief was that Christopher had become intangible. There is something about being able to feel something solid that helps soothe the permanence of loss. I knew I needed physical things to feel closer to him, to help remember him—things I could touch.
>
> During the third and fourth years after Christopher died, we did just that. First, we put a bench on the mountain near our house that he loved so much, Mount Tamalpais. We put a brick with his name on it in a community rose garden. We planted a tree in our backyard for him. I have always loved quilts— the way stories are told through them. I found a quilt artist and commissioned her to make a quilt about Christopher's life. I encourage others to do this, too. It gives you a stability; physical reminders are positive.
>
> I dried every rose petal that came into our lives from family events and presents, and I took them up to Mount Tamalpais, where we had also spread Christopher's ashes. This was a way for me to share happy family times with my son. You can leave only natural things on the mountain.
>
> While the rose petals were a sign of happy times, when they spilled to the ground on visits to Mount Tamalpais, I found myself filled with sadness. When I visit Christopher on top of the mountain, it hits me really hard that parents are not supposed to outlive their children.

Different circumstances might cause you to feel disoriented. The condition that forced Radha, a very clear-thinking individual, to feel bewildered was profound grief over the loss of her son. Again, this phase compels you to face the reality of your circumstances: "I am in this situation, and like it or not, I have to accept it." Dealing with your new reality, however, is easier on some days than on others. You may swing between embracing it and rejecting it, as if you were moving forward and then slipping backward. This frustrating movement is part of what produces disorientation.

In order for Radha to begin to accept the reality of Christopher's death, she had to confront "the unfairness of it, the violence of it, the fact that it happened in anger." The most effective way for Radha to face the truth was to channel her grief into working toward justice by joining a major political movement promoting gun control. This work felt essential to her. If she could make a difference, perhaps Christopher's death would have been less in vain.

> Three months after Christopher's death, I began volunteering with the Trauma Foundation at San Francisco General Hospital, advocating for tighter gun-control laws. Three years into my volunteering, I helped organize the Million Mom March in Washington, DC. The actual event was so healing because I was marching with so many people who cared about gun control and saving people's lives. Over a million moms showed up from all over the country to ask for tighter gun-control laws. I felt good about being involved in something that mattered.

> During this time, I also started working with families who had experienced a similar crime. My job was to help them navigate the criminal court system and guide them in negotiating their grief. It softened my grief and made me feel like I was making a difference.

During Disorientation, you vacillate between who you were before the transformative experience and who you are becoming as a result of it. This process involves identifying what is old and what is new about you, sorting out those pieces, and having the courage to step into your emerging identity by making healthier choices.

For Radha, stepping into the new version of herself required learning to say no. Instead of agreeing to every worthwhile project, as she would have done before, Radha had to honor her growing need to save her energy for only the greatest opportunities. There were simply too many worthy causes and groups for Radha to work with all of them. She had to decline some invitations in order to be able to tend to her family and personal life.

> During the Million Mom March I had been asked to be on the board, and I said yes. A month after the march, I went to my first board meeting. When I returned home from the meeting, I wanted to sit down and digest my experience and all of my years of work for gun control when, in the stillness, it came to me: "I think I have saved more than one child."
>
> I had already helped to enact local, regional, and statewide regulations to help ban the flow of Saturday night specials that entice increased sales through lowered prices. As I sat in the silence, I vividly remember looking up and saying, "Christopher, I am done."
>
> I talked to him for a long time.
>
> That's when I resigned my position on the board after only one meeting and ended my work for gun control. It was a relief to stop at that point.

This action was a very significant marker in Radha's transformation. It opened her up to shift more deeply into who she was becoming—her new identity. Despite the excitement of this step forward, though, Radha still had a long way to go on the path to transformation.

After a transformative event, it can be temporarily helpful to attach your identity to your present circumstances. At first, Radha identified herself primarily with Christopher's death and with others who had suffered a similar loss. She revealed her self-association with this group when she remarked, "We, the grieving people, have to give others a break. Most people don't know how much pain we are in. They can't read our minds." But eventually, Radha needed to be more than just a mother who had suffered the tragic and brutal loss of her son.

When you are in the initial stages of recovery after a trauma (phases 4–7 on the Map to Wholeness), your identity is false; it is tied to the trauma rather than to who you are becoming. Four years after Christopher's murder, Radha decided to stop fighting for him and against the reason for his death. She had gone from being Christopher's mother to being his advocate and the champion of his cause. Now her identity was essentially unknown, as is characteristic of the Disorientation phase.

Radha's resignation from the board for the Million Mom March signified the release of her feelings of obligation to Christopher. It also represented a shift in her priorities, from focusing on others to begin loving herself. She was still in the process of recovery, however, and she wasn't close to focusing solely on herself.

After resigning from the Million Mom March and board, I decided to put my energy into something that didn't have to do with Christopher's death, something that just had to do with helping people. I became involved with the Tenderloin Neighborhood Development Corporation, a company dedicated to helping people of low income to thrive, so I could creatively and artistically help one of the most marginalized areas of San Francisco.

I got on their board and started helping people find places to live that were safe and offered necessary social services. I knew that Christopher would really like that. It was good to take a break from thinking about guns every day, to do something that allowed me to give to others just because it was dear to my heart, rather than helping others because of my personal strife.

I knew that Christopher didn't want me to be miserable. He loved happiness and people coming together. I knew my life needed to be about serenity and happiness. He would want me not only to live but also to thrive. The way for me to honor his life was to make the best of mine.

Making my life about me, rather than being centered on tragedy, felt healthy. I felt good because ending the advocacy work meant I was getting better, that I had thoroughly completed my need to liberate Christopher's death out of the shroud of tragedy and the violence he suffered and make of it something that gave life not only to me but to others. Seeing markers of my transition, such as my resignation, became really important because it felt good to get through something. It was part of the healing process. It was important to know that life could get better; I could experience the joy in little things.

Radha made an important shift here toward embodying a new, as yet unknown, identity. Her volunteer work with the Tenderloin project was centered on empowering and educating people rather than on fighting about guns. Her progress may appear out of place in a phase called Disorientation, but an important aspect of this phase is your attempt to find your center after having been thrown way off. Your feeling of disorientation motivates you, consciously or unconsciously, to take action that helps you gain some sense of control over your health and well-being. You are driven to make changes that help you feel healthier than you were before your life-changing event.

Soon after her work with the Tenderloin project, Radha found herself moving in the direction she wanted to go. Through dear friends, she met Jacques Verduin, executive director of Insight Prison Project. He worked with inmates at San Quentin and had been looking to partner with the loved one of a murder victim. He felt he could help inmates heal by sharing with them the perspectives of people whose families had endured violent crime.

Jacques and I started regularly working together on how traumatic crime stains a family. We talked about every single thing that had happened since Christopher's murder. We looked through trial transcripts and at pictures. He really wanted to be educated.

Then he asked me to come in and speak to men in prison. When I agreed, he was surprised that I was ready to talk with the men so quickly.

Seven years after Christopher's death, I visited San Quentin for the first time. The room we met in is now condemned. It was dilapidated, with metal folding chairs, a leaking ceiling, no windows, and birds flying in. Men started spilling into the room—seventeen of them. All of them had been convicted of murder. They were wearing jeans and light blue denim shirts.

The first thing I noticed was that they had kind faces. They weren't ugly. Here I was thinking that murderers should be ugly, but it was just like other people thinking that I should look awful because I was grieving. I shook their hands; I looked them in the eye. Then they all sat down.

I told them my story, which took about an hour. Afterward, I was in a room of seventeen sobbing men—not crying, not sniffling, but sobbing. I was amazed. Maybe it was because I was a mother, or because they had a sister, or because of their brother. Something in my story resonated with each of them. The fact that I was sharing with them and talking to them as human beings also resonated with them.

My story is very tough, and it hurts. The men saw the pain I live with every day without my son, and they realized that they had created this type of pain for a family, for everyone connected to that family, and for everyone connected to everyone connected to that family. It is the "pebble in the pond" effect, and the ripple is far-reaching.

That day was as profound and moving for me as it was for the inmates. I was hooked and wanted to continue working at San Quentin.

Upon first glance, Radha's new work with prison inmates looks like she had returned to volunteer work related to Christopher's death, and in a concrete sense, it was. However, this latest endeavor is different from her previous work because instead of avenging her son, her work in San Quentin was about releasing and liberating her own grief.

※ ※ ※

Disorientation is a period in which you want to make changes in yourself for the better. Still, try as you might, little that is accomplished in this phase feels like a real success. For many, Disorientation feels like stepping on the accelerator when there's no gas in the tank. During this phase, your ability to have the better life you desire is impeded by the part of you that is less healthy—the part that can't go where you are going. Once you have encountered numerous blocks to the life you want to have, you are ready to enter the Dismemberment phase and say goodbye to the past.

10

PHASE 8: DISMEMBERMENT

We need suffering in order to develop our ideal of compassion, for compassion arises from the darkness of human travail. It is the gift of our humanness, not to be denied but rather to be affirmed, to be sponsored, to be thoroughly understood.

—JOAN HALIFAX

I often think of Dismemberment as the most easily recognizable phase on the Map to Wholeness. If you say to anyone, "Tell me about the most difficult time of your life," chances are you will hear a story about Dismemberment. As the word implies, this phase is a period in your life that you tolerate at best—and at worst, you just try to survive. The latter scenario is more common.

The word *dismemberment* conjures up horrible images of a body being mutilated or divided limb from limb. While this phase tends to have visible aspects of loss and trauma, the vast majority of the dismemberment and disintegration is usually invisible to others. This phase constitutes a time of going deep within, into your own underworld, so you can discover and recover more of who you are.

Dismemberment begins with a devastating experience that places you in a situation where you feel out of control. The terrible circumstance will typically take you by surprise: you lose your job, all of your possessions are destroyed in a flood, you learn that you have multiple sclerosis, your partner has an affair, you discover that your child is taking heavy drugs, your beloved dies, or you get arrested and go to jail.

To make matters worse, you will find that as this phase progresses, your situation worsens. For example, a father might enter Dismemberment when his teenage son's struggle with depression spirals into suicidal threats and actions. This type of crisis thrusts you into foreign territory where you are likely to feel terribly desperate and vulnerable. You may notice that those around you are daunted by the magnitude of your challenges and avoid becoming involved. Even if you enlist the help of others, you might feel as though you are lost deep in a cave without a light, or far out at sea with insufficient supplies. Because you are ill equipped to handle your situation, it is common to experience a sense of panic so strong that it feels as though your life is in jeopardy. You cannot escape your circumstances, so you must cope the best you can and endure.

The initial horrifying event that marks the beginning of this phase causes you to dis-member and fall apart. As the phase progresses, your life circumstances will help you see and eventually let go of ingrained ways in which you attempt to control others and yourself. For example, after being fired from your job, a close friend from work reveals how your stubborn, egotistical behavior contributed to your professional demise and then says he no longer want to be friends. Being fired is awful, but hearing this information and losing a trusted friend is worse. A very low point such as this causes you to let go completely and allow a part of yourself that is no longer needed to disintegrate and die.

What Is Good about Dismemberment?

You might wonder, "Is there anything positive about this phase?" The short answer is yes. Your life circumstances pull you apart, down to your core, so you can re-member who you truly are at your essence.

Even though anguish is an inevitable aspect of Dismemberment, you need not be pinned down to complete misery and unmitigated suffering. Spanish poet and Roman Catholic mystic St. John of the Cross wrote a poem that has given us a more positive way to understand our own disintegration and renewal. This work, now referred to as "Dark Night of the Soul," describes a spiritual crisis that leads to maturity and union with the divine. His poetry reveals how Dismemberment, this extraordinary experience of darkness, requires detachment from your known world and purification through ordeals, tests of courage, and perseverance. He helps us to understand that even though navigating Dismemberment is "without light or guide, save that which burns in [your] heart," the darkness can offer you something intensely sublime or even sacred.

There are two phases on the Map to Wholeness that tend to provide us with easier access to mystical experience, the divine, God, or something larger than yourself: the Transformative Experience (phase 4) and Dismemberment (phase 8). The first occurs when you ascend into the frontiers beyond you; the second happens when you descend into the mysterious depths inside you. Both give you easier access to information and experiences beyond the common run of life.

In the chapter about Transformative Experience (phase 4) I discussed the mystical potential of a life-changing event, and here I wish to examine this same characteristic as it presents itself in Dismemberment. The most significant reason why this phase has the potential to give you access to something sacred is because you have been overtaken by deep and profound grief. You have endured such great loss that you are as emotionally low as you can possibly be. In this state, you are extraordinarily unguarded and open to experiencing something beyond yourself.

The reason for this radical openness is that you have absolutely no fear, expectations, or bias. When your losses are so drastic and pervasive, the sadness makes your body feel literally and exceedingly heavy, which is helpful when the task is to go downward, into the earth. Your mind is wiped clear, and you no longer care about striving to be happy or good, let alone great. You have been emptied. In these delicate and precious weeks, you enter into an altered, bittersweet, sublime state of complete and utter openness.

Being in this acutely vulnerable situation is a mystical state wherein you have a sense of yourself as not being real, of daily life feeling surreal, of living in a dream, or of watching your life as though it is a movie. You might experience other key characteristics of a mystical experience, such as an altered experience of time in which everything feels as though it is moving in slow motion. Some people in very deep dismemberment talk about wondering, in a spiritual sense, if they are dead or alive.

Beyond the mystical nature of this phase, it provides a great opportunity to access wisdom or even to have a spiritual awakening. Psychologist Stanislav Grof and his wife, Christina Grof, coined the term "spiritual emergency" to describe times like this. As St. John of the Cross found, the Grofs posited that some crises can be opportunities to "rise to a new level of awareness" (Grof and Grof 1989, x). There is something unique and vital about the combination of profound grief, raw openness, and psychological disconnection from people, circumstances, expectations, and most importantly, social norms.

In light of this information, it can be very helpful to allow yourself to view Dismemberment as an opportunity to sit on the edge of something deeper or wiser for an extended period of time and listen to what comes to you. Instead of resisting the pain and suffering, consider feeling it fully. Entertain the richness of spending an ample amount of time dwelling in the silence of your inner world.

Making the Most of Dismemberment

When I was in my early thirties, my old car stopped working, and the mechanic said he had to take a major part of the engine out in order to access and fix what was wrong. There was no way around it. Since I had to go to the expense of taking out the big part, he explained that we might as well replace a few smaller items that lay deep inside that were heavily worn and had the potential to malfunction or die soon. Of course I agreed to the cost. It was preemptive maintenance, and besides, I was already spending quite a bit of money—what's another $75 to be safe?

Although human beings are far more complex than automobiles, this story comes to mind when I think about the opportunities that come with Dismemberment. There is something to be said about making use of the fact that because of personal crisis, you have already been opened and taken apart. Because you are stuck in this vulnerable situation that is "costing" you a lot of energy and difficulty, you might want to consider taking a look around inside to see what else needs cleaning, "fixing," or even replacing.

You can start by paying attention to your feelings, thoughts, and motivations. Try contemplating the role others play in your life. Ask yourself what you're learning from your friends, what the purpose of life events is, and what a given situation can teach you about yourself. If you are attentive to your inner world, even everyday ordinary experiences can become a great source of information about the meaning of life, who you were before, and who you are becoming.

Because Dismemberment is a rich time for learning, you can make a practice of regularly asking yourself rhetorical questions, such as "How is this helpful to me?" and "How does this circumstance teach me what I cannot see in myself?" Once you ponder and reflect for a while, let it go and allow the question to marinate in the back of your mind. You might discover that an answer comes to you a few days later when you are listening to someone tell a story, while you are watching a commercial on television, or as you are taking a shower.

Hopefully during this phase you can begin to notice dysfunctional patterns by paying attention to whatever bothers you—the things you complain about, outwardly or silently. Here is a list of common ways we can neglect, abuse, and manipulate others and ourselves.

- Disregarding your body's need for healthy foods, exercise, rest, intimacy, cognitive stimulation, or play

- Remaining silent and not speaking your truth; putting the needs of others before your own

- Attempting to control someone else by influencing him or her to make certain choices or live in a certain way

- Blaming or hurting others so you can get your way and not have to feel wrong, hurt, or abandoned

Do you recognize any of these behaviors in yourself? Recognizing your own damaging behaviors allows you to take responsibility for your role in strained relationships. If it is difficult to isolate your own unhealthy pattern in a dysfunctional relationship, you might ask yourself a few key questions in regard to whatever bothers you the most about someone in your life:

- What action have I been avoiding because it seems almost impossible to take?

- If I am really honest with myself (and others)—true to my inner self, health, and integrity—what action do I know I need to take to repair or help this situation, even though the thought of it feels almost unbearable?

If you have trouble answering these questions, ask someone who knows you well to help you. Your ego (sense of self) doesn't like being out of control, so it will obscure your ability to face deep-seated fears without the help of someone you trust.

Why the Word "Dismemberment"?

The story behind the word dismemberment can give us another perspective on the role Dismemberment plays in our development. The use of the term in the Map to Wholeness stems from a myth about the descent of Inanna, the Sumerian goddess of love, fertility, and warfare. Written on stone tablets in Mesopotamia in about 3500 BC, it is the oldest known myth about a woman's purposeful downward journey into the dark underworld and the feminine aspect of the divine.

Although Inanna was a mature woman who had achieved high status, she sensed that something was missing. This caused her to "turn her ear to the Great Below" (Hannan 2005, 289), meaning deep within, and she recognized that she had adapted herself to prosper. The solution was to descend into the underworld, or the inner chasms of her unconscious, in order to retrieve and recover aspects of herself that had been wounded or that she had shunned in order to survive and to become accomplished. The myth perfectly captures the purpose of Dismemberment. Regardless of your gender, the descending portion on the Map to Wholeness is about salvaging aspects of your inner feminine nature.

When Inanna met Ereshkigal, the keeper of the underworld and Inanna's complement, she had to face feminine aspects of herself that she had rejected, such as softness, vulnerability, slowness, and emotional suffering, as well as shadow tendencies such as volatility, manipulation, and chaos. These are often seen as less desirable features of the feminine aspect of existence that both men and women possess. She had disavowed these qualities so she could compete in a masculine-dominated world. Being forced to accept that she possessed these characteristics caused her to become dismembered or pulled apart. In the story she was reduced to a piece of "rotting meat" hung on a peg.

Relieved of all that she once was, Inanna was condensed to her essential core, her *prima materia*, which in the ancient science of alchemy is the foundation from which transformation is made possible. In psychological terms, what is actually dismembered is her personality and ego—her sense of herself—and her ideas about what is real, that is, what is possible and not possible.

Before her descent, Inanna asked a loyal servant and fellow warrior priestess to ask for help if she did not return. She instructed her confidant to ask the good father of wisdom, Enki, "he-who-knows-the-water-of-life and he-who-knows-the-secrets-of-creation" (Hannan 2005, 182), to restore her to life. Because she did not return, her servant did as she was told and made a plea to Enki, who sent two beings to the underworld to save Inanna. When they found her, Ereshkigal eventually allowed them to pour the food-of-life and the water-of-life on the rotting meat, after which Inanna rose and journeyed out of the underworld.

Having survived her ordeal, Inanna understood how the descent into darkness offers an incomparable opportunity for personal growth, renewal, and "initiation into a more comprehensive identity" (Hannan 2005, 282) or completeness. Inanna's bravery and survival show us that even though the unconscious "still holds death, pain, and intense vulnerability ... it is a negotiable realm" (Wilkenson 1996, 237). We can survive Dismemberment, and afterward, we can thrive.

Although this ancient story begins as a woman's journey, it unfolds to include the masculine. Equipped with this knowledge, Inanna asks her husband Dumuzi (who is also interpreted as her inner masculine) to complete the downward journey, too, so he does. Carl Jung explains that when both the inner masculine and the inner feminine endure cleansing (which occurs during Dismemberment and Surrender and Healing), an inner union happens, called *conjunctio*. The concept of *conjunctio*, another term from alchemy, means that you have reconciled and incorporated the opposites within you. *Conjunctio* is the ultimate purpose of transformation. This unification occurs at the beginning of the Power phase and culminates in the Integration phase as Wholeness.

Kenny: The Bottom Drops Out

Thinking that the worst was behind him, Kenny picked up the pieces of his life and once again continued to pursue spiritual advancement. Surely, this time he would be successful. He continued to read, meditate, and go on retreats.

About three months after my divorce, I was feeling like my life was going pretty smoothly. I was at an intensive in San Rafael, California, for two days when Gangaji did the strangest thing. She sent me a letter through her manager saying that I was no longer wanted or needed, would not be given any more scholarships, and could no longer come to any satsangs. I wasn't welcome.

It was a horrible blow. It hurt like a son of a gun. I was angry ... but more like devastated. Depressed. Confused. Shocked. Speechless.

I didn't believe it was really happening. I was grasping, trying to make sense of it.

The bottom dropped out for Kenny. His community, his home, and most importantly, the person to whom he felt he owed his life were now rejecting him. True to the dark night of the soul that characterizes Dismemberment, Kenny became detached from his known world and was forced to survive without his community. In a real sense, this was the first time since his release from prison that Kenny was truly on his own.

After that, it took about a month for me to get stable. Once I began meditating again, things just started taking off. I realized that all I was looking for was family, sangha, community.

I found a Buddhist place where I would go and meditate. Once I found the Buddhist group, it was a relief. I thought, Wow. I am grateful. This is perfect. I am so glad this happened.

I began looking even more and found all sorts of things, including a chiropractor and Tantra. I was learning a lot. It was a time of growing up, in a sense.

I recognized that it was quite wonderful that Gangaji had kicked me out. I realized that in a way, every retreat and intensive was really about hiding out. I could run away by achieving a conscious state of mind. It was a problem, as if nothing existed except for Gangaji.

Her letter broke me out of a trance. I had to find other ways to keep myself sane. I had to find other communities. In the end, that was the best thing that could have happened to me.

For a whole year, I discovered all sorts of things outside the satsang.

Kenny's ability to let go of resentment and to look for the goodness in the hardest of his lessons was a testament to the magnitude of his ongoing transformation.

A year later, Gangaji contacted me and said, "We would love to see you at satsang."

But by then, I no longer needed the retreats. I was in a different state of mind. I wasn't attached to satsangs, intensives, or Gangaji's programs. Before that, I had to have them. I was mesmerized by everything she did. And then, once I was kicked out, I realized that I had been hooked. I saw that I had been in a trance. And now I saw that there was so much more to the spiritual world than Gangaji.

So when I did return, everything was cool, but it was not anything momentous.

Despite his humbling learning experience, Kenny was not out of Dismemberment. This phase is tricky that way. Once the crisis that occurs during Dismemberment has ended, it is easy, even logical, to think that it's over and things will get better.

Unfortunately, Dismemberment is not one of the shorter phases. It tends to hang on far longer than you think. Its processes are also private, subtle, and unseen by others. Even when the external crisis appears to have subsided, you still must endure an internal crisis of reconciling aspects of yourself that are wounded or that you reject. For example, even though you obtain a job offer and it appears that you are recovering from being fired, inside you are still suffering from the devastation of emotional losses and the turmoil of identity crisis.

I was drifting, so to speak. Somewhat lost, without any real focus. There was a lot of drinking going on at the time. I was just hanging out near where I worked, partying, and going to clubs. I wasn't really doing anything helpful. I wasn't teaching or trying to write a book or anything. I just did my life.

During that time, when a spiritual opportunity showed up, I just went with it, but I didn't go seeking them out. I didn't have a focus or direction. I would just follow something that sounded interesting. When I learned everything I needed to learn from that particular opportunity, the teacher just fell away, and something else came up. A lot of times, it felt like what showed up was being sent just for me. And I saw how far it would carry me.

As is the case for all big transformations, Kenny pushed onward against obstacles through Dismemberment for several years. Being asked to leave the only spiritual community he had ever known forced him to branch out and to discover other groups and practices. But this type of exploration was not the kind that is fun and exciting. He was lost and just trying to survive.

Dismemberment is oriented toward survival. You are not interested in creating or achieving anything or even in engaging with others. There is a useful activity you can perform at this point, and that is to concentrate and reflect upon your feelings. The information you discover in this way will help you understand more about yourself, your struggles, and what will set you free. Some of Kenny's reflections went something like this:

At the time, I wanted to be a spiritual philosopher, a teacher, a guru. I wanted to be like all those guys. I wanted an organization and to make money teaching. I was into Michael Mead, Jack Kornfield, Malidoma Somé. They all had followings, groups of their own, and I couldn't stop thinking, "Why can't I be like that?"

So I had a deep awakening and it seemed to say, "You are a teacher." And yet I am not teaching. Why am not I teaching? How am I a teacher?

At the same time, I thought, "Well, at least I am hanging out with all these teachers." I wasn't hanging out with just anybody. But it still bothered me. I thought, "I am just as awake and conscious as they are. Why aren't people following me?"

Although Kenny did not yet see the ways in which he was not "awake" in his personal life and behaviors, he was at least asking himself provocative questions. Eventually he did arrive at a conclusion that was novel to him.

But after all that time of suffering, what I came away with was that it all comes back to letting go. Even though I did so many spiritual activities—all those retreats, ceremonies, fire dancing, whatever—it didn't matter. Nothing was going to help me to be like them. In the end, I had to let it all go and be empty. Again.

Go into what is now, what I already have.

I had to remember that who I already am is just fine.

That final statement helped Kenny arrive at an important and pivotal realization in his Dismemberment: a key source of his suffering was his own belief that he would be an instant guru, and moreover, that he deserved this status with little effort. This assumption caused him to feel entitled, which was probably off-putting for some, and to act bitter, demanding, and impatient each time he had to work hard or did not achieve his goals.

This humbling realization pushed Kenny to begin making an effort to accept his actual status, behaviors, and capacities rather than buying into his biased self-perceptions. Dismemberment is sobering because it helps you begin to see what is rather than what you want to see. Just as Inanna's ego was dismantled during her journey into her underworld, Kenny had the opportunity to let go of his ego's need to be like his teachers so he could recognize his true nature and gifts.

As reflected in Kenny's story, Dismemberment requires your willingness to meet the challenges of each moment, to ask difficult questions that help you learn more about yourself and others, and to feel your feelings as best you can. Breakthroughs like this one help you gain control and cause your troubles to begin to dissipate.

Kenny spent time with many of the renowned teachers he talks about and was a diligent student. Now that he understood that becoming a guru doesn't happen without hard work, a certain degree of internalized harmony, and a well-developed skill set, he finally decided to ask his teachers for help. One evening while sitting around a fire at a retreat center, he spoke up.

I finally asked them, "How did you get started?"

They said, "We all wrote books."

I said, "Oh, okay. Well, I need to write a book."

This was uncharacteristic of Kenny—asking for help. He was used to being in control and knowing what to do and how to act. This is another function of Dismemberment: it puts you in situations where you have to become softer in your style, slower in action, and more vulnerable, just like Inanna. Dismemberment involves a great deal of suffering unique to your own shadow and gifts. Whether or not Kenny would write a book was inconsequential. What was significant was that he continue to let go of outdated or erroneous aspects of himself so he would be able to birth his potential.

Radha: "I Just Want Her to Be Happy"

Radha is equipped with an admirable combination of inner strength, keen organizational and communication skills, self-awareness, and determination. Part of the purpose of Dismemberment is to refine such capacities and take them to another level. Six years after Christopher's death, Radha was unconsciously ready to go deeper into her interior so she could heal and accept aspects of herself that had previously been hidden, contracted, or disrupted.

As we have seen, Dismemberment begins with an unpleasant experience that is so dreadful it takes your breath away.

> On the sixth anniversary of Christopher's death, when Christina was about thirty years old, she had a mental breakdown. She was devastated by the death of her brother. When I looked into her eyes, she was no longer there; her eyes were vacant. I was consumed with fear. Here was my child in front of me, mentally catatonic.
>
> I knew mental illness existed, but I really didn't understand it intimately. I never thought it would happen in my family. When Christina had her breakdown, I didn't get emotional. I immediately went into action mode, just like I did when I got the news about Christopher. It's a mode where I dig in and say,

"I have to figure this out. What do I have to do?" I go outside myself and get all the help I can get.

Once again, the family rallied—this time to support Christina through a very difficult time. I helped her find a therapist, and with the financial support of a beloved friend, she went to therapy every single day.

After three months of intensive therapy, she started going two times a week, which continued for almost a year. Fortunately, we had the means to support her. In the misery of what was happening, I remember thinking worriedly, "What do people do in this situation if they can't pay for a therapist?"

One of the hallmarks of Dismemberment is an experience that makes you feel completely out of control. Christina's breakdown took Radha to a place of fear she had never known before, and that says a lot given that she had already experienced the murder of her son.

When Christopher died, Radha latched onto an obvious crusade for justice and a clear place to direct her energy: bringing his murderer to justice and advocating for gun control. She felt that laws allowing the easy purchase of cheap guns needed to be overturned. By combating these visible enemies, Radha was able to cope, act, survive, and eventually thrive. She funneled her immense pain into "getting a huge job done," as she put it.

But when it came to Christina's breakdown, Radha had no one to blame for the pain, no injustice to make right. How do you get the job done when the problem isn't injustice—it's simply raw pain?

Of course, I can blame Mark Taylor for Christina's breakdown and everything bad that happens to me for the rest of my life. Yes, he did take her brother. Yes, he could be responsible for her condition. But even if he is at fault, I knew that he couldn't fix her, that he was not a part of the solution, and that she had to find the strength to go forward and to be responsible for her life.

Christina's collapse brought Radha to her knees and made her face her greatest fear.

Christina's suffering was truly the hardest part of this whole thing. I was in deep fear of losing two children. I honestly thought I was going to lose both of them. I thought, "God can't be that cruel."

I was already deeply grieving—broken—and did not have my usual strength to help Christina with her pain. That was really hard for me, not to be at my best for her.

It didn't matter how transformed I became or how positive I stayed or how stable I felt. Having someone that close to me who was as delicate as Jell-O meant that I was suffering right along with her.

The worst part was seeing her suffer. I didn't know what to do. I felt helpless because as compassionate as I was, I didn't know depression or what to do about it. All of my skills barely made a difference. Even though I hired experts to help her, she couldn't see a clear path that would take her toward healing and stability. Watching her journey was incredibly difficult.

With every choice I made, I thought of Christina. I thought about how every one of my decisions would affect her, the consequences they would have on her life. I made specific decisions because of her. I rarely traveled anymore, but when I did, I had people lined up to check in on her. It was excruciating, wondering if the twinkle in her eyes would ever come back, waiting to hear her laugh. I felt like I was in a constant state of waiting.

After Christina underwent a year of therapy, Radha, Christina, and Radha's brother sat down to discuss discontinuing her treatment. Radha and her brother thought it was okay to end Christina's therapy. "It seems that we have a stable person here," they reasoned. When they all talked it over, there was mutual agreement.

I breathed a sigh of relief. Christina had reached the point where we could trust that her life was going to keep moving in a positive way. We had done something extraordinary to get her out of the darkness and into some semblance of steadiness. I felt as though I was launching her into the rest of her life, that she was going to be stable.

Although Radha was tremendously relieved that Christina had made a turn toward the positive, Radha herself was still enduring deep grief. She was enduring the horrible loss of her son, and though her daughter showed a turn for the better, Radha was at the beginning of recovery from the crisis of fearing that she would lose her only remaining beloved child.

Mirror, Mirror on the Wall

Even though Christina's health continued to improve, she still struggled, which meant that Radha still struggled. Radha's challenge came from the fact that her child was in pain, which triggered her own pain. Making it harder for Radha was that she and her daughter were so different, and now their differences became magnified. Christina activated Radha's ideas about how things should be done, how to deal with emotions, and what is important and unimportant in life. Christina did almost everything contrary to how Radha would do it.

> I move through things quickly. My daughter is the opposite. She doesn't feel like it is okay to feel happiness on the anniversary of Christopher's death or on his birthday. I feel it is very important to feel happiness on those special days.

> Christina is a procrastinator, and I am not, and that is a hard bridge for me to cross between us. She can't make a decision, even about mundane things like what restaurant to go to for dinner. At that time she was in her early thirties and didn't know what she wanted or where she was going. Christopher's murder was one of the core reasons for her stunted development.

> Christina's favorite part of the Sunday paper is the advertisements; she likes to dream about shopping. I am an "if I need something" kind of shopper. When Christina obsesses over what she wants to buy, I shake my head and think, "That seems wasteful." But she enjoys it, so who am I to say anything?

The dissimilarities between Radha and Christina had always existed, but after Christina's breakdown, they became heightened, and Radha's involvement in her daughter's life increased. Under these circumstances, Radha's own issues came to the fore. The essence of the Dismemberment phase is that your own embarrassing shortcomings are brought up to be seen by you and everyone around you. The situation that kicks off this phase is usually so overwhelming that you can't hide your faults.

During the Dismemberment phase, the situations that trigger you are generally not new to you, but they become amplified to nearly intolerable levels. Whatever your challenges are, during this phase they will become pressing and incessant. You may wonder how you are managing to survive.

The challenge that took Radha over the edge was Christina's phone calls for support. After Christopher died, Christina called a few times a day and sometimes more, and Radha could barely manage this frequency. It was hard for her to listen to Christina repeat the same problems, feelings, and frustrations over and over and then watch her continue to be unable to take action instead of being a victim to her circumstances. For example, if Christina was feeling lonely and wanted a dog, Radha thought Christina's next step should be to actively shop for dogs. For whatever reason, though, Christina spent time talking about her frustrations rather than exploring possibilities.

Radha's entire being is focused on taking action to improve whatever is problematic, so listening to her daughter do the opposite was challenging. And then it got worse. After Christina's breakdown, she called her mother four or five times a day for reassurance. Christina needed to touch base with her and hear validation that everyone was okay. As Radha puts it, "Christina was walking in new healthy ground, and I was part of her navigation." Radha had to dig even deeper for the patience she needed in order to remain supportive.

As a dedicated mother, Radha could not simply avoid Christina's calls. But every time she picked up the phone, the disparity between her and her daughter was glaring. At the start of each call, Christina would ask, "What are you doing?" Radha would immediately feel aggravated. *Which thing?* she would think. Radha was so active that she was always doing several things at once. Then she would imagine her daughter immobilized on the couch, obsessing over her emotions. Radha would feel impatient and frustrated, silently demanding, *Why don't you get up and do something?* And this was just the beginning of the conversation.

I was frustrated, and Christina could feel it. I dreaded her phone calls; they restricted the flow of my life. I had to keep going and say to myself, "I am not giving up on our relationship." She and I were very different people. We always had been. I had to rationalize it this way: "She did come out of my genes, and she is my daughter. So, somehow, I have to keep moving forward."

Radha's Dismemberment phase, like that of most people, forced her to strengthen aspects of herself that were underdeveloped, as she was repeatedly made to face circumstances that highlighted her weaknesses. Radha remained completely devoted to her daughter even though it required her to do what she was not good at doing: being patient with someone who was slow to act, had difficulty making decisions, and fixated on the negative.

If we face this process the way Radha did, it reconfigures weaknesses into strengths and turns shadow into light. The tedious, painstaking activity of overcoming our unhealthier impulses is the engine of a complete transformation. All phases lead us to this pivotal, almost sacred place where shortcomings transform into capabilities. Here, in the moments of being triggered, we make our weakness an offering to be sacrificed so we can become stronger. One of the primary functions of transformation is to shed something outdated, and doing so allows you to create something new. Therefore, the phases of transformation that precede Dismemberment all serve to get you ready to let go of some aspect of yourself that you no longer need.

Radha had to have more patience—and that was hard for her. She had to accept that she could not fix Christina. Radha's ongoing growth and present life circumstances demanded that she let go of her need to control Christina. The powerlessness she felt was debilitating:

At one point, I went to see my previous therapist. I asked, "What should I do?" I told her I was tired of being patient with Christina, and she said, "Do it. You have to find a way." So that's what I did. I simply had to continue to be patient, over and over and over again.

One of the biggest things that helped me was positivity and appreciation. I chose to see Christina's beauty. I made a practice of constantly reminding myself, "Christina is a beautiful, kind human being." I knew that I didn't need to be so worried and upset. I would give myself a pep talk: "It could be far worse. She is not a drug addict and she is not hurting others. She is just sitting on a couch watching television." I knew I needed to focus on her goodness.

Radha's session with her therapist reinforced how little power she had when it came to her daughter's life and choices. This fact is apropos to Dismemberment because a primary purpose of this phase is to help us let go of the ways in which we try to control others and ourselves. Radha did the only thing she could: relinquish her attempts to influence her daughter, listen, and mostly, let go of her own ineffective impulses to steer her daughter's life toward what she perceived as better. She began to learn to offer advice only when asked.

Think of Dismemberment as turning the light on in a room you would like to clean. The light helps you to find the dust bunnies, dirt, and stains. You might not be in the mood to clean, but once you reach Dismemberment, you have few options. Like Radha, you have little choice but to clean house.

Shifting Her Identity as a Mother

Another reason Christina's situation brought about Radha's Dismemberment was that it was devastating for Radha to feel inadequate as a mother. Being a mother was at the core of her identity. As she put it, "My mothering for my immediate family, and for the world, is an important part of who I am."

Transformation doesn't just transmute your issues; it also involves a change in identity. And Radha had to change her idea about what it meant to be a good mother.

> Before Christopher's death, Christina was on the dean's list; after he died, she floundered. Helping your child "feel better" after surviving her brother's murder is too huge for any mother. There is so much damage that isn't physical. Trauma of this magnitude is such an all-encompassing experience. The mothering impulse of wanting everything to be okay just didn't work anymore. I wanted to protect my children. I didn't ever want to see them hurt.

As a mother, you want your children to be well and happy and to thrive. When they are in pain, you want to give them love: a Band-Aid when they get hurt, and chicken soup when they are sick. You want to make things better for them. But this kind of pain does not just go away. I couldn't protect them—either one of them. I couldn't keep them from being hurt. Ironically, Christina's breakdown is what nearly killed me. Of the two events, I would have thought Christopher's murder would do me in.

I felt like a failure because the sunshine in Christina's life was out, and I didn't know how to turn it on for her. Somewhere deep inside, I knew she needed to turn it on herself. But I felt I should be able to show her the way.

When Christina had her breakdown, Radha entered new territory. Her daughter needed to hear her mother's voice at least once a day. This meant that Radha lived with the terrifying reality that her daughter had a risk of a repeated breakdown—a constant, gripping fear that at any moment, her daughter's emotional state could take a nosedive.

I still don't know how she is going to get there, to that place of being solid inside herself. Even if I live to be 102, at some point, she is going to have her mother die. I am concerned. That scares me.

After sifting through her frustrations and fears, Radha finally arrived at the core question that was feeding her terror: "Who will take care of Christina if she does not make this shift?" Like all mothers, Radha wanted to know that her daughter could survive without her. Fortunately, Radha was about to make a critical shift into the Surrender and Healing phase, where she would be able to find peace in her mothering.

✳ ✳ ✳

Dismemberment involves leaving what is familiar and going downward into your own darkness to discover that "what is missing is wholeness and a connection to the Self that can come about only through confrontation with one's shadow … and take an initial leap of faith into the unknown" (Hannan 2005, 195). This process, albeit painful, helps you let go of patterns of behavior, objects, people, places, a job, or even a lifestyle that, for whatever reason, is not aligned with who you are about to become. In order to re-member who you truly are, you must dis-member what you have been. Dismemberment is a process of taking yourself apart so you can rebuild yourself in a new configuration that can hold more love, power, and knowledge.

You will leave Dismemberment and encounter a sizable hurdle, a situation that asks you to change a deeply ingrained unhealthy pattern. Once on the other side of that, you can enjoy a shift out of darkness and into a much lighter, brighter period that brings healing.

11

PHASE 9: SURRENDER AND HEALING

Your task is not to seek for love, but merely to seek and find all of the barriers within yourself that you have built against it.

—*A COURSE IN MIRACLES*

Now that a part of you has psychologically or spiritually "died" during Dismemberment, it is time to put yourself back together again. Fortunately, you don't have to figure out how to do this or look for someone to help you achieve the task, although you can if you want. Because transformation is a naturally occurring process, life circumstances will organically arise to give you just the types of experiences you need. These seemingly serendipitous situations will help you mend, heal, and find yourself as you emerge out of the depths of the darkness.

In order to better understand the overall content and purpose of this phase, we will revisit the ancient Sumerian story about the goddess Inanna who traveled into the underworld in order to become whole. After Inanna experienced dismemberment and died, the god Enki sent two beings to the underworld to save her. When they found her, the keeper of the underworld allowed them to pour the food-of-life and the water-of-life on her, after which Inanna rose and journeyed out of the underworld.

The story illustrates that after Dismemberment we must have an event, like Inanna did, that brings us back to life. On the Map to Wholeness, the incident that saves us is a moment called Surrender, which also marks our passage into this phase. Surrender opens you to your new life and is equivalent to walking through a doorway that you had never been through before. It might take hours, or it might only take minutes.

Then the resurrected Inanna begins her ascent to the upper world. From the perspective of the Map to Wholeness, this ascent respresents Healing, the second aspect of this phase. Healing transpires over the course of months, or more commonly, several years. Although Healing offers relief from the intense suffering of Dismemberment, Inanna's process warns us that the journey is not easy. The primeval fable shows us that not only does the pathway lead ceaselessly uphill; it becomes complicated by demons from the underworld that cling to us as we make our way back.

Psychologist Sylvia Brinton Perera points out in *Descent to The Goddess: A Way of Initiation for Women* that as Inanna returns to the upper world, she must guard "against haste, staying with the endless affects and events of daily life until the flow of life energies return to [her] stricken soul" (Brinton Perera 1981, 78). It is crucial to understand this point: the Surrender and Healing phase can feel like it lasts a very long time. Thus, when you are in Surrender and Healing, it is important to be patient and to reorient yourself to the present moment. To do this, let go of your desire to rush your process by making hasty decisions, don't get lost in a fantasy about the future, and remember that the phase will *eventually end.*

Surrender

As defined by a dictionary, the word surrender does not have positive connotations, at least judged by prevailing social norms. None of the accepted synonyms of the term are particularly inviting: give up, concede, back down, cave in, lose, remit, crumble.

The term's wider historical connotations are equally unappealing, with close ties to political and military conflict where the leader of a beaten contingent cries out, "We surrender!" Because you might be a veteran or have a friend or relative who is, it might not be a stretch for you to envision what it would be like to be a great warrior who must lay down his or her sword. In this scenario, we can imagine that even though you and your soldiers fought valiantly, your efforts weren't sufficient to win or even to move forward. It would be understandable, for example, to feel profound and utter defeat and dejection. When you are ready to die for a cause or your country and then you are forced to surrender, it can feel like you are giving up a part of yourself. In this context, surrender is heartbreaking or even soul-breaking. Due in part to this ancient ancestral remembrance, the act of surrender tends to wear a shroud of shame: "I was unlucky." "I didn't have what it takes." "You outsmarted me."

Given this history and our collective ideas about the role of surrender, it is not a surprise that the term has negative associations. Consider, for instance, if we replace war images with more everyday scenarios: How many disagreements in your life went on far too long or became ugly because you would not "surrender"? In noncombat situations, we don't have someone standing there commanding, "Surrender, you have lost this battle." Fortunately, the term Surrender as related to the Map to Wholeness is not about battle or winning and losing. Instead, it is ultimately positive; it gives us new life.

Here Surrender occurs when you encounter a deeply troublesome and recurring dysfunctional pattern, and you choose an entirely new response. Your growth through the Map to Wholeness gives you the inner strength you need to make a big change and take healthier action. Instead of thinking of Surrender as a defeat or breakdown, it is more accurate to think of it as a breakthrough.

Surrender is a distinct event that marks your transition out of Dismemberment. Although the term traditionally appears to be one that asks the person to become passive, Surrender on the Map to Wholeness is not passive. Surrender involves making a distinct behavioral modification to change an outdated and less healthy habit, which might lead to having to say goodbye to a person, place, thing, ideology, or lifestyle.

To better explain what I am talking about, I will take a moment to discuss what was happening behind the scenes during Dismemberment, so you might better understand what contributes to the breakthrough of Surrender. During Dismemberment, a specific situation becomes progressively painful, going from bad to worse and making it increasingly difficult for you to cope. Your husband becomes increasingly despondent, and you become obstinate and more controlling; your boss requires more and more of your family time, and you continue to work harder and harder; or the stress you endure is now showing physical symptoms that say you must make a change, but there are bills to pay, and changing jobs is not a viable option.

You don't need to hunt around with a magnifying glass to figure out the issue that will trigger a surrender event. The cause for your surrender usually relates to the problem that is bothering you the most. Surrender is typically provoked by extreme strain in a very close relationship, such as with a spouse, child, parent, colleague, housemate, counselor, religious leader, or best friend. If you are in this stage, you can help yourself by identifying three situations going on in your life that cause you stress daily. It is likely that your surrender will pertain to one of these problems.

For example, my friend Judy is middle-aged and married, has two teenagers, and leads a successful career. Her son had been defiant for years, even though she offered him opportunities for health by providing him with a nice home, sports gear, and good clothes, and by driving him to his sports games and recreational interests. Over the years she had tried everything within her power to help her son, so when she discovered he was using heavy drugs—including cocaine and oxycodone, and probably others—she was at a total loss for what to do, and she went into the Dismemberment phase.

During Dismemberment it is important to make an honest appraisal of how your own shortcomings have contributed to your present-day misery. Judy's obvious contribution to her son's problems was her career, which required that she work long hours, including phone calls that interrupted dinners, weekends, and even vacations. Despite complaints from her children about excessive work, Judy recognized there was an even deeper contributor to the situation: her tendency to avoid conflict. Judy didn't want to upset her son by setting sorely needed limits. Afraid she would lose him if she was too strict, she allowed him to have freedom he could not handle. Dismemberment tends to have a rock bottom, and Judy hit this low point when her son went to jail and then entered court-ordered rehabilitation.

Six months later, during a pointed and raw therapy session, Judy realized that the only way she could help her son was to make three major changes: to begin to love herself enough so she could believe her voice mattered; to speak to her son about her needs and wishes, holding him accountable for his actions; and to step down from her prized executive position, work part time, and support her son's rehabilitation and recovery.

Surrender means you must actively change a deeply ingrained and unhealthy pattern. When you intentionally yield to and accept the overwhelming unhealthy circumstance in your life, your only option is to make the healthier choice, to take the "road less traveled." You must step outside your comfort zone and do what you have been dreading to do. There is a reason why you have avoided this action. Although you do not want to realize your worst fear, you are not willing to compromise whatever is at stake, what is dear to you. You have encountered a crossroads where you will no longer sacrifice your children, your body, your integrity, your lifestyle, or your livelihood because of your old pattern. Instead, you forge ahead and take a different action. This is your Surrender.

Surrender occurs when you have exhausted your ability to cope. When Judy's son walked out of rehab without completing the program for the fourth time, she knew she was done being the nice guy. She had no more energy or patience to hear his excuses or to be subject to his manipulations. Most importantly, she recognized that the problem was beyond her control. On some level, she *no longer cares* whether he goes back into rehab or not. She has let go of the outcome.

Judy's actual moment of surrender occurred when she resolutely told her son she would remove her emotional and financial support if he continued to reject rehab—and for the first time, she meant it. The experience of "not caring" about something you normally care about is an important indicator that you are at the threshold of surrender. When you no longer care, your pain outweighs your fear, and you have finally let go of trying to get your way or control the outcome. Also, you have let go of your fear of being abandoned or hurt in some way. You give up your habit.

How to Navigate Your Surrender

At the beginning of this scenario, you might have seen Judy as a victim of circumstance—a woman who had bad luck despite doing her absolute best to meet the incalculable demands of working and raising children. From the perspective of the Map to Wholeness, however, it's helpful to view Judy's situation in light of what she can control rather than what she can't. Appreciating the ways in which Judy's own unhealthy behavioral patterns might be contributing to an emotionally draining situation requires contemplation, inquiry, and honesty.

This approach leaves you empowered rather than victimized. Judy is not responsible for her son's actions and choices, but she *can* discover the ways in which she might be acting out of fear of abandonment ("My son will leave me if I hold him accountable") instead of love of self and others by telling the truth. In other words, she can learn how her son isn't the only one with issues that are contributing to the problem.

Recognizing your Surrender experience when it happens is less important than acknowledging that you have exited the darkness of

Dismemberment and moved into Healing. If you are interested, you can always retrace your steps later to determine when your Surrender happened and figure out why it was so meaningful to your development.

Healing

Like a nurse who treats an infected wound by cleaning it out, Dismemberment removes the crud stuck in your festering emotional sores by opening them up for you to experience—and for others to see. Experiencing your own inadequacies and having them witnessed by others acts as a disinfectant. To continue the metaphor, the Healing stage is like a salve applied to your tender, open, cleaned wounds. Healing gives you time, space, and supportive people so you can relax a bit, recover from being raw and exposed, and grow some new skin.

The word *healing* may seem to imply that you must seek someone or something that can help you repair yourself: a doctor, psychologist, psychiatrist, or self-help book. Receiving help from others is fantastic during this phase but is not necessary if it doesn't feel right. This phase, like the entire Map to Wholeness, is a natural process. Therefore, the Healing stage is less about *what you do* and more about *what is already happening* without your interference. In a real sense, you don't have to work hard at healing (or at becoming whole, for that matter); you need only be present to your immediate experience, because wholeness is already coming about.

I interviewed a middle-aged man named Duane who had recently moved in with his significant other and her children. As the founder of a web design company, he worked out of the home and was excited to be a stay-at-home dad. When I told him he appeared to be in the Healing stage, he was dumbfounded. "I don't see anything about my present life that is healing," he said. I pointed out how he had mentioned earlier that he always wanted to be a stay-at-home father because his own father had had to work long days. This period was very healing for Duane because, for the first time, he was living with a kind and caring partner, giving to their children, and coasting with a stable business.

Like Duane, in this phase you will encounter relationships, opportunities, and synchronous events that are deeply meaningful and therefore healing. In other words, Duane's situation was healing because on a daily basis he had the chance to give to his children in a way that his own father had never given to him. This was deeply healing for Duane even though he didn't know it.

I asked Duane, "Based on your history, isn't each day—when you greet the children, make them food, and play with them—a healing event?"

He laughed. "You're right. I never thought about it that way before."

Kenny: Healing through Hell

The good news for Kenny was that he now had concrete advice about how to achieve his goals. Writing a book about his spiritual experience would liberate him from simply trying to survive and allow him to thrive. The bad news was that writing a book is an enormous endeavor that takes a colossal amount of energy and dedication. When you are in Dismemberment, you don't have excess energy. In this challenging period, Kenny's life took a pivotal turn.

> I lost my job as a limo driver. I had been doing it for five years. So I went into window washing. A lot of my friends were highly successful at it. I bought a van and tools, put out ads, and started washing through the summer. But window washing is seasonal, and come October, the bids were drying up. No clients. By November, all the rest of the guys were ready to go on vacation to India, Bali, Hawaii. I was broke, down to my last dollars.

Kenny's worst nightmare was not being able to make enough income to survive. The threat of being hungry and homeless was always in the back of his mind. He knew himself well enough to know that without shelter he might be desperate enough to revert to crime, and if he started, it would be difficult if not impossible to stop.

Fortunately, the wisdom and strength instilled in him through his spiritual awakening and subsequent growth made him unwavering in his determination to choose honesty and perseverance over fear and crime. His only choice was to Surrender. Indicative of the characteristics of the Surrender stage, his life circumstances required that if he wanted to remain clean, without crime, that he would have to do something that went completely against his natural inclinations.

> That's when I met this real wealthy guy, and I broke down in humility. I had to beg. I said to him, "I am so broke that I can't even pay attention enough to try to help myself. I just have to get through the winter. Can you support me?"

> He got beet red and said, "I will think about it."

> Two or three days later, he called me back. He covered me $2,000 to meet my day-to-day expenses. I guess he had stayed awake at night, and it hit him hard. He said to himself, "Why can't I help him? How would it hurt me?"

> A week later he called and said, "Let's see how we can start a prison project."

> Instead of giving me more money, he paid me to build a nonprofit. We were off and running. The idea was to give back. I would be returning to my brothers and sisters. One thing led to another. We got nonprofit status, and about six months later, we came online and a whole organization came into being. Now I could share my spiritual experience with those who could appreciate it.

> We called the organization This Sacred Space, and I have been doing it ever since on one level or another. Starting the prison project felt so good. That was a very exciting time.

Surrender involves letting go and receiving help and support from a person or a group. Accepting support is often deeply humbling and even surprising. It can be hard to believe that others will give to you in your most vulnerable state. It can feel overwhelming.

The remainder of this phase, which tends to be relatively long, is filled with experiences that allow you to heal old wounds and change outdated, dysfunctional patterns. Everyday experiences can be healing, although most people would not interpret them as such. When you find yourself involved with individuals, books, or activities that make you feel free, you can bet that you are in the Healing stage.

My prison work with This Sacred Space was like a new career. I was doing what everyone else was doing: I was going to work, I was a businessman. I was designing a website, talking to people, meeting people, and saying things like, "This is my philosophy . . . ."

We also realized that the prison project could provide a way for me to realize the dream of a book. It could be a way to get the word out. Donations for the nonprofit just kept coming in, and then large donations started to come in for the book, too, but I needed a coauthor or maybe a ghostwriter.

People were giving to Kenny in a way that touched him to his core. This is how the Healing stage works, like soft, flowing water smoothing a stone, gently and beautifully, until all that is jagged falls away, leaving only magnificence.

Then I was at a weekend intensive for the Gangaji Foundation. My future writing partner, Shanti, said she wanted to write the book but wasn't in a financial situation to be able to do it for free. Another key player who was sitting there said, "Let's put the idea of your book out there to the foundation and see." So I put it out there: "I want to write a book." The response was good.

I thought it might be a good idea if I left them alone to talk, so I excused myself to the restroom. Later I learned that the founder of the conference said, "This would make a good book and would help a lot of people. I can offer financial support. I can buy Shanti's time out." When I returned, he gave me his card. We wrote for over a year.

For much of his life, Kenny had acted on his deeply held belief that the ends justify the means in getting one's needs met. This pattern arose from his early wounding. He stole, pimped, and forged checks to survive—but now he wanted none of that. He soaked up instruction like an eager apprentice.

It is very hard to write a book. It makes you dig up stuff you had forgotten all about, and it's still your shit, your inadequacies. It just has so many ups and downs. Makes you look at life. It made me put myself back in that hell again.

But at the same time, it is a healing process. It don't seem like it when you're doing it, but it is.

Activities such as sailing, fishing, knitting, and gardening can be healing; writing, whether for work or leisure, can be especially potent in this regard. Writing a memoir is emotionally grueling, and publishing one requires cultivating patience, which was a big part of the challenge and growth for Kenny.

The year after finishing the book was bad. The process of writing was emotionally grueling but also physically draining. I quit everything that year: meditation, seminars, satsangs, retreats. I just didn't go. I was tired of it in general.

When we got to the point when the manuscript was finally ready to go but not yet published, I ran out of money. The economy crashed, and people were pulling back their funding. Man, it was tough. My primary funder backed out. I couldn't find a publisher. My relationship with my girlfriend was on the rocks. I started smoking cigarettes and weed.

It was bad. All the money and support was coming to an end. Even my interest in the spiritual gatherings was gone. Something was coming to an end, but I didn't realize it.

Making the most of transformation is not for those who are discouraged by a challenge. Like Dismemberment and other phases, this phase requires the courage to see your own inadequacies and work through them—to choose healthier ways. Sometimes opportunities to heal come in the oddest packages.

And then my daughter's husband committed suicide.

She was totally distraught, and I knew that I had to be present for her through this traumatic experience. I went to stay with her for about three weeks.

I never stayed with her like that before, where I was in the role of helping her. Even though I had been a counselor to others before, this was different; this was my daughter. I felt inept. I didn't know how to be present.

All I did was listen to her and confirm that she was okay. I knew she had a lot of guilt, the fear that it was her fault. I had to hope that what I said and did was good enough to help her through this very intense period.

She was crying a lot, and I remember anxiously waiting for the right moment to go outside and smoke. When I finally got outside, I had this moment when I was standing there smoking and I thought, "Why am I standing out here when my daughter needs me? I am not helping her right now. I am only helping myself. She needs my presence." I stopped right there. That was the end of smoking. I threw them away.

Kenny's most important relationship at the time was with his daughter. During this phase, his daughter's tragedy gave him an opportunity to be a father, to give unconditionally and completely to her. Most importantly, for those weeks he placed her needs above his own.

I came back from being with my daughter, and I was very focused. It was very clear: I was going to get my book published. My girlfriend and I were breaking up, and I was moving out.

Then I was invited to speak at the Science and Nonduality Conference. I did a talk about my book and did an interview. Everyone was impressed with my presentation. "We'd like to help you get the book published," they said.

The following year, four years after Kenny and Shanti began writing, the book was finally published. It had a stunning cover, excellent reviews, and a poignant story of hope—that everyone can change for the better. Excited and relieved, Kenny had put his all out into the world.

When the book was first out, I was riding high. Then about four or five months later, things crashed. I thought the book was supposed to be an overnight success; it didn't happen. I started to sink back into my old worries and confusion.

Why can't I be like them—Gangaji, Jack Kornfield? I am like them. I have funding, I have a coauthor, I have a book. I am like them. I thought I had finally arrived.

But I didn't arrive. I did everything I was supposed to do, and it all fell completely flat. I went into a state of depression.

The central purpose of transformation is to achieve a new identity. Until your new identity emerges during the Birth phase, you will think you are further along in the process than you actually are. This means you will also think you are someone who you are not yet capable of being. Kenny reflected this struggle when he questioned, "Why can't I be like them?" and a few seconds later proclaimed, "I *am* like them." These contradictory comments reveal how his inner struggle is informed by his desire to be a certain type of person and his inner sensation that he *already is* that type of person. Behind his words, I can imagine he is saying to himself, "What's the problem?"

Kenny has two misperceptions that are characteristic of the Surrender and Healing phase. First, he imagines he will grow to become like his teachers because it is difficult at best to imagine possibilities one has never experienced. Second, the transformative experience instills a strong feeling that you have already transformed when in actuality you are not yet transformed. Like Kenny, you are still in the process of letting go of unhealthy habits and behaviors that you want and need to change.

The best you can do at this point is to slow down and remember that you are in process, and that like a lotus that emerges from the mud, you will eventually transform and flower.

Radha: "No More Walking on Eggshells"

About nine years after Christopher's death, Radha shifted out of the devastation of Dismemberment and into Surrender and Healing. Entry into this phase is marked by a significant experience of letting go, in which you are forced by circumstances to relinquish old patterns of control. Radha gave up the habit of being passive and accommodating, especially when it came to her daughter. This is a good reminder that Surrender does not mean becoming passive or weak. Instead it requires a great deal of strength, courage, and self-love to end a long-standing unhealthy pattern and choose a healthier option.

Radha's moment of Surrender was so embedded in the fabric of her everyday life that she didn't register it as anything special or unusual. In fact, it took several hours of discussion with her to finally uncover the exact moment when the Surrender occurred. Radha, Gary, and Christina were about to go on vacation together when it happened.

> Gary and I were at the house, getting ready to leave for the airport. We were waiting for my brother to arrive to pick us up, and waiting for him is always stressful. He always comes early. You tell him to arrive at eight o'clock, and he will arrive at 7:45. I told Christina, "He shows up early, so come early." But she was late. We were stressing.
>
> When Christina arrived, I freaked out. She said to me, "Why are you doing this?"
>
> I blurted back, "Why are you doing this to us? You know that being on time is a real big thing for me. Do you think you can accommodate? Do you think you could try harder?"
>
> I am phobic about not being on time, and she finally got how important it is to me. After that, she did try harder, and I settled down. I'm sure it is a huge effort on her part, but now she mostly comes on time.

While this interchange might not appear significant to others, it was pivotal in Radha's transformation into a new person. Radha violated her own unspoken, and perhaps unconscious, promise to herself: "I will not upset Christina." Since Christopher's death, Christina had struggled to accomplish even basic tasks. Radha had learned that if she asserted her own needs by asking Christina to act differently, Christina might have a breakdown.

> Through the years, I had learned to choose my battles. I couldn't change the fact that it took her forever to decide what to order in a restaurant. In those types of situations, I learned to just take a deep breath. When I had other things, more important matters, to talk to her about, it was very important to choose a good time so she wouldn't go into a tailspin—or worse, a depressive episode.

Given that Radha had spent six years walking on eggshells, fearful of upsetting her daughter, we can begin to understand the huge risk she took when she demanded, "I want this from you, I want you to do it my way, I want you to accommodate me, and this is why." By asserting herself to Christina, Radha feared jeopardizing her daughter's mental health. Even though Radha knew the chances that Christina would ever attempt to hurt herself were slim, the thought was still in the back of her mind. The fear of losing both of her children had prevented Radha from raising her voice, asking Christina to change, and, most importantly, requesting that Christina meet her needs.

This event in Radha's journey constitutes Surrender because, for the first time, she violated her own unspoken rule to never place her child at risk, even if it meant disregarding her own needs. Surrender happens when circumstances force you to break out of a deeply ingrained dysfunctional pattern and take a different action. This is so because what you normally do, your unhealthy tendency to try to control others or yourself, is no longer working. Your suffering becomes greater and greater, and you realize the only way out of it is to choose the healthier action you have avoided until now. Doing so is usually petrifying, but Surrender is also very exhilarating or freeing because you become released from your self-created prison of misery.

Radha helps to illustrate what this means. This was the first time she had ever asked her daughter for what she needed without first making certain that Christina was in the right frame of mind. For the first time, Radha didn't coddle Christina; she just announced how she wanted her daughter to change. She was tired of having to carefully plan the requests she made of Christina, because it required so much energy. When Radha stood up for herself in this way, she also demonstrated an unconscious awareness of Christina's developing strength. On some level, she knew that Christina could handle the request. More significantly, Radha was ready to ask for what she needed—and she did it.

With Surrender complete, Radha could move into the Healing stage. One of the hallmarks of Healing is relaxation. Relaxing happens after you surrender. After letting go, you settle down. While the sting of Dismemberment still lingers, life becomes gentler, softer, and easier. You can breathe a bit and can sometimes even do activities you might have done before Dismemberment happened. The pain and challenges aren't over, but your daily life becomes lighter and less consumed by anguish.

Once you go through Surrender, your confidence in your ability to repeat similar actions of self-care is much greater. For example, Radha began to make strides toward personal healing by putting her foot down at work. She said no to some opportunities to help organizations, just as she had started to do in previous phases—only now she did it more frequently and for more personally significant reasons.

This phase brings very specific experiences that are soothing after the ordeals of Dismemberment. As Radha created more space in her life by declining invitations to assist various groups, she received more requests to work one on one with people whose lives were touched by traumatic loss. She very much wanted to do this type of work. At the same time, seemingly serendipitous opportunities kept arising that gave her ways to serve others in ways that soothed her pain.

I was granted the most amazing opportunity: to cook Thanksgiving dinner for the inmates with whom I had been working. Thanksgiving is my favorite holiday, and I wanted to acknowledge how much my working with them over the years had meant to me. As a mother who loves to cook for her family, I offered the best of me, the deepest of me, to others. To cook Thanksgiving dinner for a group of inmates at San Quentin who had not, in some cases, had a home-cooked meal in thirty-three years was the most humbling and sublime of experiences.

We all sat at a table like we do at home. I baked bread, and the men were astounded that I did that for them. One man had never seen sparkling water and refused to try it. Another said he had not had fresh meat in twenty-five years. We went around the room and listed the things for which we were thankful. I had to remind myself to breathe.

One man said, "All my family outside have died, and this is my family now. I cannot find the right words to express how much this means to me to sit around a table like a family." He was sobbing. I cannot express the magnitude of healing that happened for me on that day. For this reason, I did this dinner *for three years until a new administration came along and wouldn't allow it anymore. We were grateful to have it as long as we did.*

The visit ended with an inmate playing "Amazing Grace" on his handmade flute. When the song was over, one man said, "I only have one word for you: grace." I was in tears, and I was humbled. We don't often get the opportunity to see how the steps we take in life reverberate through others' lives, and here were seventeen men telling me I had made a difference in theirs.

During this stage, Radha's most painful wounds were touched with love—the ultimate transformer. Radha boldly opened her heart and sweetly gave her love to people who, like Mark Taylor, had violated the lives of others. In so doing, she became more comfortable living with the fact of having endured her son's tragic death.

In her day-to-day life, Radha continued to volunteer with the Insight Prison Project. One day, she had the opportunity to meet with inmates at San Quentin who were working on an exercise called "letter of permission." In this exercise, the perpetrator writes a letter (that is not sent) asking for permission to meet with his victims or the survivors of his victims for a dialogue. In the letter, the inmate explicitly admits his guilt and expresses his feelings of shame and remorse.

An inmate named Richard read his letter, addressed to his victim's family, out loud. I started to cry uncontrollably. I felt he was addressing me, and when he finished reading the letter, I was compelled to hug him. It was a totally instinctive act, and it affected both of us. Richard later told me, "Radha, when I read my letter of permission and you hugged me, it was the first time I truly felt human in over twenty-six years."

My experience that day made me want to know if my son's killer, Mark Taylor, could also express his remorse and accountability. For the first time in eleven years, I wanted to meet him.

Through this unexpected opening, Radha took steps toward the ultimate act of healing that also had the potential to be damaging: to meet and talk with her son's murderer. One year after listening to Richard read his letter, which was also twelve years after Christopher was killed, Radha would sit down face to face with the man who had taken her son's life.

> I felt like I needed to meet him—to walk the talk. If I am going to be about forgiveness, I ought to go all the way. Before our meeting, I kept asking myself, "How can I find a comfortable place in my soul for this unstable person, so that every time I think of Mark Taylor, it doesn't eat me alive?"

Although visiting your perpetrator is probably a rare desire, Radha knew herself well enough to recognize the type of action that her heart and mind needed in order to be at peace.

Before engaging in this extraordinary dialogue, both Radha and Mark Taylor went through six months of preparation with Rochelle Edwards, head of the Victim Offender Education Group program of the Insight Prison Project. This training asked Radha to delve deeply into her present-day thoughts and feelings about her son's death, Mark Taylor, the impact that Chris's death had upon her family and her life, and what she needed from the meeting. Similar to the way in which writing a book forced Kenny to revisit and mend painful childhood memories, the process of preparation asked Radha to open herself to her implicit grief and sift through what was important and unimportant for her to say to Mark Taylor in order to be at peace.

Getting healthier in one area of your life tends to ignite action toward health in other areas. It didn't take long for Radha's attention to turn toward taking care of her body.

> Through this whole experience, I really developed respect for my body, because it had held up for me. It protected me. I realized that it was this incredible capsule for my soul, and it was strong and it was there for me. I have really been trying to give back to it by eating healthier, exercising regularly, and getting enough rest.

Radha was feeling truly grateful. She was doing all she could do to empower herself. But she knew there was little she could do to help

Christina rebuild herself. Serendipitously, though, a friend of Radha's gave Christina the gift of a group session with a woman named Karen who has psychic abilities and specializes in working with the bereaved. Little did Radha know this gift would provide the breakthrough she had desperately been wanting for Christina.

As a medium, Karen has the ability to hear, see, and feel people who have died. During sessions, Karen gets messages from people who have passed, often things only their loved ones on earth would know. The gift Christina received proved helpful, as Radha witnessed in person when she attended Christina's session with Karen.

Christopher showed up near the end of the session, with his ever-present humor. But even before he showed up, I had begun feeling very graceful and patient, realizing that if Christopher's spirit did not communicate with us that evening, I would still be fulfilled, because the smiles on the other parents' faces made me so happy.

As I sat listening, feeling quiet and reflective, Karen asked, "Who here has a connection to chocolate milkshakes?"

Christina and I laughed. It was Christopher; we used to have contests to see who could make the best chocolate milkshakes. (The secret is a dash of nutmeg.)

"I don't care if you gain twenty pounds," Karen relayed. "You haven't had a milkshake since I died. Go have one." Then she commented, "This one is real funny! That means he is very comfortable where he is."

Then she asked, "Was there something about an argument?"

Christina shared that the last time she saw Christopher, they had argued. She asked, "Is he holding on to that?"

"Of course not," Christopher assured Christina through Karen. "Let it go."   •

During that session, Christina's heart and mind relaxed and shifted. She finally had a chance to connect with Christopher, to feel close to him, and to get permission to begin letting go of her anger and pain about the fact that his death was so unfair, unjust, violent, and abrupt. It wasn't until she felt like she heard from Christopher himself that Christina could start to recover and heal.

After the session, a huge weight lifted from Radha's shoulders. Although this was by no means an instant cure, it really helped Christina. "It was time for her to let go of the anger, the uncomfortable feelings," Radha said. She decided that every year for Christina's birthday she would give her a session with Karen. Radha reported that the evening after the encounter with Christopher through the medium, "Gary and I went out and had chocolate milkshakes and made a toast to Christopher. They tasted so delicious!"

Radha had successfully broken through her fear of losing Christina and was taking action to discover and meet her own needs for health and happiness. She experienced healing by preparing to face her son's murderer and offer him love. In order for her to feel complete, her integrity required her to go to the extreme of meeting and being kind to the man who had taken her son's life. She had control over this aspect of her healing. When Christina got a chance to connect with Christopher, Radha's deepest pain subsided. She could now release herself from the heaviness of the past and birth her new self.

Surrender and Healing is the last phase of traveling in darkness. From the story of Inanna, we learn that "the journey back to the upper world can be disorienting" (Hannan 2005, 202) because you are recreating yourself. The Healing path upward asks you to incorporate—to put into your body—both what you have known before your descent into the underworld and what you learned about your hidden self once you were there. In other words, the next two phases—Birth, and Abundance and Creativity—help you to "integrate, accept, and live with [your] new consciousness," the new self (Hannan 2005, 202).

As the Surrender and Healing phase draws to a close, you will have fewer and smaller troubles and more confidence and support than ever before. The suffering will be over, and your life will become easier with each passing day. When Inanna completes her ascent and reaches the upper world, she is seen for the first time as a totally different woman. So too, in the Map to Wholeness, when you emerge as the newly recreated self, you exit the Surrender and Healing phase and enter the phase of Birth.

12

PHASE 10: BIRTH

The death of a seed is the birth of a plant;

The death of gametes is the birth of an embryo.

Salts die to form cells; cells die to form salts.

In each growth, form death and birth of matter.

—RM. SHANMUGAM CHETTIAR

Years ago, you started a journey beyond the boundaries of who you were. It began in the Seed phase on the Map to Wholeness, when your unconscious had the impulse to grow. During the life-changing event that occurred at the apex of the map's figure eight, you conceived your new self. This new self gestated inside of you through the next six phases in which you descended into the underworld. Now, in the tenth phase, you give birth to your new identity.

You have completed the hard work in your transformational journey. At this point, daily life will get easier. It might be difficult to believe, but it is true. You are rounding the base of the figure eight, signifying a great transition: the ending of dwelling in darkness and the beginning of living in the light.

It is difficult to portray the extraordinary nature of the Birth phase, but this story might help explain it. Once when I was attending a professional conference, the keynote speaker made an ordinary comment that struck me as profound. In referring to a famous person in the field, she said, "I knew Geoffrey Canada before he was *Geoffrey Canada.*" She placed particular emphasis on the second instance of the man's name to let us know that she'd had some sort of personal relationship with Geoffrey before he became widely recognized.

It was almost as if time stood still for me. I looked around. Most people were smiling and nodding, and a few chuckled, yet I was lost in her statement. I repeated the words several times very slowly in my head: "I knew Geoffrey Canada before he was *Geoffrey Canada.*" Adrift in my own world, I had many questions:

- Why do we say we knew someone before he or she became widely known, and imply that the individual is a different person now?

- What does this statement really mean?

- How can this seemingly facetious statement quite literally be true?

- When we say it, are we acknowledging the greatness of the transformed self?

Everyone recognized the social meaning of the speaker's remark, but I still thought to myself, "It's not as though Geoffrey 'wasn't himself' *before* he became famous." Surely, he still possessed many of the same characteristics, interests, and problems he'd had before gaining national attention. I continued to be perplexed for a number of minutes as I heard more about Geoffrey Canada's life.

He grew up in Harlem, New York, and against all odds was accepted into Harvard Graduate School of Education. He became a leader in the areas of social justice, nonviolence, and accessible education. His pioneering vision, counseling, and creative interventions transformed his community, which in turn influenced educational opportunities for many more communities. In 2009, the Obama administration chose to implement Canada's programs in twenty cities across the nation.

When I considered his history, I could see how there was truth to the implication that a dozen years ago, he actually *wasn't* the man now known as Geoffrey Canada. If we assume he wasn't the same man when the keynote speaker met him in 2002, what should we call him? "Geoffrey Canada in the making"? Clearly, Geoffrey Canada had transformed; perhaps that was the meaning of the cliché? Maybe this is why my research shows that we probably can't reach the heights of human potential, of being a positive force for change in the world, without transforming. It is probably the case that Canada's creations and successes resulted directly from his journey to wholeness, as is true for you and me.

When we look at the Map, it is clear that transformation is a process. Yet there comes a distinct point when the new you is recognized. For instance, the Geoffrey Canada whom friends and family knew and loved became *Geoffrey Canada* during a pivotal circumstance in 2009, when key stakeholders—including the President of the United States—*noticed* him, not only for his brilliant ideas, abilities, and fervent dedication, but also for his inspirational character, all of which developed through his journey. Being noticed meant that people in positions of power could assess the high quality of his work and his abilities, and they gave him opportunities accordingly.

The significance of *being detected* can't be underestimated. For example, the Grammy Award for Best New Artist recognizes a performer who releases "the first recording which establishes the public identity of that artist," according to the official guidelines. In other words, a star is *born*, and the birth occurs as a direct result of a credible source assessing and designating that person as the best new artist.

In a real sense, being discovered and recognized by an expert creates something new. You are seen in a way that reveals your truth, your essence, and your gifts. Even though most people who transform do not become famous, they are still discovered by important people in their lives. When this happens, a magnificent new you, endowed with unique gifts and talents, is born to your community.

When you go through the Birth phase, you adopt a new identity. This identity denotes your individuality, which once lay dormant as potential and now is beginning to blossom. Your new identity is archetypal and may be an aspect of yourself that has been present but latent in your life. Examples of identities that a person might birth include leader, businessperson, healer, teacher, artist, mother, father, veteran, survivor, doctor, wise one, immigrant, lover, genius, writer, expert, caregiver, farmer, and so on. Even though some of these identifiers represent jobs, within the context of transformation they also signify an important part of your essence.

Once you have a new self, you will naturally see and experience yourself and everything around you in a new way. Your world has changed because you have changed. Just as a baby leaves the environment of the womb and enters into this realm, so too will you leave behind your previous reality and enter into one that is new to you. As with the example of Geoffrey Canada, once he was recognized as a leader in social justice and liberating education—that is, once he was birthed—he found himself in a world where he was instantly given more respect, resources, opportunities, and power.

In addition to finding yourself in a different environment, don't be surprised if you also see friends, family, and coworkers from a new perspective. You might even wonder if they have changed.

Birth is quiet and would scarcely be recognizable were it not for three distinct events, which parallel the phases of childbirth:

1. Birth moment #1. You are ready to come out into the world, and an opening occurs. This moment is comparable to dilation, the first stage of labor.

2. Birth moment #2. You are seen by others. The equivalent in childbirth is that the baby's head comes out. You find yourself in a situation where your cumulative gifts can be shared at a new level of expertise for you. Key people see your uniqueness and your achieved mastery.

3. Birth moment #3. You are called by your new name—the baby emerges entirely. Key people can now see all of you, and they

literally—though unknowingly—say your new name out loud: "Look at the *elder (accomplished athlete, famous artist, respected council leader, religious teacher, visionary, etc.)* coming over here!"

In addition to knowing the three moments, you can detect the milestones of this phase because they possess distinct qualities. The Birth phase functions a bit like a physical, psychological, mental, or spiritual test. Just as countless leaders throughout history have tested warriors, students, and apprentices to determine whether they have achieved the capacities worthy of a title or status, so too will you be tested by the circumstances of your life. On the Map to Wholeness, the Birth moments ask you to step up and become your wholeness, because you are ready. You will discover that these moments demand all of who you are and have become. For this reason, Birth involves dichotomous extremes of disbelief and awe, trepidation and exhilaration. These remarkable moments can make you feel like time is standing still or that you are watching yourself from a short distance away. Your life circumstances literally ask you to become more alive, and so you do.

The entire Birth phase might occur within the span of a few hours but tends to arise across several days, weeks, or more rarely, months. As you live through the Map to Wholeness one time, it becomes increasingly easier to recognize these phases when they happen to others and yourself. Below are the details of how it unfolds.

The First Birth Moment: You Reach an Opening

Birth moment #1 happens when you first become exposed to your new, emerging self. Because you have radically changed, you experience the world differently, so in a real sense, you also begin entering a new world. This experience is very private. No one else has any idea that a new you is coming (birthing) into form. But you get a sense of your new identity through a very distinct experience in which you have the intimidating opportunity to step into shoes that are one size too big for you, so to speak. For example, the Birth phase might begin when your boss invites you to a meeting of higher-level managers that you typically would not attend. You are nervous yet excited about the opportunity to share your ideas and be seen for who you really are. When you enter the situation, you may immediately feel disbelief ("This situation appears way too challenging and important"), trepidation ("Do I belong here?"), or even alarm ("I don't feel right here!"). In the example of attending a high-level meeting, years later you might recall how this event was directly responsible for your promotion.

I once interviewed a young man in his thirties, Kaito, who perfectly described his first Birth moment:

> I had this moment when I was teaching a breathing meditation class by myself in a gymnasium in San Jose. I realized that a year or two before, I would have been terrified. I didn't have much prepared for the class, yet I was hearing words come out of my mouth that really engaged the people and helped them move forward. I thought, "How the hell is this happening? This isn't me." But it was me.

You have been preparing for this instant for years by developing a stronger belief in yourself and your ability to realize your true potential. After it is over, you may wonder, like Kaito, "Did I really just do that?" You don't see yourself this way because you haven't yet identified with the self that has shown up.

Others usually don't notice this transitional experience as anything significant, yet it is monumental to you. No one in the yoga class knew Kaito was just becoming recognized as capable after much effort. It probably looked like he had been facilitating and teaching like that for years.

The centerpiece of the first Birth moment is experiencing an opportunity to make use of your gifts. You recognize that you have the knowledge or skills that the moment demands, yet you are likely to question whether you are the one who best meets the needs of the situation. It's a bit like the age-old warning, "Those are some big shoes to fill." In the near future, you will discover that the big shoes you stepped into in your first Birth moment were actually your own.

The Second Birth Moment:
You Are Seen

During Birth moment #2, the knowledge, skills, and abilities you developed along your journey become visible to a person or a group specializing in the area of your expertise. These authorities understand what it takes to be the type of person you have become, whether you are a gardener, counselor, manager, or humanitarian. Most importantly, these experts can accurately judge the degree to which you have attained mastery.

Let's say you were ordained into the priesthood a few years ago but did not feel totally comfortable with that identity until recently. Your openness is a signal that you are ready for Birth. At about this time, a tragedy hits your community. You rise to the occasion skillfully and compassionately, leading your congregation toward the type of healing that transforms suffering. Your leadership is exactly what the people need, and they respond with overwhelming trust and gratitude. The congregation embraces you as its spiritual leader in a way it had not before. From this point, there is no need to question whether your gifts are valid, interesting, or needed.

You are ready to meet the moment by claiming your authority and allowing others to see your talents instead of hiding them. The second Birth moment asks you to move into a position where you are ready to do a task, not only because you are the best person for the job but because you are quite possibly the only one.

The Third Birth Moment:
You Are Named

The third and final Birth moment occurs when a person or a group literally calls you by your new identity or archetypal name. Most such instances do not occur on stage—"And here is our community leader, Sally Johnson!" Whether your naming occurs on a larger platform or a smaller one, you probably won't recognize it as Birth moment #3 until later, when you are assessing your own transformational journey.

Birth moments tend to be camouflaged in the garb of daily life. Despite the miraculous meaning of the third Birth moment, when it occurs, you do not hear a voice coming from the sky or see a lightning bolt discharge from a cloud. This moment is much more likely to occur on an ordinary day when a person casually speaks your archetypal name. It might come as a compliment: "You are really brave, a true *explorer*." It is often said nonchalantly: "Wow, your home remodel and new landscaping have turned this place into a palace. It's finally fit for a *king*." Or it might be matter-of-fact: "Yeah, that person over there is a *painter*." Your name tends to go undetected because, in the moment, you are not thinking about your identity; you are immersed in a playful, flattering, or mundane experience.

The person who casually says your archetypal name has made a genuine and accurate observation about your gifts and the essence of who you are. This person may not emphasize your name, because naming you is not his or her intent. Moreover, whether or not anyone, including you, recognizes the significance of the moment is inconsequential. Within the context of wholeness, the third Birth moment has been accomplished.

Examples of archetypal names include the following:

- Advocate
- Artist
- Athlete
- Caregiver
- Child
- Creator
- Explorer
- Gardener
- Hero
- Intellectual
- Lover
- Magician

- Maverick

- Orphan

- Performer

- Royalty (king, queen, monarch)

- Trickster

- Visionary

- Wise one or sage

An archetypal name might be related to a career (*artist*), social status (*community leader, pioneer in thinking or creativity*), or unpaid talent (*social justice leader*). Some archetypal designations may have negative connotations. For example, *servant* may initially sound like a horrifying title, but the term *servant leader* has been retooled by contemporary business philosophy. According to the concept of servant leadership, a leader helps others succeed by sharing power and tending to their needs, and in so doing, he or she contributes to the prosperity of the whole.

The key to recognizing your third Birth moment is to pay attention to your feelings, your intuition, and what happens around you. If you are fortunate, you will hear your name called—and with that name comes direction.

Kenny's Birth Moment #1: "No More Trying to Be Something I Was Not"

Kenny was struggling to bridge the giant gap between knowing spiritual truths and actualizing them in his daily life in order to live a balanced existence in which he could take care of himself and have healthy relationships. Without a job or enough cash to survive the winter, he thought of Bali. Over the years of hanging out with spiritually oriented friends, he had heard that Bali was a place imbued with spirituality. It seemed his only hope to get out of the rut of simply surviving. Instead of waiting for a savior as he had done for so many years in prison, Kenny took himself on a pilgrimage to find God. He gave his landlord notice and purchased a plane ticket to Bali with the little money he had.

I didn't know why I was in Bali; I just knew I was supposed to be there. When I got there, I met a friend, and we went on a motorbike ride. It was like God told us to go to this place, Tampak Siring. I didn't know what to expect.

When we arrived we found out there was an ancient temple there called Tirta Empul, built around a sacred spring. It had many pools and fountains of holy water. The temple was all about purification, rebirth, and baptism.

I just ran and jumped in. I said to myself, "Oh, this is why I came to Bali." There were thirteen fountains, and we bathed in and drank from each one.

Bathing in the holy waters was sacred. The Hindu god Indra had dropped his pitchfork into the earth, and from that spot up sprayed these waters so he could be reborn. I was there to get baptized and be born again, to come home to these holy waters to give thanks to the mother, to give thanks for saving me from prison.

I came all the way back to the mother. The Muslims go to Mecca, and there is Kumbh Mela in India; I had to do my pilgrimage to Bali. Whatever happened in that moment, from then on, I started speaking in a different way, almost from a place of knowing, of surety.

When Kenny told me this story, I was amazed at how beautifully this baptismal ritual set him up for his first Birth moment. The soul knows the ancient and natural rhythm of transformation. The culture and place allowed Kenny to feel comfortable being himself fully.

I got the opportunity to speak in Bali at a poetry event, a place for the spoken word. It was interesting to see the different energies present in the room. The vibe seemed open: "Okay, let's see what he has to say." I spoke for about thirty minutes.

The crowd was diverse, with people from all over the world: London, Bali, Holland, Austria, India, Germany, all over. The people were too diverse to please them all, so I decided not to worry and just to be myself. I was just being matter-of-fact: "This is my experience as a teacher." For the first time, I was no longer hesitant or trying to be politically correct.

My talk was totally different than any time before. More relaxed. No more apologizing or trying to be something I was not: This is who I am, this is what is going on, this is how I am doing my life, this is my awakening, this is my spiritual experience, like it or not. This awareness of my own situation gave me permission to be fully me. I just shared my inner experience.

The people were really quite grateful, because I ended the event with a moment of silence. Everybody in the whole place stopped and became almost still. That stillness is universal.

It was interesting. I did three or four more talks, and each time, the crowd got smaller and smaller. I can see why. Bali is not a place where people do talks. It is a place of constant ritual and ceremony but not of dialogue.

Birth moment #1 is very private. No one knows that you are transitioning out of an old self and into a new one. Kenny stood before a diverse group of people (as opposed to the Caucasian-dominated audiences that tended to attend his previous talks), and for the first time, he told his story as Kenny Johnson, the black man from Star City, Arkansas.

The liberation that Kenny experienced in Bali made his return to the Unites States painful and even perplexing. How could he accept himself in a country where he didn't feel totally accepted, absolutely free? He talked about his feelings and thoughts once he was home.

Bali was very quiet, loving, inviting, and ritualistic. I fell in love with the scenery, people, rituals, and outdoor satsangs. In Bali, every day I could wake up and there were people taking action in the service of truth. Wherever I turned, people were serving God. I didn't have to go to the chapel. It was just there, everywhere. Being back home, I realized how daily life in the United States was dominated by activities of the mind and not of the spirit.

In Bali, I felt literally free to come and go. When you got on your motor scooter, there were no police to monitor you or tell you what to do. Law enforcement was virtually nonexistent. Once back in the States, I sensed how much I was always being monitored and watched—all the highway patrol, city police, even citizens, all policing each other.

I realized that for my entire life, I was trying to make people like me or love me. That is the best word for it: trying. I would bend over backward to go out of my way to make someone else happy or approve of me. I realized I was causing a lot of suffering for myself and discomfort for other people because they were being placed in a situation of having to deal with me.

Now when I talk to a group of people, I walk up, say what I have to say, and walk away. They can like it or hate it. What I say might fit within their understanding of truth, or not. Doesn't matter to me anymore. I am okay with that. I'm done trying to be like Gangaji; her husband, Eli; Adyashanti; Rupert Spira; Swami Vivekananda; "Ananda"—anybody. Let it be me, and let it happen.

Because of this awareness, I decided that I wouldn't do impromptu talks. I would only talk when I was invited. I wouldn't promote myself when I was in these spiritual places. I would just go and enjoy the holiday.

International travel is a potent way to gain a new perspective—especially one that is radically different from your typical outlook. Kenny's travel to Bali helped him see the ways in which he had limited his own happiness and potential. This revelation was liberating because he now understood that he was sometimes his own greatest obstacle. But his travels also created an awareness of a condition that was the opposite of liberating.

When I returned from Bali, I tried to do a couple of satsangs, but I was very depressed. I was very, very sad. I saw so much that I hadn't seen before. I realized that a lot of our suffering was around class. I got to see America as it was. I could see what was making people suffer and how most didn't know it.

I realized I was in a class struggle, that there was a higher class than me, and that my friends unconsciously embraced me according to status. I was born to an untouchable class. Even people who read my book didn't trust me. I have asked for help marketing my book, and some have said, "Are you hustling me?" Someone even said, "The name of the book should be The Next Hustle."

How was it that I was interpreted as hustling, whereas if a white man were to begin marketing his books, he would be bringing his eggs to market? What *made me different? Yet there was a difference. I was seeing things I hadn't seen around class.*

Kenny was completely overwhelmed by his first-hand experience with oppression. How could he ever be socially and emotionally free (beyond the spiritual freedom he felt while in prison) if societal divisions that came from a different era restrained him? His disillusionment was compounded by being very poor and, therefore, totally vulnerable.

> *When I got back from Bali, a very loving couple gave me somewhere to stay until I could make enough money to get my own place. I was very grateful. It was humbling, embarrassing. There I was, a sixty-two-year-old man, and I didn't have a place to stay. You hear about how writers and musicians are struggling, doing great work in certain aspects of their lives but not able to feed themselves, clothe themselves, or buy a car. I am grateful I went through that experience.*

This dejecting episode may not sound like it belongs in a phase called Birth, yet birth itself isn't always about celebrating. For example, when a mother gives birth to a second child, the whole family experiences the loss of a certain quality of relationship that exists when there is only one child. The arrival of the second child means that all family members must adjust to the change.

After his first Birth moment, Kenny had to let go of what remained of his pride by asking for help with his basic needs. He also had to face realities about classism and racism in the United States, which he had not previously seen. When you greet a new reality, there is always a loss of innocence, and that often evokes grief.

Kenny's Birth Moment #2: They Were All in Attendance

Only a month after his return from Bali, Kenny traveled to the Bahamas as an invited guest speaker at a prestigious venue. Thankful for the diversion but mostly for the humbling opportunity, he left for a satsang at Swami Sivananda's yoga retreat center.

It was really an honor that Swami Sivananda, a founder of ashrams around the world, had invited me there. In order for that to happen, these sages had to okay it, giving me the right to come and speak and touch so many lives. Wow.

I got there on a Sunday, and I had to wait one day, two days, three days almost, until it was my turn. I listened to the teachings and did the meditation.

The meditation hall was like a cave. A lot of meditation and yoga had happened there; ritual and ceremony took place there all the time. It was really, really beautiful. We watched a video of Swami Sivananda and some of his teachings. In the video, they showed him flying in a plane around the world, across boundaries, to spread peace. He flew over the Berlin Wall, and fighter jets scrambled to shoot him down. When they flew next to him to take the plane down, he held up a flower.

I thought, "Wow, this is one powerful cat." I realized that he was one of the few teachers who got up off the chair and actually did something. Most of these gurus sit on a stage and say, "There is nothing but love ... give me the money." I was really impressed by that.

This swami broke the guru mold. Kenny realized he did not have to be like other teachers. The example of this radical spiritual guide with a peace plane allowed him to accept that what he had been through in his life qualified him to be a spiritual teacher, one with a unique way of expressing truths. A few days later, it was finally Kenny's turn to talk.

At this point, Kenny had given many talks in front of spiritual groups. But this one was different. He had the chance to speak as a teacher of teachers. Standing as an equal among leaders who were recognized as enlightened, he was utterly humbled as he entered the venue.

It was my turn to sit down and speak to the whole ashram, Swami Swaroopananda, his consort, and all the other swamis. Typically, everyone didn't show up to all the talks, but the night I spoke, they were all there.

Then I realized that so many other people had come up there and sat in those same chairs, in that same seat, from around the world. Wow, man! It was a momentous occasion. It was a special time for me. I had to represent, as they say, my teachers Ramana Maharshi, Papaji, Gangaji, and also my African American lineage, ex-convicts—all wrapped up in one.

Being able to sit there and just take it all in for a moment, and then speak, was really quite amazing.

I talked about the prison program. I told my spiritual experience.

The essence of Birth moment #2 is that you are in a situation for which, knowingly or not, you have been preparing for years. Despite the fact that you are, in a sense, an expert, during the second Birth moment, you enter the big leagues—a large and important group or situation. It is an absolutely thrilling boost, as it was for Kenny, and you may want to shout, "I am finally here!"

It was an amazing talk, as far as I was concerned. I was able to speak to a group of people who had seen speaker after speaker after speaker. Powerful men and women had gotten up there to speak, and I was able to do the same thing. I got a standing ovation. It was something to get honored by the swamis in attendance.

I may never be called to go there again. I made the most of it while I was there. My heart was just wide open. It made my heart fly. If they wanted me to return there right now, I would.

Like a baby coming out of the birth canal, during Birth moment #2 you literally enter a larger world that is more complex, challenging, and rewarding than where you came from. You might wonder for a brief time, as Kenny did, how you got there—even though deep within, you are aware that you got there because you endured the losses and growth of transformation. Although others are there to welcome you into the new realm, as they did Kenny, they do not know you or your journey well enough to understand just how intimidated and humbled you feel.

Kenny's Birth Moment #3:
"My Chocolate Chief"

In order to tell the story of Kenny's third Birth moment, I need to provide a bit of Kenny's reflection about the meaning of his his travel to Bali and his talk in the Bahamas.

> *The Bahamas turned everything around, because I was meditating; I was around a lot of awake people. I hung out with black people in the government of the Bahamas. I saw that black people had value, and they had meaning. Being down there, it just turned me around, put me on a new trajectory.*

The combination of experiencing freedom in Bali and accepting his ethnic and spiritual identity in the Bahamas was nothing short of liberating for Kenny. The weight of internalized classism, racism, and self-defeat had been lifted.

> *I came back and found a new part-time job, and then another one, and started saving money so I could move out of my friends' house. I was energized. I was fired up. I came to peace with what I had learned about classism. I realized that I could belong anywhere. I realized it was all divine.*

> *I realized that there is an equalizer called consciousness and that meditating and praying matter. You can experience something that transcends color. Waking up in consciousness transcends everything. Waking up allows you to be in the subculture of conscious beings.*

> *I saw that love brings people closer and closer, and all I had to do was bring others closer to love. Do my part. That was all I had to do.*

In the weeks that followed his return from the Bahamas, Kenny used video chatting to reconnect with several people he had met in Bali who were deeply affected by him and his talks. An encounter with one person in particular gave him his third Birth moment: being addressed by his name.

> *A young lady, Pilar, had come to three of my Bali talks. Like others who wanted to stay in touch with me, she affirmed that I was a wise teacher, a good teacher. She was totally supportive and complimentary, so unwavering. Even though I'd*

heard that before, it was still strange to hear. She kept calling me "my chocolate chief"—her guru. I had never really heard that before. I said, "Wow. Okay ... all right ... cool."

Kenny's Birth name, "Chocolate Chief," made us both chuckle when he said it out loud. I had never heard someone receive a name of that nature because it was so personalized. I questioned whether "Chocolate Chief" was truly his Birth name, but after many rounds of interviews, it was clear that before that point he had not been recognized as anything else but *teacher*, and that name didn't seem to fit. It was clear that what had been missing from his identity as a spiritual leader was the fact that he is African American.

I was trying to appeal to white people. The spiritual field that I was hanging out in was Caucasian-dominated. People were trying to get me to fit into their boxes: "This is how your awakening should look and how you should talk about it."

Bali gave me permission to be fully me: "This is my cultural background. This is my inner experience." I felt freer.

Naming not only recognizes your newly revealed essence but points to your purpose. Being in Bali introduced Kenny to a new type of spiritual community in which each day was permeated with ritual and prayer. His baptismal experience sacralized his journey and gave him permission to be himself. He had spent years trying to match his teachers, none of whom had had his type of upbringing, spent decades in prison, or was African American. In Bali, he spoke for the first time without the burden of emulation, and in the Bahamas, elders acknowledged Kenny as one who holds wisdom.

Radha's Birth Moment #1: Just to Be Open

Radha's first Birth moment occurred when she met Mark Taylor. After twelve years that included recovering, learning, doing prison volunteer work, and participating in the Victim Offender Education Program, Radha was well-prepared. She approached it with a feeling of openness and curiosity about what would happen and with no expectations about how her son's murderer would behave. To do otherwise would not have been healthy for her. She did however, hold open the possibility of actually helping Mark Taylor heal.

On the day of the dialogue, she was accompanied by her dear friend Jaimee, whose job it was to provide emotional support and even to help Radha communicate if she was unable to find her words. After an hour of passing through security checkpoints, Radha, Jaimee, and Rochelle Edwards, head of the program, arrived in a cold, empty, and stark room. Shortly afterward, Mark Taylor's sister arrived, and then Mark Taylor was escorted in.

Sitting across from each other at a metal table, Radha and Mark's dialogue consisted of telling each other about the day of the murder and the effects trauma had had upon their lives. They both had a chance to ask questions of clarification about the details and about their thoughts and feelings. Radha showed Mark pictures of Chris at various stages of his life and told a few stories so Mark could get to know Chris a bit more.

The two roommates had only known one another two months when the tragic event occurred, so Radha didn't know Mark other than from the trial. She asked him to tell her about his daily life, and he told her he worked 8:30 a.m. to 3:30 p.m. Monday through Friday. He watched television after work, and he owned a heater pot that he purchased for $15 in prison that he used to reheat food in his cell. When she asked him if he helped others or himself along the lines of personal growth or reading self-help books, he said he did very little of that kind of thing. Jaime and Radha offered to bring him books to read and he agreed.

As expected, the dialogue was an intense experience that ran the gamut of emotions. Some moments were flat and unremarkable, and others caused Radha to weep. There were several times during the hour-long talk that each person got a chance to reveal a bit of their character. As the time was drawing to a close, Rochelle Edwards asked both Radha and Mark if they wanted to have future contract. Then the following series of poignant moments happened.

I asked him how he would like our relationship to be in the future, and he said he would be an unwelcome guest in my home. I was not expecting that type of response. Then the facilitator skillfully interjected and tried to help him to understand that he had the power within him to change for the better. Her words were almost poetic, something along the lines of: "There are things you can do to become welcomed. You can grow into yourself, become whole in the places where you think you are broken, where you are wounded, where you are scared and angry. Becoming welcomed requires some work, some healing, and as you do that work within yourself, the doors of people's homes and the doors to their hearts will open for you."

Without a thought, I jumped in and said, "My heart has been open to you for a long time, regardless of the way we came into relationship, and also your family. This was true from the beginning. I will say, you are not on my top ten, can't-wait-to-be-with people, I will give you that."

He responded, "I am probably on the bottom ten."

I said gently, "I wouldn't be here today if you were on the bottom ten."

During this and many other moments during the dialogue, Radha demonstrated her uncommon character and awe-inspiring ability to extend unconditional love to even the most unlikely person in her world.

In addition to the content of what was spoken, Radha satiated her deep-seated need to do everything within her power to liberate the pain and suffering in herself and Mark by getting to know him, telling him the truth, and offering him support, love, forgiveness, and compassion. Even though she would have like to have Mark make attempts to grow as a person, the meeting allowed her to put her hopes to rest and her heart at peace.

I was open to any outcome. But I went in with great hope that he would take responsibility, to own up to what he did in a genuine way, to say something like, "I am sorry I made a horrible mistake." I understand horrible mistakes. I would have given him a hug and said, "I get it."

But the dialogue confirmed my beliefs about his character. It was like getting a fresh report card ten years after the trial, and the grades had not changed.

He even accused our family of bribing the jury. It was so appalling that I just had to sigh and say to myself, "I know there is nothing I can do about this." I can't help him.

Despite my disappointment, I felt a deep sense of relief afterward. I knew that Christopher was proud of me. I walked away finally comfortable about my relationship with Mark Taylor. During the dialogue, I tried many times to offer him a bit of help, but he did not open that door for himself. I offered him forgiveness on a silver platter, and he didn't accept it. Yes, he would still be a presence in my life, but now my own eyes and ears told me that he needed to work on his life and that I could not help him with that.

Despite real disappointment, this pivotal meeting offered Radha unparalleled healing and peace. She did what was, for most, unthinkable: she sat down with her son's killer, and she did it in a way that was true to her vow to approach each moment with grace.

What made me saddest was that two lives had been lost: Christopher's and Mark's. Mark had chosen to live his life in prison without adding anything positive to the community there. All I could do was let go.

I had to come to a certain place for me to blossom in my own spiritual traumatic journey. I finally accepted that I wasn't responsible in any way for Christopher's death or his murderer's rehabilitation. That was a relief.

Radha's feelings of guilt ended. She had to know resolutely that although murder is never a valid solution to a dispute, if her son had contributed to his own demise (and, secondarily, Mark Taylor's suffering in prison) as the result of any choice or action Radha had made, she could now put it to rest. She knew with certainty that she had put forth more than the necessary effort to make it right. All was done.

Shortly after the meeting with Mark, Radha recognized that something was very different about her.

Afterward, a calm grace came over me. I realized then that I was in touch with myself and feeling kind. I realized how important it was just to be open.

The change was not immediate. It took a week or so to detoxify from the intensity.

At this point, she understood that she would no longer waste energy that could be directed toward her own health. Now was the time to release her hopes for Mark Taylor. Letting go is an important activity throughout the descending aspects of the Map to Wholeness, but it is particularly crucial during the Dismemberment and Surrender and Healing phases, because the purpose of those phases is to cleanse and clear what is no longer needed.

Radha's Birth Moment #2: Unsuspected Witness

Radha and I exhausted ourselves twice trying to discover her Birth name. There is evidence that Radha birthed herself as a *teacher*, because when she was nonchalantly called this name by many people (but in particular by a participant in a group she led about grief), she immediately rejected it. Initially rejecting a title is a sign—but not a guarantee—that it is your Birth name. Radha was certainly teaching others, but this identity seemed too narrow, considering her character, stories, and activities. She had blossomed into a civic leader, inspirational figure, and compassionate guide, as well as a teacher.

The very last story she told me provided the clincher. The event happened about a week after her dialogue with Mark Taylor. As it happened, Radha's second and third Birth moments occurred within the confines of about an hour as she sat with a group of incarcerated men in San Quentin. Having both moments within one experience is relatively common, because as you emerge and others witness who you are, it is probable that they are really captivated by you (in Birth moment #2). Because of the momentousness of the occasion, it is likely that one person will summarize their experience of you in words.

Right before the meeting with Mark Taylor, I talked about the pending dialogue with my original group of inmates in the Katargeo Program (San Quentin prison's in-house rehabilitation program), with whom I felt a particular bond because I had been working with them for years. I shared with them how I felt about it, how I was apprehensive, and how I was worried I would have the heebie-jeebies when I saw Mark Taylor.

After the dialogue, I met with them again. We were sitting in a circle. One man said, "I knew where you were going the day of the dialogue. I was incarcerated at that prison once. I know you had to be there early to get through security. I was praying for you and imagining it when all of a sudden it came to me: What if I had this opportunity? So, I had a conversation in my mind with the mother of the person I killed. I realized that I was so proud that I had grown so much, that I could express my remorse in a genuine way and mean it. I would never have been able to have that experience had it not been for you."

This man's sincere compliment was unexpected, and Radha was deeply touched by it. In the context of having just met Mark Taylor, the inmate's words were even more meaningful. Radha did not receive the gift of genuine remorse from Mark Taylor that this man implied he would now be able to give to the family of his victim; but through this interchange, she was granted the ability to understand what she had done to help another so profoundly. Until that moment she didn't truly comprehend the impact of her years of giving guidance, support, and most importantly, love.

Radha's Birth Moment #3: A Mother's Love

In order to understand Radha's third Birth moment, you need to know what happened to her during the fourth phase, called Return, shortly after Mark Taylor's trial had finished.

After the trial, I wanted to get close to the ground, back to my body and soul. I went to an upscale hiking retreat on the San Mateo, California, coast. On one of the excursions I met a barefoot Hindu hiking guide. He was so excited that my name was Radha. My namesake is Radha, the Hindu goddess of selfless, endless, unconditional love—Krishna's consort.

When I gradually opened up to the guide about my reason for being on the hike, he said, "Do you realize that it is your responsibility to go out and love the world? Do you know that?"

He was very impassioned and at some point said very intently, "You know you cannot love your husband more, you cannot love your daughter more, or your friends more. What you have to do is find a way to pour the love for your son somewhere."

The words from that Hindu hiking guide have stayed with me all this time. I carry them around in my heart.

Ironically, Radha did exactly as he foretold. Over the course of twelve years, she spent thousands of hours pouring her love into countless others through her efforts to change gun-control laws, help groups of inmates, and provide support to the San Francisco Food Bank, to name a few of her many worthwhile endeavors. She cannot ever know how far the impact of her efforts will reach. Through her trauma, Radha's burning heart was unleashed, and like the Hindu goddess Radha, it became endless.

This story of how Radha lived up to the calling of her namesake provides the background necessary to appreciate her third Birth moment. As mentioned in the previous section, about a week after Radha met Mark Taylor, she facilitated a regularly scheduled group at San Quentin. The group consisted of men she knew well—and as it turned out, they also knew her well.

I had told my story of meeting with Mark Taylor, and most of the men wanted to share their thoughts and reactions. I was already inspired by what they had to say when one man said something that floored me:

"Radha, you never know what happens with the seeds that you plant." Then he said something that just got me to the core of my being: "You also may want to consider that that might have been the first time in his life that Mark Taylor sat across the table from a mother's love."

I felt like I was hit with something. Wow. What he said really blew me away.

Incidentally, both those men who said such powerful things to me that day are now free, and the first is married and has a child.

Radha has a keen ability to feel the nuances of her feelings and to express them through precise use of words. There are a few ways to describe what being named feels like, but her account does a great job of it. It feels like being hit with something. The words you hear make you stop internally, even though your external actions may continue fluidly forward as if nothing has happened. Perhaps this is what happens when the truth is spoken out loud: it brings the mind to a halt, if not the body. You might question yourself in a fleeting second: *Did something just happen?*

If we take a closer look at Radha's Birth moment, we can also see that the incarcerated man characterized her essence in a very unusual way. His specific words did not even refer to Radha as a person. He did not say words such as "sat across the table from a woman who could offer him motherly love" or use more commonly heard phrases such as "unconditional love." Instead he said Mark Taylor sat "across the table from a mother's love," almost as though Mark were sitting across from love itself, rather than a person. The inmate in Radha's group witnessed her as love itself—and this naming could not have been more true.

Fourteen years after her life-changing experience, like a baby coming out of the womb, Radha had become herself.

You see, it took me a really long time to feel comfortable with myself. Every time I went through a breakthrough in life, I felt like I was more comfortable with who I was and what I was capable of being.

I realized, "I have survived this transformation well, and I can actually give to other people to make it a little bit easier for them."

By the time you claim who you really are, you are already there, and it feels good. It doesn't feel so uncomfortable or foreign anymore, so why not just acknowledge it? The bottom line is, it does feel comfortable. I am Radha, and it feels really good to be me.

The days, weeks, and months that followed would be easier and happier than Radha had been able to imagine until that time. She had passed through the darkest parts of her life, and any challenges she encountered during the remainder of her transformation would be far less extreme.

About a month or two after the victim dialogue, Radha pulled out the transcripts, read them slowly, and had a revelation.

> My opening really occurred when I read the transcript of my dialogue with Mark Taylor for the first time.
>
> It isn't very often that you get to "hear" yourself speak by reading your communication word for word. I was very impressed with myself. I could see my kindness, my mothering, my caring even for someone who had murdered my son. I had to come to this place to blossom in my own spiritual traumatic journey. I even said out loud to myself, "Damn, you are good!"

Interestingly, Radha describes her inner experience of the Birth as an openning. It is difficult to recognize the major internal shift that occurs as a result of your own Birth experience, but Radha had the benefit of having transcripts and a keen ability to sense her feelings and bodily sensations.

Her response of "Damn, you are good!" is appropriate. Your new self is truly awe-inspiring—almost unbelievable. Of course, Radha was impressed! She had done many amazing things before this time, but she had never exhibited her compassion, openness, and integrity to this degree. She saw her new self in its glory and could not help being delighted. She had the great fortune of witnessing her own Birth—her transition from who she had been to who she had become.

※ ※ ※

On the Map to Wholeness, the three Birth moments are sandwiched between the Surrender and Healing phase and the Abundance and Creativity phase. The Birth phase is, no doubt, the most difficult one to identify, because it is usually camouflaged as ordinary and is over within minutes. During these brief moments a new self is born, the one that was conceived many years ago during your transformative, life-changing experience. The new self emerges with the skills and personal traits you developed during your journey. It is the first time you are exercising those fresh, new skills and traits as a whole, and so they are perhaps not that different from a precious newborn—delicate, dependent, and ready to grow. During the next phase of Abundance and Creativity, you will be like a flower bud bursting forth from the soil and growing exponentially. With the sun shining upon you, you will experience the joy of the support of others and engage in an activity you love to do.

13

PHASE 11:
ABUNDANCE AND
CREATIVITY

*If you step into exactly who you are, then everything
that you are, you attract.*

—TRACI THOMPKINS, ENTREPRENEUR

The new you has been birthed, and uplifting experiences await you! As
the abundance and creativity of this phase unfold, the hardships you had
become so accustomed to in earlier phases dissipate significantly and will
eventually resolve. Your daily life shifts from being centered on adversities
to enjoying delightful changes in your relationships, career, health, and
home life. In this phase, you encounter opportunities to immerse yourself in creative projects that accentuate your gifts.

Although this phase is affirmative and uplifting, the new you has not
yet matured. In this phase you are like a young person who must develop
and define a sense of identity through daily choices: "I am willing to do

this but not that," or "I am attracted to a person that has these characteristics, values, and interests but not that person," or "I want to spend
my time and energy in this way but not that way," or "I will decorate my
space with this item rather than that item because it better reflects my
style." These types of decisions offer you a chance to discover the new self
and define who you are now.

In addition to mundane choices, you will also face a few naturally
arising ordinary challenges that ask you to make the "right" choice, that
is, the one that aligns with who you have become and what you think
is right and just. Similar to the tests of the Birth phase, these situations
are also tests that help to reinforce your identity and develop your integrity. What will you do, for example, when you encounter a situation
that gives you the opportunity to either choose love, openness, kindness, generosity, wisdom, and self-love, or else fear, greed, and desire
for domination-based power? When you choose a love-based option you
become increasingly intact, integral, and whole. Developing your integrity is an essential part of integrating your life-changing experience and
becoming whole.

Although this word *integrity* is often equated with morality and ethical
behavior, the origin of integrity comes from the Latin word *integer*, meaning "entire," which is the basis of the words *intact* and *integrate*. The term's
origins point to the idea that when we are intact or integrated, we have
integrity. This information helps us understand that integrity has less to
do with knowing right from wrong that derives from your upbringing,
a religious text, or law and has more to do with the degree to which you
know who you are.

International attorney and expert negotiator Julian Gressler has exten-
sively examined the concept of integrity. In his book *Piloting through Chaos:
The Explorer's Mind* (2013), Gressler defines integrity as "a sense of connect-
edness, coherence, wholeness, and vitality" (9). This aspect of the definition reinforces that idea that when you are whole, you will know what is
morally right and just, not according to something that is written or proclaimed, but according to you. Gressler also explains that integrity is "the
capacity of every living thing to maintain its hold [cohesion] in the face

of entropy, disorder, and uncertainty, its link to the living world, and its ability to carry on its life, however humble" (Gressler, 9). From this perspective, integrity is a demonstration of the ability to remain "together" in the face of inevitable and ongoing chaos and adversity. Integrity and wholeness are one and the same. We can't have one without the other. Although you have not yet arrived at the thirteenth phase, called Integration, you will get to that phase by building your integrity as naturally occurring circumstances in the Abundance and Creativity phase allow you that opportunity.

Abundance

An interviewee of mine in her early forties described her experience of the Abundance aspect of this phase after having survived a medical condition that prevented her from walking for four months. When we spoke, she had recovered entirely, and her life had changed significantly.

> My body feels better than ever. I have a wonderful home, a great boyfriend, a nice plot of land, and a huge garden that I have always wanted. I have a family, but the children are not my own, which is just what I need. I have always wanted a family but have never been interested in the responsibilities of being a mother.

This phase isn't a fairy tale, pipe dream, or wishful thinking. The abundance you find is a direct result of your years of hard inner work. The personal growth that comes from letting go of old ways of approaching life that no longer work and being who you are meant to be gives rise to new possibilities.

One thing you will notice right away in this phase is that, with very little effort, you meet people who better match the person you have become and who appreciate and support your gifts, interests, and talents. They are the types of people you have always wanted to have in your life. During this phase, meeting your future spouse is quite common, and I have yet to encounter someone who doesn't make healthier, happier friends.

Another interviewee had amicably left her husband and their twenty-five-year marriage. After passing through the trials of Dismemberment, Surrender and Healing, and Birth, she had the following to say:

> I left a life where I was not feeling good about myself, a life where I attracted people who reflected my weaknesses. Now I am meeting all these really cool people who are becoming part of my daily life. It is really amazing! Things are happening fast. I have met more women in the last five days than in the previous eight years. I needed to detox, literally and psychologically, in order to be so receptive.
>
> Before, I was resistant to exercise, but now I do forty-five minutes of fast walking every day. I have lost thirty-five pounds through a great program, and I have gone four months without eating sugar.
>
> I feel great. I look good. I have renewed energy. It feels like I am turning back the clock. I am in a really great place in my life. I love waking up every day.

It is also common in this phase to receive objects, information, or money that makes your life easier or more enjoyable. This bounty comes out of the blue. It might be a promotion, funding for a project, cash to do or purchase something you have always wanted, or long-deserved recognition. For instance, your business might relocate, cutting your commute to ten minutes; a new neighbor might move in and offer low-cost child care for your kids; or the bank might discover an accounting error and credit you $500. One woman I interviewed was writing a book, and during this phase, her friend, a professional author, offered to edit her manuscript pro bono.

Creativity

One of the most prominent characteristics of this phase is the overwhelming need—and desire—to use your creativity to do something that brings you joy. Seemingly out of nowhere, you are given an opportunity to do something that makes your heart sing, such as rebuild your home, investigate your lineage, create a small urban farm, begin a nonprofit, or start a new business. The conditions are just right for this endeavor.

I had the fortune of interviewing a renowned author, Carol Adrienne, whose second Birth moment occurred when her good friend, an accomplished and savvy literary agent, made an offhanded but serious comment. She made a suggestion that encouraged Carol to combine her love of personal growth, helping others, and spirituality with her ability to write well: "Why don't you ask James Redfield if you can collaborate with him to write a guidebook complement to The Celestine Prophecy?"

Carol replied, "Oh, no, I can't do that. Are you crazy? That's his thing."

Creating during the Abundance phase is compulsory. You can't help but create any more than you can squelch the impulse to eat when you are starving. Creating is a natural by-product of becoming a new person. Your body, mind, and spirit want to be a wellspring that gushes forth with gifts to give to others.

After a brief reflection that same day, Carol decided to step outside her comfort zone and her limiting self-talk. She had to admit that, deep down, she felt an instinctive resonance with the Celestine material. She had already begun to apply the principles with some of her own counseling clients. Perhaps she could take a leap of faith and come up with a proposal for how to apply the principles in real life.

She purchased a manual for writing book proposals, sat down at the computer, and started writing, following along with each chapter. She kept her project to herself, fearing her friends would think she was a little too ambitious or would be rejected. Several weeks later, Redfield readily welcomed her support.

It was sheer joy to do the writing. I was happy about the work we did but didn't really know how much of an influence it would be on my life. Once The Celestine Prophecy: An Experiential Guide was published, it was all about keeping up with the abundance.

Once the Abundance phase is underway, you will find opportunities arising at a pace that could have you working long days. Prior to her

Celestine Prophecy book, Carol, like most Americans, was trying to make ends meet. Her client base for numerology consultations had always been small, and she was accustomed to constantly working hard.

When *The Celestine Prophecy: An Experiential Guide* was published, Carol became completely committed to responding to and attending to the many individuals who wanted to work with her. Her teaching and consulting work was so energizing and satisfying that she didn't even notice a massive opportunity when it appeared unexpectedly.

> I was still living in my little cottage in Richmond when I got a call from Oprah Winfrey's producers. They wanted me to come on the show. I was intensely immersed in my work, so I told them, without a thought, "I am booked to teach that week, so I won't be able to make the show."

Carol had never entertained going on her local nightly news, let alone Oprah Winfrey's show. She confessed to me, "It's a humiliating story—oh my God, can anyone be that dumb?" For the first time in her life, she felt fully utilized for her most intimate purpose. How could she stop doing that for a television interview? It didn't seem practical.

> I was so busy I could barely keep up. I really felt a commitment to do all the things I said I was going to do. And going on Oprah … well, I didn't have that in my mind. Of course, some time later it dawned on me what a faux pas I had made. When The Celestine Prophecy was the top-selling book in the world, and I said no to Oprah?! Being on Oprah was so outside the realm of possibility that I didn't even register what I had been asked to do. I only thought, "I am just keeping up with what is coming in," and "I love the work."

> Can you believe that?

I can. Carol's is the ultimate story of what happens when you are genuinely dedicated to your work. Her example is an important reminder to think big—and bigger yet.

About that time, Carol received a call from her publisher: "We want more books from you, and we want one now." When the bounty of the Abundance phase happens, watch out!

I wrote the books The Purpose of Your Life *and* Find Your Purpose, Change Your Life *in four months. I had intensely focused consciousness and stamina to write, work, and teach. How did I ever do that? It truly felt like somebody was giving me extra help. The words would flow so well. And if I needed an inspiration, the phone would ring, and boom, a client consultation or inquiry would often turn into a perfect story for one of the books—a synchronistic gift out of nowhere.*

I was constantly traveling to do workshops in the United States, Italy, Portugal, Mexico, Canada. I was very happy and enjoyed the teaching a lot.

When I came home, I got right back into private practice in person or by phone. By then I had hired an assistant who helped me with scheduling, bookkeeping, and fulfilling orders for my numerology charts. We still did paper charts in those days and mailed them at the post office! During that period, I wrote the book When Life Changes or You Wish It Would.

Abundance might as well be called the "busy phase." With massive transformation come opportunities that seem too good to be true, and they require work at an intensity you may have never achieved before. The phone will ring off the hook, and emails will blitz your inbox. And if you miss a big chance, hopefully you will get a second one—as Carol did. Oprah invited her again.

Oprah had received a galley copy of my book The Purpose of Your Life *and raved about it. Her producer called me to come on a show featuring the concept of synchronicity and intuition.* The Purpose of Your Life *wasn't even in stores yet, and she held up a galley copy in her hand. Oprah's enthusiasm, kindness, and wisdom are amazing. I was very honored to meet such a powerful force for healing and all things empowering.*

One of the challenges of Abundance is learning to accept goodness, fortune, and happiness. Having the capacity to graciously and authentically receive bounty is a skill that, for most people, requires practice. How can you begin to mentally process an invitation to the Oprah Winfrey Show?

More difficult than receiving money, objects, and opportunities is accepting the love others show toward you. Accepting adoration from others is a learned skill for most people, even for those who are relatively happy with themselves. The skill you can practice is your ability to accept the idea that you are inherently worthy of being loved and experiencing goodness and abundance. Because the heart has limitless potential to grow in capacity, the learning curve never ends. You will encounter opportunities throughout your life to open your heart ever wider and deeper and let love in.

The Abundance phase, while invigorating and sometimes hectic, is basically sweet. Still, this phase involves resolving a remnant from the past. You may notice the presence of naysayers—people who do not support or acknowledge your personal growth, or who may not be happy about your abundance and creativity. Their lack of encouragement (or your perception thereof) can trigger your inner critic, as well as old patterns of self-sabotage.

You are not sliding back into the past or reverting to a previous phase, however; the existence of internal and external criticism simply means that you are getting close to being done with the healing required by transformation. The presence of critics in this phase reminds me of doing dishes. If I am cleaning a complex item, such as a cheese grater, I always double-check to make sure it is completely clean. Upon inspection, I usually find a little piece of cheese still stuck somewhere. Healing the human being is similar. Even though the Surrender and Healing phase is over, a few unresolved issues related to fragments of your former self still remain and need to be cleared out before the job is done.

In this phase, real or imagined underminers may make a final effort to halt your progress—but to no avail. Remember Carol Adrienne, who moved forward despite having thoughts like, "I can't do this!" and "James Redfield will never say yes to me; I am just another one of his million fans!" You have the choice to listen to your inner knowing and accept your true qualities and abilities: "I can do it! I know what I am doing! I know who I am and what I deserve." If you can embrace the strength of who you are, your detractors will no longer have power over you.

Kenny: Simply Living

After Kenny's return from the Bahamas, he lived with friends until he could save enough money to afford a place of his own.

The Abundance and Creativity phase involves new relationships. Six months after Kenny returned from Bali, he was still talking via Skype with Pilar, a woman he had met briefly there. When the two were overseas, there was chemistry between them but also something much deeper. Spirituality was centrally important to both of them. Over the months, they spent hours and hours sharing about their lives and discussing philosophies. They felt a familiarity with each other that was comforting, sweet, and exhilarating. Their mutual feelings deepened and they wanted to see each other again, so Pilar traveled to see Kenny in the United States.

> That was an amazing, beautiful time. We were just happy to see each other and be with each other. Grateful for each moment. We weren't making any plans or anything.

> I just knew I had finally found myself a friend, someone I could trust, someone I could love. I could finally relax. I just knew when I met her, that first day in Bali, that we would be together and that I loved and cared for her.

> When you live in a world this big, it is hard to find a friend that you can really trust. Up until we met, I hadn't had anyone I could trust. When I found her, I said, "Ah, an ally." She is my ally. She complements me perfectly. I don't have to look for anybody else.

> We have both had our spiritual awakenings. We don't have to teach each other, help process each other. We don't have to fix each other, go through any of those gyrations or gymnastics just to have a relationship—tantric workshops, therapists. We love life. We love consciousness.

Instances of abundance tend to enter your life during Surrender and Healing. But at the beginning of the Abundance phase, something overwhelmingly wonderful happens. Like Kenny, you find yourself experiencing goodness beyond your dreams.

After spending a month with each other, Kenny and Pilar decided to live together. She went back to Bali, gathered her possessions, and returned a month later to move in with Kenny. Even though they were enjoying the excitement of a new relationship, their joy was dampened by a pressing major life decision: Pilar's green card was about to expire. Although Pilar had been living in Bali when they met, she is a citizen of Spain. Her expiring green card forced them to confront stressful decisions in the midst of the instability of a brand-new relationship.

We didn't know how to deal with these huge decisions after having known each other for such a relatively short period of time. We didn't know what to do. Should we get married so she could have U.S. citizenship? Or should we move to Bali? She had already lived in Bali for six months. Before that, she was in Thailand for eight or nine years. So being in the U.S. was a major, major shift for her. It was very challenging for her to adjust to the American psyche, to the Western mind.

After living in Bali and Thailand, she was used to stillness, quiet, and simple things. She was not used to the U.S. lifestyle—people working day and night, literally moving around all the time, being in cars a lot, driving here and driving there. She was used to being in one spot for days and days and days and days. Even though we wanted to be together, she had strong trepidation about getting married to me, because that meant moving to the United States.

I kind of understood, 'cause I knew the challenges I had coming back to the U.S. after Bali, and I was only there for two months. So I could only imagine her challenges, 'cause she had never lived here.

Even though this phase is characterized by positive experiences, Abundance and Creativity contains important experiences that trigger your deepest issues. These situations give you the opportunity you to work though the changes you have been working on all along. The difference between the past and the present is that in this phase you will be able to approach your problems from a position of strength. For example, a situation that once would have made you spiral into fear or anger now has far less control over you.

When we got together, we thought it was going to be all sweet and loving. But because of these issues, it was really stressful. Our relationship was acrimonious; we argued, we fought. It was just uncomfortable. Over the course of a few weeks, though, we settled down. She decided to spend a weekend in LA to be with a girlfriend and sort things out. That was when I bought the engagement ring. It was just very clear to me. I knew she was the one.

A week or so later, we went to a New Year's Eve party at a friend's house. When we got home, she was looking on the dresser for something and spotted the pink, heart-shaped box. "What's this?"

I didn't intend for her to have it at that moment. She grabbed the box, and I said, "Oh, shit." She opened it up, and there was the ring. And she immediately said, "No, no, no, not now."

She was totally surprised, not ready. She had been thinking, I am leaving here. I am arguing with him. I hate this country. It's cold.

I said, "You don't have to answer now."

She woke me up at two or three in the morning and said, "I accept."

Everything shifted for us. She knew that I cared for her.

Kenny's first marriage, to Inga, had been a disaster, so it might seem a bit surprising that he felt comfortable proposing to Pilar so quickly. But it was not that shocking because Kenny has always been a person who doesn't waste any time.

The apartment was too small for the two of us. We didn't want to live in the East Bay, definitely didn't want to live in Marin. I had lived in Sonoma before. I asked her, "You want to look at that?" She said, "Yeah." We looked at one apartment, which she liked. I came back a couple of days later to look at it in the daylight. We met with the landlord and said yes.

It was amazing that we found what we wanted on the first try. What was even more amazing was that when friends heard we were moving, they said, "I've got furniture," "I've got a couch," "I've got this," "I've got that." Next thing you know, we had everything.

During the Abundance phase, it is common for people to appear suddenly and unexpectedly, sometimes even people you don't know, to give you what you need. At the same time that Kenny and Pilar decided to marry and find a new home, he needed to secure a stable job that would allow him the kind of economic freedom he needed. Doing so turned out to be surprisingly easy.

I knew this guy who was buying and selling cars. I called him and asked him a few questions, and he said, "I will teach you what I know." I started making money, losing money, making money, losing money. Eventually, I learned.

Kenny needed a steady, honest income that had flexible hours and allowed him to be his own boss. Although he did not aspire to be a used-car salesman, this type of business offered the flexibility he needed and accentuated his strengths. Kenny's lifelong love of cars combined with the skills of intuition and persuasion he had acquired on the streets helped give him the confidence and success he needed.

As the Abundance and Creativity phase progresses, you will notice that like Kenny, your relationships and lifestyle become healthier and a better match to who you have always wanted to be and who you have become.

In Sonoma, I didn't have to prove anything. I didn't have to do anything unless I absolutely wanted to. I didn't have the pressure to go meet and hang out with certain friends. I knew people, but I didn't have a social life. I never really had a social life; I am not really that type of person. If I am invited, great, but I am happy just doing whatever comes up.

I enjoyed married life, learning to take care of myself. Everything was more natural. Just living, doing business. Not having the pressures to go out and teach spiritual anything, not having to prove anything—just enjoying life.

You know Jack Kornfield's saying "After the ecstasy, the laundry"? I was doing the laundry. I was selling cars. And it was okay.

Despite the job, I did feel financial pressure in my own head. I was carrying more of the weight as far as bills were concerned, and then Pilar got her visa so she could work. I would have preferred that she move a bit faster to get a job, but she was afraid to get back into the workplace, and I didn't want her to act from that place. When I get worried, I just go inward. I relax, watch, witness. I relaxed, knowing I was going to be okay.

I was living the teachings, as opposed to going to another workshop, going to another satsang. For years, I had gone to all these satsangs, all these retreats, and after a while, I knew I should embody this stuff; it should be a way of living.

I began to live.

Kenny's words perfectly describe the sweet satisfaction of Abundance. After an era of intense change, loss, and suffering, life without the heaviness takes on an almost surreal quality. In the first few months of this phase you might wonder if it is wise to lower your defenses, wondering whether the difficult times are really over. Like Kenny, you might feel as though you can finally enjoy life, and even the smallest positive events are delightful and uplifting.

In addition to experiences of abundance, you will also find yourself in situations that give you a chance to be creative—to use your talents and knowledge. The beautiful aspect of this process is that the opportunities tend to find you, as was the case for Kenny.

A woman named Amerika Sanchez got hold of my book. She decided to use it as a teaching tool to restore men to their rightful place in society. She wrote up a curriculum using my book, to teach restorative justice.

Amerika is a schoolteacher for the San Francisco Unified School District in a program called Five Keys. They are taking education to jails in a formal way. Men and women who are incarcerated are given the opportunity to go to school every day and earn credit, as opposed to lying in their beds all day. Now that it is popular, LA and San Diego want to learn about it. It can help people get a GED.

Once I got to know more, I thought she did a good job. The point is to restore the individual back to balance. If he is robbing, raping, or killing, he is out of balance, because he has not been acknowledged by and talked to and valued by society. The process is about reading, seeing how their thoughts cause their own suffering, and how they can change their thoughts. It's based on recognized teaching and psychology.

She invited me to be the keynote speaker for one of the program's graduations. My speech was only about five minutes long. The occasion was all about the guys being with their families, taking pictures. It was their day. I didn't want to hog up the limelight, so I said just a few words.

Whatever I said, it was enough. They came up to me and said, "Kenny, we want you to teach in the program." And I said, "Ah, well ... okay." I had no idea what I was saying yes to, of course. I ended up having to be fast-tracked. I have been on a fast track ever since.

The fast pace that Kenny got thrown into is very common for the Creativity aspect of this phase. The opportunity usually requires immediate and intensive action. Kenny enrolled in a training program to prepare him to teach the curriculum based on his book.

I had to be educated on what the hell I was going to be doing, just within a few hours. The other teachers knew what they were doing and why they were there. I wasn't aware. I was saying to myself, "Why do I need this training? Why am I here? What am I going to teach?"

I had absolutely no education about how to do this right. But after three days of going to class, eight hours a day, slowly, I thought, "Oh, this is why you gave me a computer to use. This is why I have a combination lock. This is why I have a classroom. This is why I have twenty-five students. This is why I have a curriculum. Oh, this is what I am going to teach ... and I am going to teach from my book! Wow, this is kind of cool. You're taking my book and turning it into a teaching tool to change people's thinking process!"

I learned. I didn't understand how powerful a curriculum could be if taught in jails.

When I started teaching, aw, shit, I was nervous and excited, saying to myself, "I am going to be a teacher, and I am trying to make money at the same time. I got to find myself a car. I'm not sure how this is all going to work out. I am just sitting here trying to wrap my mind around what the hell I am going to teach for the next five weeks."

If I could teach this, and learn it also—wow, I might be onto something. It could be my next step into who knows what! If I could understand it, if I could teach it, I could also market it, package it for all the jails around the country, for whoever teaches restorative justice.

I had a curriculum, based on my book. I was teaching me! Wow. That was really powerful! That was really, really, really fun.

Like Kenny, you don't need to look for opportunities or wonder if you are qualified once they arrive. You will be eager to work hard because you can finally have a place or forum to express your gifts. You are quite literally the best person for the job.

When I glanced over the course materials and thought about how we could work together as a group, I had a euphoric experience. I said, "Wait a minute here. If I got euphoric just by glancing at the materials, what is going to happen when I work with a group? Not just a single person having a transformative experience, but a group of people having that experience?"

I realized that the more qualified and awake the teacher is, the quicker the principles can be implemented, and the transformation or the desired effect can happen quicker. I could really be a vehicle to help shift the consciousness of the men more quickly.

It made such a difference that I already knew their thinking process, their criminal behavior. I knew the prison experience real well. To help others go on this journey of transforming, of shifting consciousness, was something that could also help me! Mmm mmm.

It was totally unique. It really was. Something I never expected.

Everything seemed like it was coming toward me. I was thinking, "I can become a teacher. Wow, man!" Because I knew I couldn't keep buying and selling cars forever. I felt like I was getting too old for that. I wondered, "What can I do? What is next for me?" I could teach from my own life. That was really exciting. How did this happen? Oh, man. Times do change.

This unique program helped Kenny recognize that there were other options besides offering satsangs and his prison program, This Sacred Space. In this new setting he had the chance to help men and women by drawing from the wisdom of his spiritual awakening *and* from a lifetime of survival in and out of prison. This type of teaching meant that Kenny didn't have to abandon the lessons he'd learned through crime, prison, and harmful actions. In fact, it allowed his testimony of survival to become recognized as contributing to his development just as much as the heights of his bliss.

Until this point, Kenny's spiritual awakening had been the focus of his attention, notoriety, and career planning. But from this time forward Kenny could let go of relying on his life-changing event to pull him out of economic turmoil and emotional distress. He had much more to offer than he had previously imagined, and there were potential audiences for his wisdom that he hadn't imagined. Kenny's story highlights an important clarification for understanding transformation: accepting all of your experiences as valuable and contributory to your development is not only healing, it is the foundation of wholeness.

Kenny's Unique Version of Abundance

The Five Keys program with the San Francisco Unified School District gave Kenny the opportunity to be joyfully creative in ways that are typical of this phase. However, Kenny's experiences of Abundance also show that the wealth of this phase does not always mean excessive money, status, or recognition. His process did not yield a wildly famous book, hundreds of devotees, or a greatly improved income and lifestyle. If we take a closer look at his transformation in the context of his lifetime, we can better understand why Kenny's journey unfolded in the way that it has up until now.

For sixty-six years, Kenny woke up each day with worries about his ability to survive. He was never free from fears of not being able to make enough money to feed himself or to pay the rent, and he was not in a situation to be able to rely upon anyone else. Although he never seemed to have problems finding a girlfriend, he did not yet have the skills to create a relationship that was healthy enough to trust.

But during the Abundance and Creativity phase, Kenny experienced what it was like to wake up without these tiring doubts. Instead, for the first time in his adult life, he began to experience living instead of surviving. It was a big change to become accustomed to waking up rested and to feel the comfort of knowing he had the ability to earn a steady income. He was in control of his life without taking control away from others.

For Kenny, this was nothing short of monumental. If survival is the only way of life that you have known, transformation does not mean being rich or famous; it means simply living. From this perspective, we can see how having a "normal life" was a more natural culmination of his growth than becoming a spiritual guru—especially when being a sought-after and beloved spiritual teacher requires anything but an ordinary lifestyle.

Abundance for Kenny meant that he could wake up, kiss his best friend and wife, make coffee, and do some laundry. Then he could drive out of his quiet and quaint neighborhood to earn money through honest means. This kind of life might not seem abundant to some, but for Kenny it meant transformation. He was becoming free.

Radha: Becoming Her Own Masterpiece

Fourteen years after Christopher's death, Radha turned another corner in her journey of transformation. She could finally relax into some semblance of normalcy for the first time in a long time. Instead of having to deal with moment-to-moment psychological survival, she began to have enough space and perspective to look back at the darkness from which she had just emerged.

> Time is a wonderful, gentle healer that people don't give enough credit to. It becomes a thick, woolly blanket against the pain. In the beginning, I just

wanted to be able to walk past a picture of Christopher without bursting into tears. Now I walk past his picture and smile. Time has been good to me.

Abundance is a welcome change. Radha's first salient experience of abundance happened when she was given the opportunity to contribute to the inspirational self-help book *Courage Does Not Always Roar: Ordinary Women with Extraordinary Courage.*

A woman called me up out of the blue and said, "I am writing this book— would you consider being in it?" I said, "Sure!" How could I not get excited about that?

I sent her a short piece I had written, and it went in the book! I wasn't even sure it would happen. And then she emailed me and said it was published. I wasn't sure it was something I would be proud of, but when it came out, I was just delighted.

At its core, Abundance is about receiving unanticipated positive experiences. It involves opportunities, like Radha's chance to be published, that manifest from the inner work you did during the earlier phases of transformation. Gifts like these confirm that a new you has emerged. They are also inherently therapeutic.

Radha cherished celebrations. She loved to affirm the good things in life, especially when it came to her family. When her niece announced that she was getting married, Radha saw an opportunity to do something she loved—to create an enormous event filled with beauty, awe, and connection. This would not be one of Radha's typical affairs, for the general public. As with the elaborate party Radha had planned for her brother's birthday, her family would get to enjoy the results of her passion and dedication.

About a year before the wedding, I went to Santa Barbara to visit my sisters. I said to Sheridan, my oldest sister, "Why don't you let me take care of the wedding?" Sheridan cares for my second-oldest sister, Michele, who has cancer, and Sheridan was thinking she was going to plan the wedding for her daughter, too. I told her, "What you are doing with Michele is very important. It would be easy for me to do the wedding. It is no big deal—in fact, it would be fun for me. I love putting on events." Sheridan was thrilled. She didn't want to learn how to be good at throwing a huge party. From then on, I was the one who made sure it happened.

I had a great budget. The wedding was held on a beautiful piece of private property, a second home for the groom's family, because it was where he had grown up. His family were caretakers for a prominent family.

We had to bring everything to the location—every fork, spoon, and knife; the caterer; the photographer; music. I arranged everything. I was the hostess with the mostest! The bride and her mother figured out the flowers, and my other sister put together the gift bags for people's rooms. We bought local foods and bottled water and stuff like that for the people who were visiting from out of town. There wasn't anything I wasn't involved in, and I have pretty high standards.

Radha devoured the tedious work of planning a wedding. She was fueled by an insatiable love and desire for family to be happy and well cared for. The wedding gave Radha an outlet to express her innate talents and her growing mastery of orchestrating events that inspired healing and love.

The wedding took my organizational skills to a fun new level because I was managing an event that was to be two states away, in Washington. My whole family was blown away by how flawless it all was. I felt very gratified!

My sisters couldn't believe it. It was more than they ever expected. I felt good about it. In fact, right here next to my computer is a letter from the groom's mother:

Dear Radha,

What a magical wedding you created—a true masterpiece. And it was self-evident that your love permeated every last detail because the joy felt by all could not have been reflected otherwise.

Claire was the belle of the ball, sublimely beautiful; Galen was her shining prince; and you were the godmother who made it all happen with a hell of a wand.

I am in gratitude to witness the love you have for Claire, the love you have for your family, and now the love you have for my son. Thank you for an extraordinary weekend. I will always look forward to seeing you.

The Abundance phase involves a labor of love—a task done not for compensation but for enjoyment. You dedicate your whole being to it. The outcome is deeply satisfying and an exquisite display of who you are. Even though Radha had, in the past, helped countless people through her fundraising, organizing of national advocacy efforts, speaking engagements, and counseling endeavors, there was almost nothing more gratifying than giving to her family.

About the time that Radha seized the chance to plan her niece's wedding, she was asked to lead Insight Prison Project's first large-scale fundraiser. She accepted.

The fundraiser was very successful. Our goal was to raise $30,000, with $10,000 to cover expenses and $20,000 for the organization. We ended up incurring and covering $9,000 in expenses, and we raised $44,000 for the organization. The success was particularly impressive given that the event was scheduled for the same time as a big parade for the local major league baseball team, the San Francisco Giants.

Working with the investors was the biggest challenge, because this fundraiser wasn't as fashionable as donating to the ballet or the symphony; this was restorative justice and working with inmates. We had 170 people RSVP, and we thought, "Oh well, the whole room might not show up." But 160 came—that was pretty amazing! And the good news was that all ten who didn't show up sent money!

It was the most successful fundraiser they had ever had. I was the other speaker, with Jack Kornfield, whom I had never met but who is quite the somebody for a lot of people. So it was great to be the other speaker with him.

At the end of my talk, there were lots of tears. We gave a copy of the book containing Christopher's story, Courage Does Not Always Roar, to everyone there. Inside each book we put a bookmark we had made that encouraged them to make a donation.

I was extremely happy about the fundraiser. It was a beautiful, heartfelt, spiritually wonderful event. What more could you ask for?

I was so high and happy. Someone came up to me afterward and said, "Radha, not only do you share your story, but you share yourself. You don't hold anything back, and it is so evident. It is so great to hear, and it makes such a difference."

During the fundraising event, Radha was approached by Nancy Mullane, a nationally renowned independent news reporter. Nancy had interviewed Radha years earlier for a radio documentary about life in prison.

Nancy reminded me of the interview we'd done, and she told me she was going to use that interview in her forthcoming book about the prison system. The book, called Life after Murder, tells the story of inmates who got out of prison and what they did right before they got out. I guess I had worked with some of the men in the book, and they talked about me.

As illustrated in this situation, one aspect of the Abundance phase is unexpected visibility or recognition. It is as though you have been working underground for years, and suddenly you and your efforts are being noticed. For instance, for seventeen years Radha had been volunteering for the San Francisco and Marin Food Bank, an organization that provides healthy meals for thirty thousand families per week. In the recent past she had started a Planned Giving department for the food bank. Because of her many contributions, during this phase she was asked to step into a distinct leadership role.

I was ready for a new challenge before they figured it out. I was thinking, "Okay, what's next?"

The development director and major gifts officer of the San Francisco Food Bank approached me and asked me to chair the Champions Circle, an advisory board of past board members and high-level donors. My verbal response was, "That's a great job for me." But I was thinking, I have been waiting for this! The organization had been benefiting from a lot of coaching from me. This new post was a real acknowledgment of the work I had done before, and it was something I could get really excited about. I love working with high-level donors and developing relationships with people. It is all about the people for me; I am very blunt and bold, and I love having people invest because they really want to.

My major task would be to run the twenty-fifth-anniversary event that would take place in two years. I did the fundraising event for the twentieth anniversary, and we earned $650,000. They knew I was an asset.

External acknowledgment of your gifts, even from friends, is integral to this phase. You won't necessarily win awards, although doing so is not unusual. Rather, people around you recognize your talents, knowledge, and character. You have worked hard to do something with your unique abilities—even if, for example, you are simply a remarkable artist or chef in your community. It is inevitable that, at this point, others are attracted to you and what you do best, and they want more of it.

The Abundance and Creativity phase is the diametric opposite of the Dismemberment phase, in which you can barely take the pain—and then more pain happens. Instead of accepting the pain of loss, here your work is to open yourself to new possibilities. In addition to her fundraising efforts, Radha expressed her creativity through writing.

Everyone kept asking me to write a book. While this was flattering, I wasn't up to the task. When someone suggested I write an article, I immediately took to the idea—it seemed more practical. So, my writing started with the article "50 Things You Can Do to Help an Organization You Like Raise Money."

It was so successful that I was asked to write a similar article, so I wrote "50 Things You Can Do to Help Someone in a Health Crisis." People kept asking my advice about how to deal with grief, so I wrote the article "50 Things You Can Do for a Grieving Person."

The writing was really wonderful, so I decided to start a blog about Christopher and my process of living despite his death. It has really helped people. I get emails from people who tell me how much my words mean to them. In the *process of writing, I learned that a central way to dance with grief was to "be open to the process," because no one knows what tomorrow will bring. I am ready with open arms.*

Each time Radha chooses to write something new, she breaks down internal barriers that have kept her from the joy of helping others as a writer. This type of change is a continuation of internal work but is less about letting go of the outdated self and more about accepting the new self. During this phase opportunities arise that ask you to take action that will make your gifts increasingly visible and able to affect others. Just as Radha accepted each occasion to write, you too will discover pivotal occasions that ask you to exhibit the new you.

In addition to opportunities to show others who you have become, during this phase it is important to refine your ability to swiftly make choices that are in alignment with who you have become—your integrity—and this usually means you must place your needs first. For Radha this meant becoming completely adept at removing herself from commitments that were not in alignment with her emerging identity. Although this was a change she had been working on over the past several phases, during this phase it was time for her master that skill. One endeavor that had to go was her leadership role in a large local art festival featuring regional artists.

I told the director, a friend of mine for twenty-five years, that I was resigning after the September meeting. He asked me to stay on the board until December. When I told him I would, that I would complete my term, I thought, "It will only be a few more months. I can handle that."

At the next meeting we had a horrible discussion in which they asked me to make an uncomfortable phone call to a board member, a longtime friend of mine. It was very frustrating because I knew the phone call would affect our relationship, which I treasured. When I took the position on the board, I had made a deal with that friend. We agreed that we would not let our positions negatively impact our relationship, and the idea of making that phone call forced me to do just that. It was brutal. I didn't want to have conversations like that.

Their request to Radha pushed her to an extreme. What would she do—compromise again or choose her integrity?

> I thought, "Life is too short for this. I don't even want to do this until December. I am out of here." Besides, given the choice, I didn't want to spend more time on that board, even though my friends on the board didn't feel like they had a choice to stay or go, and I did. I thought, "I leave too many meetings feeling like my head has been in a vise for three hours. I don't want to feel that way." My decision was clear. It was not where I belonged, and I needed out.

> It was hard for me to tell the chair of the board that I didn't want to continue, but the rest of it was easy—it was a huge relief. I made a choice, and it was a good one. They were emailing me for advice after I left, but I finally stopped answering them. I figured, "It is your job." I had to make a separation, a demarcation. I had to really end it.

> After it was over, I thought, "Okay, I just got this off my plate." I imagined myself finally getting a chance to do more writing and gave myself a pep talk: "Now I am making space for writing my book."

Radha had always been choosy about which volunteer efforts she agreed to participate in, but like most people in this phase, she refined what she was willing and not willing to do. Once your new identity is named and claimed, you are likely to be more selective about how you spend your time and energy. Your actions can be more deliberate now that your purpose has been made more clear. It has to feel right inside. Additionally, when she made these decisions, Radha showed herself and others that she would not violate her integrity: the promises she made to her friend about friendship and to herself about writing a book.

Additionally, Radha's stated intention to make space for writing her book shows the connection between our integrity (wholeness) and creativity. When she chose to be true to herself, despite the consequences of upsetting her colleagues on the board, she was freed to dedicate her energy to a deeper joy and more intimate purpose. Her book would be the means through which she could exemplify her namesake by pouring love out upon people who are suffering.

As mentioned earlier, there will be naysayers during this phase, or at least those you imagine are talking negatively about you. Radha's external naysayers (as opposed to her internal critic) sounded like this: "Working with prisoners is a waste of time." In response to these voices, Radha exclaimed, with her typical resilience, "This doesn't deter me on my path!"

Abundance can also take the form of positive events in the lives of those we love. It is not surprising, then, that during this phase, Radha's daughter began to blossom. Christina landed a good job, and "her spirit was shining," Radha said.

During this phase, you will notice the arrival of new relationships and the deepening of a few long-term ones. The new friends did not know you during your transformative experience, possibly not even during Dismemberment. Radha was no exception to this phenomenon.

> I now have a bunch of friends who weren't in my life during all those intense years that followed Christopher's death. We hadn't yet met. When they find out about this tragic part of my life, they are really stunned because they see how I am full of life and have a happy life.

The arrival of these friends is an indication of just how far you have come. The quality of these relationships reflects your hard-won new capacities, values, and strengths. Your new friends are healthier and happier than the friends of your past. The select friendships that have remained with you through the entire transformation process, especially through the Dismemberment phase, are now deep and rewarding.

✳ ✳ ✳

In the Abundance and Creativity phase, you stabilize your integrity— your ability to be true to who you are as you handle more complexity, responsibility, and challenge. Most importantly, Abundance helps you to become more yourself. Because you have shed your old patterns of fear, anger, and sadness, and you have let go of relationships that no longer reflect you, there is plenty of space for a new life and a new you. With supportive relationships, a flourishing occupation, and a thriving lifestyle, you are ready to live your dreams in the next phase, Power.

14

PHASE 12: POWER

Be not the slave of your own past. Plunge into the sublime
seas, dive deep, and swim far, so you shall come back
with self-respect, with new power, with an advanced
experience that shall explain and overlook the old.
—RALPH WALDO EMERSON

In the previous phase, you became creative in ways that accentuated your strengths and superseded your goals. During the Power phase, you rise to the pinnacle of your pursuits and become a master of an activity of your refined and combined strengths. For example, in this phase you become a coach that leads your team to championship, a well-loved local news anchor, a grandmother who has successfully mentored her community and cared for three generations of family members, an award-winning manager of a respected department, a hair stylist who attracts people from a hundred-mile radius, or a successful full-time photographer getting paid to do what she loves. You are wholly competent. Your knowledge and skills are so honed that you have become known for your gifts, and others seek you out for your expertise.

The type of power you acquire and exhibit in this phase is not the result of domination, force, spite, withholding, manipulation, or revenge. Instead, what you achieve during this phase might best be described as *authentic* power, or power that is the result of knowing yourself well rather than knowing the outcome of what you can do. When you endure a long, healing, educational, and humbling journey, you become familiar with and at peace with who you are, what you are capable of doing and being, and what matters to you. This self-awareness and self-acceptance is true power.

You can recognize the beginning of the power rising in you when the hectic lifestyle of the Abundance and Creativity phase calms down and you can settle into a routine. The new pace is possible not only because you've overcome your learning curve about what to do and how to get the job done, but also because you have unprecedented support. If you are like many, you will have spent years doing many jobs at once with little or no help from others. During this phase you will have acquired a strong group of capable helpers and leaders who are invested in you and your endeavors. With their assistance, you no longer need to do every little job in order to maintain or grow your creation; instead you coordinate those to do significant portions of the work for you.

This means you have more time to rest, take care of yourself in ways you could not when it was chaotic, and enjoy some leisure. It is time to reward yourself. In this reprieve, it is common to take a step back and feel proud of your accomplishments. New friends, a select few longstanding friends, and key family members believe in you and your dreams, and they celebrate your creations.

Despite hefty responsibilities, you are essentially satisfied with your progress, invigorated with what you do each day, and unwavering in your certainty about who you are. You are no longer controlled by lower impulses to be fearful, pompous, controlling, greedy, or needy. Your life is the healthiest it has ever been in every respect: finances, relationships, work, and play. You might still pinch yourself every now and then and say to yourself, "Is my life really this good?" Because of who you have become in your process, your immediate internal response is, "Yes, I *can* believe this. I worked hard for this."

In order to further describe the Power phase I will share part of the story of a woman I interviewed named Sumiko. She is a financial analyst in her forties who spent years feeling unsatisfied working for others. Despite dabbling with being self-employed and having a near-genius IQ, she lacked the confidence to go out on her own. In addition to her career woes, she also struggled with relationships. She tended to deny her intelligence by avoiding others whose brainpower closely matched her own. It was easier to hide and not rise to her potential.

During her Abundance and Creativity phase, she finally accepted her cerebral gifts and married a man with comparable intellect and interests. Shortly thereafter, she started her own business. At the time of our interview, she was in the Power phase, so I asked her to talk about how it felt to do her work now, as opposed to during phase 6, her Disorientation phase. She said:

> I am not with my clients in the same way. When people used to call me and want my advice, my first thought was, "I can't help them. What if I tell them the wrong thing? I am not an expert." I had all this garbage in my head. "Should I be saying this?" and "Was I too pushy or forceful?" I would have to tell myself, "Calm down."

> Now, I don't have any trepidation. Before, I thought I couldn't talk openly. Now I don't have any doubt. It feels like me. I feel comfortable.

> I used to ask clients, "What do you want to do?" and "What do you think?" Because I thought I couldn't possibly know how to help them. Now I believe in my own abilities. I have realized that my clients don't want me to ask them questions; they need me to give them a direction, to tell them what to do next.

This illustration describes what transpires through the process of becoming whole. If Sumiko hadn't transformed, it is likely that she would have spent her career working for others or being an unsuccessful entrepreneur because she lacked the necessary confidence and skills. Power comes from having endured transformation. Sumiko revealed some of that process for her:

> In years past, I was busy convincing myself that I wasn't worthy; that I couldn't give direction to myself, let alone others; that I couldn't take charge and tell them my opinion about how they should proceed.

> Now I don't have any of that baggage. If someone says something off-key, instead of second-guessing my own knowledge, I feel confident asking them for more information or admitting, "I don't know what you are talking about." This is how I have always wanted to be.

One way you know you have accessed your personal Power is when you have feelings of self-confidence that come from apprehending yourself. Self-apprehension means you have grasped or touched who you are at a feeling level, at your core. For Sumiko, the process of becoming whole occurred through years of Dismemberment, and Surrender and Healing, that asked her to face self-doubt, surrender, and heal, in order to access her true nature of being extremely smart and completely capable of leading others financially. Freed from the burden and of fear and doubt, she could claim herself, the fullness of her identity, which is another way to say she assumed her Power.

Another aspect of your Power is the happiness you feel. At this point you are the expert in a creation that makes you feel thoroughly fulfilled. How could you not feel happy? You get to do what you love, make enough money while doing so, and spend time with people who make you feel truly delighted. These positive feelings are attractive and draw the attention of others, who say to themselves, "I want to be near that!"

Author Carol Adrienne, whom we discussed in chapter 13, told me about her Power phase:

> I was down at the Esalen Institute, a retreat center in Big Sur, California. I had done a few workshops there, both on the Celestine principles and on life purpose, intuition, and synchronicity. This time was particularly fun because my daughter, Sigrid Mathews, had joined me to include yoga in our program. We were getting some food at lunchtime. A Japanese man, who I later discovered

was another presenter, came up to me and said, "You are Carol Adrienne. My name is Toshi Yamakawa. You are very famous in Japan!"

I thought to myself, "Really? Is he joking?" No one had said anything like that to me before.

He said, "Your book, The Purpose of Your Life, *is a bestseller."*

Soon after, I did a book with his wife, one of the top gurus in Japan. They have a huge following.

This connection led to a few years of wonderful experiences in Japan, the pinnacle of which Carol described as follows:

My Japanese publishers were celebrating a hundred years of being in business, and they were choosing to showcase The Purpose of Your Life. *They asked me to facilitate a workshop for select attendees, which took place in the penthouse of a very exclusive high-rise building. It was an amazing place, chosen for its propitious location. I found myself looking down, and there is the emperor's palace. I couldn't help thinking to myself: "How did I get here?"*

Carol experienced the surreal nature of reaching the zenith of transformation—pausing at the highest point—literally, in her case—of a personal creation. The transformational journey tends to engender humility, yet admitting that you are genuinely proud of your accomplishments is a sign of healthy self-love. Carol reflected on her achievement.

I grew up in a little town in Northern California, where a lot of people tended to be conservative and fairly xenophobic. I grew up not expecting to travel abroad, let alone to Japan. If my parents had lived long enough to see me in this role, they would have been quite shocked. For me the chance to see the world, meet the most wonderful people, and do what I love to do has been just unbelievable.

It was electrifying for Carol to achieve this level of recognition and use her skills and knowledge in this way. It was also humbling to be so adored and admired. She had arrived at this place of Power, where the friction and the hard work of transformation helped her to become a version of herself that she might not ever have become had it not been for her painful, hopeful, and driven journey.

Kenny: "Doing Normal Things Is Miraculous"

A woman who worked in the prison system in Oregon discovered Kenny's book and invited him to visit several correctional facilities and a halfway home in two different cities in the state. When people in the spiritual communities there heard of his pending visit, he also booked a satsang with them.

> The inmates were excited to ask me all sorts of questions. Some were lifers and some were going home. The lifer group was looser, not structured, just a bunch of guys who wanted to meet me. For two hours we just had a talking session. They asked me all sorts of questions, like, "Why did you write the book? How does it feel to be married? I want to get my life together, what kind of advice can you give me?"

> Today, when I talk to men and women in prison, I am more into sharing how to be a better human being. They don't have to have enlightenment—wake up and see God or find Jesus—just be a basic good human being. I share how to be a basic good human being.

Kenny's purpose had undergone a fundamental shift. There was no more wavering about his message or his purpose. He was no longer wrapped up in the mystique of his awakening experience in prison and the pressure he placed on himself to help others awaken too. In this phase, Kenny relaxed into the Power of his crowning achievement. He was no longer an ex-criminal. He had become a man living an ordinary life.

Giving Together

During the Power phase, aspects of your life that have long been separate or even segregated come together, causing your life to be more integrated, less splintered. For Kenny, this meant that his teachings in Oregon included Pilar.

> Pilar has a soft spot in her heart for men and women who are incarcerated. She loves visiting jails, and the men and women enjoy her coming in. This is the work that she loves. Work that I love, too. We are on the same page about working with the incarcerated and seeing how maybe their lives can change just from receiving love and attention from someone.

> Unlike all the other lovers and girlfriends, she supports the work that I am doing 100 percent. The others had their own game plan; they weren't really on my team 100 percent. Their response to my work was, "It's nice what you are doing ..." but they had another agenda. Pilar is very supportive, is right there all the way.

> As soon as she knew I was going to the jail, she said, "Get me cleared too!"

> When we got there, she was excited and nervous because she didn't know what to expect. She hadn't been to major prison, only in jail, but just for overnight, not as a permanent state. She was curious, didn't say much, wondering, "What are they thinking and feeling?" I like that she can go together with me.

Kenny's delight in Pilar's presence was deeper than the pride that came with bringing her into the world of incarceration, with which he was truly familiar. For the first time in his life, he felt partnership through their shared altruistic passion.

"An Exercise in Futility"

Throughout his journey, Kenny wanted desperately to be liked and approved of by others, especially those whom he admired. He also wanted to learn to like and accept himself completely. In the Power phase, Kenny's steadfast efforts to release this entrenched pattern caused a shift.

> I discovered that when there were certain people who didn't like me, I would go out of my way to try to get them to like me. I kept repeating those same old habits, personality traits, which I consider to be negative. Over time I learned

what I was doing, and I realized that my strivings were an exercise in futility. I stopped doing it on a slow basis. That was an ongoing process. Now I recognize, I see now and I catch myself and I stop. Whoa. I put on the brakes.

Now I can catch it because I recognize it. I know the flavor or tone, so when it comes up, ah, here this is again. Now I can stop, back up, and give the other person space to breathe and myself space to heal and relax and really assess: "What am I trying to get from the other person?" I discovered that it didn't work. I was slowly recognizing, and once I recognized it, I stopped doing it.

Kenny's desire to be loved and accepted by leaders in his life is a feeling expressed by many people. Deep within, he carried leftover hurts from childhood stemming from a disconnect between the ways in which he needed to be loved and how he actually was and was not loved by his parents. Becoming freed from these fears and hurts caused Kenny to possess power that comes from being his own source of love, from loving and accepting himself. This important internal shift is the central crux of the Power phase because self-love and self-awareness are raw power—the source of one's power. This means that when we gain more self-love and self-awareness, our power grows.

Finding Happiness at Home

Kenny's sense of confidence in his work and within himself included his relationship with Pilar. Their capacities to deepen their relationship were maturing, and their learning and growth together allowed Kenny to open into a realm he had previously only dreamed of.

Being in a healthy, conscious relationship is a very foreign thing for ex-convicts. When I got out, I didn't know what a healthy relationship was like. I was just trying to find a girlfriend. That's it. Who I could hire, who I could have, that's all I could think about at the time. Ex-convicts want a happy life after they come out of hell.

That is what I am doing right now. I am living a happy life, a life that I never, ever, ever, ever experienced before. I didn't even know it existed. How can you know it even exists until you actually experience it? She has never been in a relationship such as this either. She has been in other relationships, but they didn't really go deep compared to where we are going.

We are two people building something we've never built before. There are lot of tears; we're experiencing everything. I am grateful to have gone through all the challenges I have gone through with the opposite sex to be where I am now.

Every day I wake up and I am so in love with my wife, and also knowing, one day this is going to end. I am not going to sleep to the reality; like the Buddha says, attachment brings suffering. If you are really, really attached, it brings suffering because you know it's going to pass away some day.

The Power phase does not equate to flawlessness nor yield only joys. Inherent in this phase is resounding assuredness about one's self, relationships, work, and play. Kenny has entered completely into a newfound reality of what it means to be in relationship, to love, and to be loved, which translates into increased inner power.

Taking Responsibility

For the vast majority of his life, Kenny was accustomed to disregarding the rules of society. He learned at a young age that he could skate through the system and avoid being responsible for taking care of his needs through honest work. To make matters worse, now he was in his sixties, and he lacked the formal training or education that most people use as a way to get and keep a job. It was during the Power phase that his love-hate relationship with the need to work was overcome.

Pilar is angry at the American way: work work work, go go go, do do do. She wants to go to the islands and hang out in the jungle, but that doesn't work for me. I don't want to go hang out in Thailand or Bali or wherever. That's a deal-breaker for me right now. My job right now as a sixty-six-year-old man is to patronize myself financially. You gotta make the money in order to enjoy the money.

Pilar has been saying, "Do what you have to do to pay the bills, but I want you to do satsang. I still think you should be teaching." And I am thinking in my mind, "You need to get a damn job! You need to go to work too. I am good with teaching, but that is not going to pay the bills this week. No one is going to write me a check 'cause I wrote a blog."

And last night it came to me: "Wait a minute. She doesn't need to do anything. No matter what, I still have to earn a living. If she wasn't here, then who would have to pay the bills? Who would feed me? I finally realized, I don't need others to take care of me; I need to take care of me.

I realized, she doesn't have to do anything but wake up in the morning and do whatever the hell she wants to do. My job is to make money and pay the bills no matter what she does, because I've got to live no matter what she does. I realized that the universe has sent me this beautiful woman, and so I will do all I can to take care of her, notice her, protect her, and make sure she can relax. As a man, I can go out and make the money, and I don't have to be the pimp and make her go out and do the dirty work.

All that matters is, "What can I do? What am I going to do?" I have to depend on my skill set. I know I can't expect anything from her except what she decides, because I love her for who she is and not what she can do for me.

Up from the depths of his being came his capacity to seize control over his life. For the first time, Kenny fully understood that being healthy and whole means earning a living through his own labor and not through the gifts or resources of others. Kenny fully accepted self-responsibility. By the end of Kenny's Power phase, Pilar began working because she felt ready to do so, not because Kenny influenced her to do so.

Decent Enough

Breakthroughs regarding self-love and personal responsibility brought Kenny into the center of his being. He now felt firmly anchored in a clear understanding of his unique purpose, capacities, skills, and place in the world as being just right for him.

I am trying to have an ordinary life. I don't have to be a guru—I call them popcorn gurus. They pop up every day. They are out there sharing the message, and so I can just relax and enjoy my life, being Kenny Dale, and that's it.

I have been in that world and I have had my decent success, not what I expected, but decent enough. I have a few friends who appreciate me, call on me, benefit from who I am just by hanging out with me. I am okay with that. It is just enough for me. I am happy with the status of things right now.

I am not trying to emulate anybody. What is coming up is to share how I feel: "I'd like to share this with you, I hope it touches you." I don't worry too much any more about how I present or how I look. I know what I have to say is very powerful and effective. I am going to say it and see what happens. It feels good inside when I say, I can do this.

Kenny assumed he would transform to become a well-known teacher such as Gangaji, helping others as she did. When this aspiration did not materialize at the magnitude he expected, Kenny concluded that he had not yet transformed, or worse, that he had somehow failed. Instead of becoming a leader, an exemplary individual, Kenny transformed from being a professional criminal with a life of deceit to an ordinary person leading an honest life. So mundane was his sublime arrival in this phase of Power that its simple beauty escaped my initial detection.

Learning How to Enjoy Life

Power is exhibited through our strengths, clarity of consciousness, knowledge, character, love, and relatedness gained through the journey of transformation. The process fundamentally shifts all aspects of life, including one's personal life. Kenny accomplished all of the arduous work required of transformation. Dwelling within the seat of his power, he could relax and enjoy the bounty of daily living.

My life now is about wanting to just enjoy life. And so that's exciting for me, because I never really knew how to enjoy life, take walks, do this, do that. I was always trying to outlive life, outrun life, out-snooker life. I never thought about just trying to enjoy life. That is where we are headed now, and I am excited. Because why? I never had a chance to do that.

Pilar was raised in Spain, and Spaniards know how to enjoy life. They have a lot of practice in it, as opposed to Americans where it's all about work. And I am a part of that. She's teaching me to slow down and savor the moment. Not run from the moment, not flee from the moment, but stay for the moment. I made enough money last week to enjoy the moment, rest for a few days.

Against all odds, Kenny Dale now lives an ordinary, extraordinary life— nothing less than triumphant.

Radha: "I Really Felt Like We Could Do It"

Radha's journey on the Map to Wholeness was coming closer to completion. She had developed remarkable abilities for loving, learning, and giving. At the beginning of her Power phase, Radha revealed her one vulnerability.

> I am still constantly nervous that Christina's mental health is going to change, and I am very cautious around anniversary dates, especially Christopher's death. I still call her regularly to make sure she is taking her medications.

One might think that at this point in her transformation, Radha would have been free of worries; however, uncomfortable emotions still come and go. What does change as you move ever closer to wholeness is your ability to remain stable and relatively undisturbed through challenges and even crises. Because you know who you are, you can act from a place of clarity and confidence. Your self-awareness allows you to take precise action. This is your power.

The Parole Review

Radha's Power phase had interesting timing with a major looming challenge: Mark Taylor would soon be considered for parole. When a person convicted of a crime is up for parole, the victim has the right to state his or her position on whether it should be granted. This occasion was momentous for Radha because she had to revisit everything: the details, the memories, the pain, and the man who killed her son. She devoted herself to preparing the statement she would make to the parole commissioner.

We had to touch all that stuff again, and I am a full-feeling person. It was very different from the first time in court. When Christopher was killed, I was in shock. I was in that state where everything is different, and you don't have the ability to fully feel.

I am very proactive when it comes to a big job like this, so I made sure to get my ducks in a row. I did my homework. I surrounded myself with people who could support me.

I don't do anger. I never understood anger, but the injustice that I had to take time out of my life to prepare for and show up for was trying, to say the least. There I was, sixteen years later, thinking, "Can't this just be gone? Am I going to have to prepare for parole every few years for the rest of my life?" That part sucked. I did it because it was important to me, but it's not like going to visit your grandmother; it's a big deal.

By going to parole, I was doing my job as Christopher's mother. I miss Christopher the most when I am really happy and want to share with him: when we are all sitting around laughing, having a great dinner, or going to Hawaii or to some incredible concert or play. It's not when I'm having to participate in the criminal justice system, like this.

I was pretty good about telling everyone that I was having a hard time going through the process. Christina really had a compassion for me that felt very good. She made a point of checking on me and asking, "How are you doing with this?" She knew it was hard and I was doing so much grunt work.

Everybody knows how strong and brave I am, but I would say, "This is a tough part." There was a day, for instance, when I didn't have enough to do, and I could see how I might get into a depressive state of feeling sorry for myself and wishing it could be different. I could see it looming on the horizon, and I thought, "No. I am not going there."

You know you are in the Power phase and can exercise the power inside of you when you are able to handle experiences that, in years past, would have been completely overwhelming or debilitating. With all of her gifts at her command, Radha was ready.

Radha spent months preparing for the hearing. To ensure the best result, she knew she had to "go with it, keep going, and be accepting," she said. The magnitude of what you are asked to do during the Power phase challenges you to the core but in an invigorating way. During this phase, you understand the implications of the challenges that lie ahead of you so that when they arrive, you respect those circumstances as pivotal in your own growth and change. You understand that all of who you are is at stake, and this is your moment in time to be fully prepared, alert, aware, and deeply rooted in your experience of who you are. Radha could feel the intensity of what was demanded of her.

I didn't sleep for about a week before the hearing, and I am not like that.

Originally, Gary could go, but then the parole date changed, and he couldn't. My best friend, Jaimee, had a fever at the last minute, and she was still fighting cancer. It would have been too much for her. We had to go the night before, because it was half a day's drive.

I was in task mode, making sure everything happened as planned. I made sure that Christina and my dear friend Lori showed up on time and left on time, not at the height of traffic.

I felt like I did a really good job. Everything I put into play worked. That was a relief.

Radha mentioned that she didn't "do anger"; in fact, during all my years of interviewing her, I never heard her angry. Since anger is natural, I got the sense that Radha was able to quickly transform her anger into heartfelt, impassioned action. The only time I sensed a heated tone in her voice was when she described the parole hearing.

There I was, across the table from someone else's child, who was really not with it, and thinking about how unfair that seemed. It took me back to all children, not just the one who murdered mine, and how we need to make sure they are loved, have what they need, and are nurtured instead of turned into violent people who don't understand how the world works.

He felt screwed over by everybody—that he was convicted by the DA and twelve accomplices, meaning the jury. The jury didn't have anything to do with what Mark Taylor did. He did it. He could have stayed in his room and locked the door. There was a phone in his room; he could have called 911. There were so many things he could have done. He said that Christopher was coming after him. But Christopher was not coming after him; they figured out that Christopher's back was to him when they did the bullet analysis.

He had so many chances to be different. The worst that might have happened was that they wouldn't have been roommates anymore, or someone would have had a bruised ego. It could have turned out in a totally different way.

Radha paused, and we sat in silence. "Four times," she finally said. "Why did you have to shoot someone four times?" The words were piercing, and the injustice of Christopher's death was in the air. These were the intimate utterances of a mother who had lost the deepest part of herself. I bet she could have counted on one hand the number of times she had ever talked like that. In typical fashion, Radha then turned to the idea of personal responsibility.

It certainly makes me want to walk in the world in a gentle, loving way, no matter how small or big our resources or abilities, because the way we act is all we need.

Then she talked about the hearing itself and her victim impact statement.

A lot of victims will talk about the gross and disgusting details of the crime, but I didn't want to go there. That was my first challenge. I decided that the fact I was sitting in that room because this man murdered my son was enough to say, "This isn't okay."

I live with the "victim impact" every day. I didn't want to slog through the icky stuff. I just wanted to say, "Until you do the work, Mark, I am not going to support your parole."

Here is part of the statement Radha read to the commissioner that day:

> My name is Radha Stern, and I am the mother of Christopher Robin Hotchkiss, who was murdered by Mark James Taylor on March 21, 1996, a day when my life, along with the lives of my family and friends, was changed forever.
>
> Mark does not comprehend that there has not been a picture of my son, Christopher, in sixteen years; no birthday smiles, no hugs, no sit-down talks about the challenges of the world, no family vacations with everyone, no "What's for dinner, Mom?," no wedding, and no grandchildren. Christopher would be thirty-eight years old. Mark cut his life short at twenty-one. What was he thinking?
>
> I requested to have a victim-offender dialogue with Mark that was approved by the California Department of Corrections and Rehabilitation, and I met with Mark in March 2008 to give him the benefit of the doubt and to assess for myself if he had embraced the reality of his actions. Sadly, Mark had not.
>
> In our conversation several years ago, Mark did not take full responsibility for the crime, nor was he aware how his life had led him to take a life. Instead, Mark was still blaming others for what he had done.
>
> I think that this quote from the Dalai Lama is significant today: "When you think everything is someone else's fault, you will suffer a lot."
>
> If he continues to refuse to deal with how his life led to the murder of my son, then two lives have been wasted. Even if Mark remains in the prison community for the rest of his life, he can be a positive change maker—if his heart is opened. Mark does not have to be defined by the worst thing he did in his life. I don't want Mark to do this for us. Mark needs to do this for himself.
>
> I have been volunteering in prisons for eight years now with Insight Prison Project. I have addressed groups of inmates in classes such as Victim Offender Education Group; GRIP, Guiding Rage into Power; and Katargeo, which is, in part, an emotional literacy program. I speak to inmates who wish to understand themselves better, how their life experiences and decisions led them to prison, and how their crimes have impacted their victims. I also help offenders

understand and take responsibility for the impact of the crimes they have committed.

Mark does not seem to have this desire. It pains me that two lives are being wasted. My son is no longer here, and Mark is not being a productive and positive member of his community, by not taking responsibility for his life and his crime.

I would like to stress during this hearing that I, along with my entire family and my friends, oppose Mark James Taylor's parole being granted. Until Mark can open his heart and take responsibility for his actions, I will continue to oppose parole.

Radha participated in Mark Taylor's parole review in a way that gave her a feeling of dignity and satisfaction.

Regardless of the commissioner's ruling, Radha was centered in the truth of her identity. She had the wisdom to let go of the outcome, which she couldn't control. More than ever, the only thing that mattered to her was to act with the strength arising from her compassion and integrity.

We all thought Mark would get a five-year denial; he got a seven-year denial, which was a good result. It meant I didn't have to deal with his next parole hearing, technically, for six years (you have to start preparing a year ahead).

In prison, he had two violent offenses and two other write-ups, which added fourteen months to his time. To even be considered next time, he has to have a perfect record and go to programming.

The human being who killed my son is so lost, so clueless. He was actually given the opportunity to speak at the parole hearing, which most prisoners would give their eyeteeth for, and he didn't say anything. Later, he said to the commissioner, "I am the same person that I was when I came in here, and I am fine." Even if you think that, you don't say it.

That makes me sad. Really sad.

Radha had spent years providing smart and compassionate service to people in prison. She had helped countless inmates learn and grow. Driven by the desire for redemption for everyone, she wanted the life of the man who had killed her son to become productive, or at least somewhat healed, so that two lives would not be lost.

> Time will tell. I explained to him that my forgiveness is irrelevant if he doesn't first forgive himself. The thing I know, beyond a reasonable doubt, is that it is all up to him now.

Although she may never witness this result, she finally could let go of her burden, and by letting go she could finally be at peace. This internal shift is an important aspect of this phase because inner harmony, and the lack of internal conflict, occurs when you accept and know who you are. And knowing who you are is your Power.

An intriguing phenomenon that occurs on the journey to wholeness is that those closest to you experience healing by virtue of being connected to you and your momentum.

> I am so proud of how Christina handled herself through this whole thing. When we went to the hearing, she drove four hours both ways. She was a partner with me and not a drain. She was supporting the process, and that was really positive for me. I felt incredible about that. It was the best it could have been. If I got this out of the hearing, I am one happy mother.

> The fact that Christina maintained this change throughout the whole hearing, and seems to have kept it up since, is wonderful. It would honestly be one of the biggest gifts of my life if this continues for the rest of her life. We will have a lot more fun. I can't tell you how huge it is for me.

This type of experience is the icing on the cake—a bonus of transformation. If it is important to you that your loved ones become healthier and happier, set out to transform yourself! Like Radha, you will discover that because of your bond, they will begin to change, not because you influenced them but because they are part of an environment that is improving because you have the courage to become whole.

Radha Comes into Her Authentic Power

No longer weighed down by the past, you can enjoy what you love in the present. Radha turned her attention to writing, not just about recovering from her son's murder but, more importantly, about living. As mentioned in the previous chapter, people had been telling Radha to write. In order to develop her skills, she started by writing helpful articles and moved on to blog posts with the goal of eventually writing a book that would encompass all she had learned.

> I don't want murder to define me or be the only thing people know about Christopher's short life. I am actually tired of murder. When I go to San Quentin, I get bombarded with murder. When I work with other people, I get bombarded. I am about being hopeful, healing, and walking around and being a positive person in the world. I am not defined by that horrible act. I don't want that to be the whole equation of my life anymore. I want to be done with that.

She was at last breaking free from the mental weight of Christopher's death.

> I have written about the parole hearing because it is a big deal, but I don't want to write about murder. It's not even on my blog. I want to write about the hopeful stuff, even some current events. I wrote about my sister and other things. I don't want to go backward any more. I have done enough of that.

> I almost see a visual wall in my head. "That's enough," I think. "I am tired of touching that part." That is not what I want to touch upon with my friends, family, even Christopher. Yes, that is how he died, but come on—there is so much to live for now!

During the Power phase, your outgoing identity loses its final hold and drops away. You stand in your fullness as the new you. The identity "Radha Stern, mother of Christopher who was murdered in his school apartment" was no longer relevant or helpful. The sadness of her loss will always be in her heart, but she had grown to become the master of love, a woman who embodies motherly love.

Through the phases of Dismemberment, Surrender and Healing, and Abundance and Creativity, Radha transformed her pain by giving to others. Now, at the pinnacle of her abilities, she was given the greatest task of her career: to lead a high-profile campaign for the San Francisco and Marin Food Banks.

> I aimed to raise $1 million for the food banks. Five years earlier, we had raised $650,000. There was no question in my mind what we could accomplish, but I needed to drive it. I really felt like we could do it, even though I had to convince others who were a bit hesitant. I just knew it. There was just no question in my mind.

> My enthusiasm became contagious. My approach for the campaign was, "If we are going to do this for a year, we damn well better have fun. We have to be excited, use our time well, get stuff done, and be kind, and it's all going to work out." And that is exactly what happened.

> The work was constant. There was something to do every day, and the work increased as we got closer to the event. We worked together, and we worked really well. After a year of hard work, we raised $1.4 million. It was a team effort, and the results far exceeded our expectations. Our expenses were less than 10 percent of the total raised, which is a big deal when you are trying to raise money.

This fundraising event was far and away the most aggressive and successful of Radha's career. Her reputation was firmly established, and her skills were honed. She knew who she was and was genuinely proud while still being keenly humble.

> The fact that I did it gave me a huge sense of accomplishment and made for a big positive internal transition for me. I realized that I was better than I ever thought.

Authentic power emanates from you when you become a leader in your trade, you are put to the greatest of tasks, and you triumph for all to see.

Afterward, I felt like I was done. I didn't have to raise any more money ever, unless I really wanted to. I helped raise money to help my friend Jaimee pay her medical bills, but that was a personal thing among intimate friends and family, so it was a little bit different.

People ask me all the time to raise money for them. I say no because (a) I don't feel like I really want to do that anymore, (b) I want to concentrate on my book, and (c) maybe there is something else I need to make room for. I've done that. I know I can do that. It's not something you lose.

The successful fundraising campaign gave Radha a sense of completion that moved her to resign her position as chair of the Champion Circle. Now that she had proven to others and herself that she could accomplish a task of this magnitude, she was mindful of being true her purpose. She had been commuting forty-five minutes each way, and she realized that the excessive driving and minimal workload did not seem to the best use of her time, energy, and talents. In years past she would have been fine with a situation that did not fully maximize her strengths, but now, apropos to this phase, doing so was intolerable. Poised with the necessary will, ability, and time, she dedicated her energy to writing. Then she was met with a major challenge.

Christina

Four days after quitting her position with the Food Bank and only minutes after completing her debut as a keynote speaker at Insight Prison Project's fundraiser, Radha had the following experience:

My husband and I weren't even back to our cars when the phone rang. It was Christina, and she was absolutely hysterical. She had been diagnosed with chronic lymphocytic leukemia.

It hit me like a whack on the head. This disease usually hits sixty- to seventy-year-olds! First, I screamed in my head, "Shit! Fuck! Goddamnit!" Then I yelled at God in my head, "What am I supposed to learn from this?"

Radha was forced to face her greatest fear, the worst possibility she could imagine: outliving both of her children. News like this might not seem to belong in a phase that has to do with becoming an authority and entering into an easier and more enjoyable lifestyle. Knowing Radha's deep dedication to her children, everyone around her thought this information would take her down a path of further suffering. But Radha had a new aptitude for dealing with crises.

> I kept thinking, "Oh my God. This is so strange." I kept working it over in my head. I would say to myself, "It is going to be okay. You can make it through this—you have the skills to make it through this."

> After the initial shock, I digested the information. I decided, "I am going to follow the sunshine." There is a lot of hope in this disease.

> I was unexpectedly clear, and that felt good. I even surprised myself. I was actually calming my other family members down. I was amazingly composed and accepting of all of it.

> Partly, I knew how fortunate we were. I said to myself, "Here we are, a loving family who cares about each other. We have medical and technical resources right here in our own family if we get in a bind. How much luckier can we be?"

> We had caring friends who were all over this. I couldn't believe the support and energy that people were sending my way—it was phenomenal. I had been giving, and it really came back. Even though there was nothing anyone could really do but send good energy and prayers toward Christina, everyone was all lined up to fight anything.

> The day of her diagnosis, that Wednesday, was an incredible day.

Such an experience of inner resilience and clear thinking signals the beginning of the Power phase. This extreme situation is a challenge that would previously have been overwhelming. Radha's transformation to this point helped her develop inner resources to meet this moment. How you feel, act, and respond shows you and others how far you have come.

As was characteristic of her personality, Radha began to plan. She considered how she could channel her stress, fear, and pain into something constructive: "What am I supposed to do now?"

When the leukemia thing happened, I immediately began to wonder, "Am I supposed to raise money for leukemia?" After a few minutes of contemplation, I knew. "I don't think so. There are so many other people doing that. I am supposed to take care of my daughter."

Relieved that she didn't feel that she had to thrust herself out into the world and give to tirelessly to others, she again dedicated all of her attention and energy to letting go of her fears so she could be present to Christina's needs.

Within the first week of learning about Christina's diagnosis, I was calm and accepting. My feelings about death had evolved, which helped. Christina's situation didn't seem as big as Christopher's violent death; with her, we had time. It sounds a bit strange, but I felt that if Christina did pass, I knew she would be happy with her brother. Maybe, given her depression, she would be happier there than she was here.

Radha had successfully absorbed the shock of the news about her daughter's health. Once stabilized, she knew that things weren't likely to get tough for about a year. She learned that her daughter's condition could slowly worsen to the point of having to have aggressive chemotherapy. After chemotherapy was the option of a bone-marrow transplant that would mean several months of pathogen isolation, during which Christina would have no immune system and would be extremely vulnerable to sickness or even death if a pathogen entered her environment.

Later, Radha said, "My reaction, my whole response to the diagnosis, was really different for me. In the past, I would have been in a panic, and I would have gone into fix-it mode." Radha was referring to the way that she would cope with suffering she perceived in others around her and herself: the many years of working on gun control, hunger among the homeless, and even advice and counseling for Christina.

Christina wanted to have a child. I was afraid the diagnosis was really going to push things—that she would rush into it and make a bad choice. At first, I was pretty freaked out about it. It was killing me, and it wasn't bothering her.

But I figured, "I am certainly not in control of that." I realized I was there to support Christina. I called my friend Karen, who is a medium, who reminded me that people on the other side—people who have died—are here to support us, but they can't do the work for us. I was exactly like that for Christina: I could support her, but she had to do the work herself. She had to be the one to embrace life and say, "I am going to manage this. I am going to have the best life I can possibly have."

In the Power phase, you finally clear out the last remaining remnants of your former self, which show up as inner voices and habits that used to tempt you to shrink into old fears. This situation with Christina triggered Radha's long-held fears that Christina was unable to think through the consequences of her decisions. In this phase you confront your core fear one last time—but now you move through your fear once and for all and anchor in a solid sense of self. Thankfully, about a year after Christina's diagnosis, Christina's CLL continued to have no symptoms and was deemed dormant. The whole family was overwhelmed with gratitude. With the ordeals of parole and threat of CLL behind her—at least for now—Christina's vitality and outlook were the best she had experienced since the loss of her brother. For Radha, this change of events brought nothing other than pure gratitude.

Now, after having spent so many years trying to help Christina, she knew from experience that it was time to let go completely and trust.

I thought, "I am not sure how I am going to make my story and the lessons it taught me into a book, but I am determined to do it." I spent months really cranking out a lot of writing, the best that time would allow. I had to pace my work so I could be there for people I loved, because a lot of other work and demands came my way.

My book manuscript was a herculean effort. When it was finally done, I wanted to touch it, so I printed it and put it in my lap. When I read it, it was so beautiful that I started to cry. I didn't think I wanted my own book, but when I saw it and I held it in my hands, it was so beautiful.

The manuscript was eventually turned into the book Griefprints: A Practical Guide for Supporting a Grieving Person. I dedicated a portion of the proceeds to the Compassionate Friends group, the ones who helped me so much in the beginning. I just wanted the information out there; fortunately, I didn't have the pressure of needing to make my livelihood with the book.

Radha's journey had given her information, stories, and experiences that others wanted to hear. But writing was only half the task.

At first, I thought writing the book was the hardest part. Not so.

I sent out a bunch of proposals and got rejected. I got tired of getting turned down, so I published the book myself and found myself thrown into the process of publishing. I had to react to things incredibly fast, almost on a daily basis. I picked the hardest kind of book to publish—full color with graphics. I couldn't do print-on-demand, which made the process way more difficult.

Even after we thought we had everything figured out, we didn't. Every day I had to learn something new, like what an ozalid is (it's a special photocopy you make during the process of placing original artwork on a page). I learned all this stuff fast, and thank God I had the best graphic designer. I also learned that promoting myself is not my forte. I do very well at promoting people I love, but not myself.

Every day I try to do something to move the book forward in the world. I have to remind myself, "It took me seventeen years to get here." I am very impatient. My hands and heart are open and waiting for how the writing will unfold.

I am very proud of the book. It is extraordinarily beautiful. I had to put my foot down when the color was wrong on the last two proofs. I didn't want to put anything less than my best foot forward. This decision delayed the book by over a month, and it cost me money. It was the right thing to do, though, because the final product is so well done. That makes me happy.

During the Power phase, there is nothing that impedes your ability to be yourself fully. You are not restrained and do not restrict yourself in any way; instead you are fully supported and you know what maximizes your strengths. This phase involves arriving at a very clear understanding of who you are now, nearly transformed.

> *I know I am different now, in a positive way. I realize I am not your average woman. And I don't feel uncomfortable with that anymore. I totally embrace it. I will use myself in the most positive ways I can. I don't know what all those things are, but I am ready. I am so ready.*

Radha was replete with the fruits of her labors and at peace with the past. She accepted herself fully. As a result of her journey, she was able to act authentically, love deeply, and simply be.

❋ ❋ ❋

Power builds quietly. It stems from assuredness brought by inner knowing and strength to resist external pressures or endure the hard work of building something that exemplifies you, combined with thoughtful, heartfelt action. Power arises from having endured the journey of transformation, and it influences others because of your dedication and passion. Your ability to have accomplished something personally great is grounded in humility gained through the many times you saw your own faults or had to give up control. Once you achieve this command of yourself and your life, there is only one more thing to do: relax into the experience of being integrated, in the final phase on the Map to Wholeness. It is your time to feel fully rounded and whole—and to simply be.

15

PHASE 13: INTEGRATION

Living union ... is arrived at by an arduous psychological and spiritual process ... entailing the complete remaking of character and the liberation of a new, or rather latent, form of consciousness.

—EVELYN UNDERHILL

You have traversed the entire Map to Wholeness. Over the course of many years you have experienced a gamut of experiences: wishing for happiness, tolerating the peak of transcendence or the horror of trauma, longing to go back in time, searching your psyche for the self you seemed to have lost, enduring inward pain, encountering healing, receiving support and love, and realizing your inherent power and potential. Although at times it might have felt like it would never end, you have finally arrived.

Integration is your final destination, the place where you achieve a state of completeness. It is the culmination of a journey beyond what you thought was possible and inward into deep chasms of the self, so you could arrive here, reinvented. From this place you get the chance to relish the reward of contentedness that comes after having endured your process of becoming yourself.

Integration is both a process and a state of being. As a process, it encompasses the lower half of the figure eight: all that you have endured between phase 5, when you returned home from the transformative experience, and phase 13, the endpoint of being wholly you. Integration as a process refers to the activities of combining all aspects of yourself, especially parts you may have initially rejected or didn't know existed, so you can become something grand and cohesive. For example, Kenny didn't initially recognize that he was unable to manage his anger or that he was ordinary just like everyone else when he learned about his Enneagram type.

Integration as it occurs during the thirteenth phase is a state of being that is achieved when you are unified. It is the reward at the end of your journey. Here you are open to all parts of yourself, accepting them equally and without restriction. You have a sense of identity that gives you a foundation of stability, clarity, certainty, and focus. You demonstrate capacity to cope with daily challenges because of your refined resilience, perspective, awareness, and compassion. Because of the voyage you've taken, you are now better able to pay attention to your feelings, thoughts, physical sensations, and environment—and to inquire about the meaning behind the present moment.

During this phase you are liberated from searching or grasping for experiences that you once believed would make you feel happier: material possessions, money, relationships, drugs, working all the time, acknowledgment, or status. You no longer feel the compulsion to possess or be anything other than what you already embody and own. There is nothing to do now except to enjoy your life and being you.

This major shift occurs because once you are integrated, you will experience yourself as paradoxical rather than homogeneous. This means you accept yourself as comprising internalized opposites. You can say without discomfort, "I am capable of being masculine and feminine, hard and soft, moral and immoral, taking charge and allowing nature to take its course, active and still, receiving and giving," and many other seemingly conflicting qualities. As a result, from here onward you are better able to regulate and maintain healthy functioning regardless of what is going on around you. You are joined into a single entity—present, available, eager, and participating in life. You experience peace and balance.

This does not mean you are perfect or free from hassles, challenges, inadequacies, or mishaps. Instead you will find that in comparison to all of the other phases of transformation, now you will have only minor and infrequent problems, and you have mastered healthier and more effective ways to respond to them when they do arise.

Author Carol Adrienne—whose transformative journey involved the pains of surviving divorce, cancer, single motherhood, and financial desolation, and whose heights involved being hosted by Oprah Winfrey and being an acclaimed author in the United States, Europe, and Japan—had this to say about her Integration.

As my career developed, I could see that everything I had gone through previously—cancer, divorce, motherhood, financial stress, career confusion—all had provided me with the direct experience and knowledge that I needed to be able to relate to and help other people. Now in my seventies, I am so grateful for the wealth of experiences I've had. I feel very content now in living simply, being able to enjoy my grandchildren and my twenty-year relationship, and pursuing my passion for painting. Like many people, I'm sure, each period of my earlier life felt uniquely different—almost like another lifetime.

My partner, Robert, and I recently downsized to a smaller home, and this move has brought me even more happiness and freedom than I anticipated. I still travel for pleasure and am always eager to come home.

The most important distinction of this phase is its culmination: the uncommon and short-lived experience of perfect homeostasis—a calm state in which opposing forces are in balance and equilibrium. You have achieved internal stability, where all that is within and without is in harmony. You are in a rewarding relationship with yourself, your career, and all of your primary relationships.

Like the moment when a flower has completely blossomed and its petals are outstretched to the sunlight, you get a chance to rest in a fulcrum where your entire life, as it were, sits in the balance between one humongous journey and the next.

A different interviewee, Carol Fischer, had a spiritual awakening in 1993 when she was at a retreat and locked eyes with the yoga master Baba Hari Das. She saw swirling light, and then:

> I burst and became everything. That was kind of it. When I came back into my body I discovered that four hours had passed and the room was empty. I couldn't move, and I thought, "Can I get up? Should I stay here? I think I died."

After this peak experience Carol survived divorce, years of excruciating strife with her troubled teenager, financial destitution, and three close brushes with death due to colon cancer. Seventeen years later she found herself at the completion of the Map to Wholeness, in the Integration phase. She described what it felt like to be in that place:

> My life is my life now. I am five years out from the cancer. It has taken this long for the chemicals to get out of my body and for me to recover emotionally and physically.

> I am calmer overall. With cancer, there is an immediacy of possible death. I feel that I am far enough away from the crisis now that I trust I am going to be here for awhile; I won't die next week.

> I lead guided imagery sessions in an oncology unit once a month, unpaid. I don't want to volunteer any more than I am right now; it's just enough. Work has been real stable. I know that my work is truly effective. I love coming to my office and seeing the people here. I don't know if everyone else likes coming here, but I do, and since it's all about me, it doesn't matter.

> I feel satisfied.

> I have accomplished what I need to accomplish. That is a really good place to be. I don't have to try so hard. I don't have to struggle upstream. I can just turn around and shoot down the rapids. I don't even know what I was struggling

for anyway. It was always as though there was too much to do. I feel a sense of relief.

My kids are doing wonderfully. They are content. They are happy. What else could you want for your kids? It was all worth it. Well ... not getting cancer; that wasn't, but I made it through that, fortunately. Not everyone does.

I have stability within myself. I have myself back.

Now I want to watch the flowers open.

Integration is a state of contentment in the fullest sense, and Carol's words express this. She has no need to anxiously run from her experience, complain of deprivation, or try to fix or change anyone or anything—and most especially herself. She is residing in her own body in a way that acknowledges her perception of things being just right and reveals how she is in harmony with her life circumstances and herself.

What she describes is a state of inner and outer union. She has achieved this state by learning to love aspects of herself she had previously rejected, which allows her to love people she judged in the past. This quality of love means you accept others and yourself more deeply, and when you can do this you have full access to peace and inner union.

If you are at peace you are residing in love, but also in power. Integration means that your energy, attention, and consciousness are concentrated and organized instead of being diffused and scattered. When you are in such a state you have fully mobilized and actualized your latent potential. This is why the Christian mystic Evelyn Underhill said, "Living union ... is arrived at by an arduous psychological and spiritual process ... entailing the complete remaking of character and the liberation of a new, or rather latent, form of consciousness" (Underhill 1974, 81).

When we say we want to have a better life, be closer to God, or lead the good life, we are actually saying that we hope to live in peace with all that is around us and within us. This state of living union is achieved by experiencing our own journey of transformation, both the catalytic heights and disintegrating depths, so we can liberate a part of us that used to lie dormant and let it become fully real.

Kenny: "I Am a Living Example of That!"

Integration is a quiet phase of peaceful revelry. The lack of drama is evident when I ask people to describe their experiences; there are always fewer words spoken about Integration than any other phase. Perhaps this is because of the tranquility or ineffability that accompanies the experience of living out our own unique version of heaven on earth. Here's what Kenny has to say about it:

> Pilar is working at H&R block. She is happy, she likes her colleagues. Work is fine, family is family. I was in Kansas City back in November. It was the first time my family met Pilar. That was okay. Family is always a challenge. Pilar enjoyed herself. I was happy she was there to meet them.

All aspects of one's life enter into a state of balance or homeostasis that is hassle-free, conscious, and steady. When a person dwells in this integrated state, others around them benefit from this serenity, even though the inner experience is private. Kenny's integration is particularly astounding because during this phase he had the fortune of speaking at two satsangs as an invited speaker to more than two hundred yogis, a swami, and his assistant at the ashram in the Bahamas where he had spoken before. The theme of the gathering was "Yoga: Spiritual Transformation and Redemption."

> It became clear that I was there to do one thing: to inspire and motivate the people in the ashram. So I adopted an attitude of quietness, of silence. It became clear that it wasn't my job to come there and be an ambassador of peace but to hold myself in a swami position, because they look up to the swamis. Even the outfit I wore that day of my talk was the color orange, the swami's coloring. Everything was designed to give them the air that, "I can't really approach him because he's quiet, he is not saying anything, he is not even looking at me, he is not giving me any energy."

> Because I held myself like that, I knew that when I spoke, people are going to see the love that's here. They're going to see the joy that's here. They are going to see the openness, the accessibility that's here. They are going to want it and

they are going to want to come up to me. It was more of a calmness, solidness, groundedness. I was calm and relaxed.

It was perfect the way I did it, or that it happened the way that it happened.

On the first night, a film director showed his award-winning movie about a guy in prison who was convicted for murder, how he met a woman and how he got out of prison. On day two, he talked more about how she changed his life. Once the guy got out, he realized he didn't have enough abilities for a relationship, so he went into meditation and an ashram in Canada. Now he is in healthier relationships.

I thought, "I am a living example of that!"

In this circumstance, Kenny's worlds merged. When he watched the film about a man who so closely mirrored his terrible and triumphant journey, he saw his life reflected, coming alive before his eyes. He witnessed the grandeur of his miraculous transformation from an external perspective. He literally *saw* himself. The profundity of this experience cannot be overestimated. The movie quite literally became an integrating agent, a cause and an effect of Kenny's years of personal growth.

They introduced me to the audience: "Kenneth Johnson who will talk about being incarcerated." I felt comfortable. I knew what I was going to say.

In all of the years I interviewed Kenny about his life, I never once heard him utter these confident words. Throughout his journey he had in fact, struggled immensely with self-doubt that came with not knowing what he would say to groups of people. Now, as a transformed individual, Kenny possessed perfect clarity.

I gave a powerful talk. It surprised me that I held myself in a different position. It was like, "Okay, I am here. I am natural. I am here in this situation as a motivator." I spoke sturdily, directly.

My talk was so well received and then I was given a standing ovation. The remainder of my visit was spent answering spiritual questions and prison questions.

Later on, I was sitting in nature and someone came up to me and said, "Wow, you have changed. You are totally different. The last time you were here ... you are more professional now." She kept saying, "You have really, really grown in the last two years."

I remember that when I spoke at the ashram before, I was all over the place, happy and excited. I had just gotten back from Bali. I was happy to be back. I was broke. It was nice to see the change from 2013 to 2015. I was two different people.

Being in an integrated state involves such spaciousness and clarity of mind, heart, and body that it can be easier to observe oneself. The state of integration is paradoxical, oddly peaceful while also being entirely natural.

When I spoke two years ago, I was excited to be in the Bahamas. I wanted people to like me. This time, I wanted people to like the message.

In addition to the potency of the content of his talk, his energy as a wholly integrated person residing in homeostasis imbued his words with his state of being. For this reason, his mere presence no doubt played a role in how he was received and the effects he likely had among those in the room.

"I Am at Peace"

A few months after his travel to the Bahamas ashram, Kenny was still in the Integration phase. This is what it was like to be him then:

I am more relaxed, more at peace. I not trying to prove anything, don't have to compete. I am just being Kenny. I am at peace.

I'm not trying to be a teacher, somebody that wrote a book and is trying to impress people. Not having to make a living teaching, being a guru, being a writer.

I am just saying, "This is Kenny, and this is what I am doing. Hello, how are you doing? Can I help you?"

I don't need to make people like me anymore. I feel good inside. I feel excited, at peace, relaxed, confident.

Kenny's life was by no means perfect, but he did become whole—wholly himself. Over a period of twenty-one years he endured profound challenges and savored magnificent accomplishments. He integrated the light of illumination and transformed, not from sinner to saint but from pilgrim in the darkness to master in the light.

Radha: "It Doesn't Really Matter What's Next"

When Radha entered the Map to Wholeness she was already skilled in self-analysis and communication, with an open heart and connections to her feelings. One might think, "What else could she need?" At her journey's end, Radha illustrated that transformation through adopting new skills and dropping old patterns is the means by which to become a different person.

> I feel fortunate, settled, that I have the ability to do a lot of good in the world.

> I have a very calm sense, a serene consciousness. It's not like shouting from the mountaintops. It's a calmness, sort of like feeling grown up in the most wonderful sense. It's not like, "Well, I am an adult now." It's more like, "Oh, I get it."

This seemingly nonchalant observation gives us a glimpse into Radha's complete internal shift. The old self took a parental and cognitive approach to development and internal stability. Her old self would have assessed her situation rationally: "Well, I am an adult now," as if to say, "You are X number of years old now, you are officially an adult." The new self no longer needed the guidance of her mind. Instead she felt the truth of what her mind had been saying all along.

> I feel very stable, rooted, comfortable, and conscious. I feel privileged to be together on the inside. Not in an egotistical way but to have the awareness of how to walk gently in the world, to make a difference—to have the spiritual ability, physical ability, and financial ability to do that.

It just feels like it doesn't really matter what's next. I am prepared for anything. I have this conscious self that can make a difference, be present, love deeply, and go on smiling.

Radha can now relax and enjoy her relationships, career, possessions, and recreational activities. In this phase, not only are you very stable; others in your life who were previously the source of stress have either miraculously exited your life or become healthier too.

Christina is doing amazingly well. She looks incredible. She wants to settle down and find a guy but refuses to go on a dating site. She is holding down a job and about to get a puppy.

She doesn't need me to tell her what to do. She is forty years old, for Pete's sake. I am mother to everyone around me. There is a point where you have to say, "That is not my job." Unless she specifically asks for my opinion, it is her life. It's not my job, in the most positive way.

It is difficult if not impossible to imagine how drastically your life can actually change until you see it for yourself. Radha is about as positive a person as they come, and even she had serious doubts that her daughter would access the type of aliveness that she was just beginning to exhibit when Radha arrived at Integration. When you become integrated, your transformation is finished, and you are complete. In this state, a driven, active, and passionate person can be at ease.

I feel happier, healthier, and more settled in my soul than I ever have in my short life. I would not want to be younger or living in any different way—so far, anyway. I have a sense of well-being and stability that I have never experienced. I have fortune—not money, but the experience of being fortunate in life itself ... even with our tragedy.

This is the first time in my life when I felt like the next project didn't have to be for someone else, like the Insight Prison Project, food bank fundraisers, or the Tenderloin project; it could be for me. Maybe it's time for me to take a language class or mosaics class. I have never done anything like that, ever.

Well, maybe that will be next. I've got some time to make that decision because the holidays are here, we have a big trip around the world coming up, and who knows what we will find when we come home.

I felt I was constantly on the road of change, and now I feel transformed. I am open to whatever comes next. For now, it's kind of nice to just be.

Radha's description further clarifies many aspects of Integration. The overall theme of contentedness shows up most prominently in the way that she wants to spend time. During a good portion of her journey, Radha spoke about the desire to focus on her own health and took action such as engaging in more exercise and quitting positions that were not aligned with her emerging identity. Now, in this culminating phase she implies a radical shift. Radha is clear that spending the majority of her time correcting injustices is now over, and she is ready to enjoy herself rather than to enjoy giving to others—two very different lifestyles.

Notice too that although she acknowledges this major shift, she is quick to say she is in no hurry to act. As we've mentioned, being rather than doing takes precedence during this phase. This state of being shows up throughout her sharing. Notice for example that she didn't say, "I feel open"; rather, she said, "I am open," which is distinctly different. Now that you are free from the need to get something done, Integration will cause you to be in a state of openness toward thoughts, people, situations, opportunities, ideas, and places.

If you are afraid that your conditioned habit of always being on the go will cause you to feel guilty and to prematurely leave the beauty of Integration, turn your attention to your body. Radha's impulse to act was only a weak thought form that was quickly consumed by her body's desire to sink back into the pleasure of being. Resisting the impulse to do something is as difficult as defying the urge to get out of the delightful, steamy waters of a hot tub. As soon as the harsh, cold air bites at your skin, your body will beckon you to quickly retreat back into the enchanting and enveloping waters for a few more minutes of delicious lingering.

It is with these delicate words—"For now, it's kind of nice to just be"—that Radha's massive transformation came to completion and herself into wholeness. Looking back through the years and across the phases she endured, one could scarcely have imagined the horrors of her profound loss, the depths of her learning and change, the far-reaching expanse of her giving, and the richness of her concluding state. Radha now resides in a state of being that will remain as a reservoir of wisdom, compassion, and power for the rest of her life. Although she cannot bring Christopher back to life or undo the wrong that took his life, she has lived and will continue to live fully and to indulge in the joy of traveling with her dear husband, sharing life-giving outings and conversations with Christina, planning parties for relatives, and savoring the personal meaning of the ways in which her efforts have positively affected the lives of thousands of people.

Making the Most of Integration

As your transformational journey draws to a close, take time to indulge yourself. Savor the experience of being free from struggle.

Being in a state of integration is different from feeling calm for a day or at ease because you are at the beach for a week. These experiences are fleeting. Once you are integrated, you can perceive the differences between being, acting, and reacting. Integration allows you to appreciate what it is simply to be—to reside in your own presence, devoid of any impulse to act or react. Once you experience this state, you can more easily call upon it and reside in it as you wish. As life moves forward into ever-evolving cycles of transformation, the capacity to simply be becomes increasingly informative as you make important and mundane choices about how you want to act and be each day.

Grace and ease may trick you into feeling like all of your troubles are now over and you can put your feet up and enjoy the good life. But this, too, shall pass, and you will eventually enter into another cycle of transformation.

For now, you might feel as if you are standing in a place that allows you to gaze far across the horizon, both backward and forward, appreciating the ugliness and beauty, your weaknesses and strengths, tragedies and triumphs. When you are integrated you have the capacity to recognize and trust that your journey is always in service of becoming a healthier, happier version of you. As poet Audre Lorde said, "When I dare to be powerful, to use my strength in service of my vision, then it becomes less and less important whether I am unafraid" (Lorde 1980, 13).

Because the Integration phase is about a state of being, not doing or action, it is much more difficult to describe. Like the Transformative Experience and Dismemberment phases, words cannot adequately express its essence. How long can you talk about the fact that you feel at ease and peaceful and that things are just right? Feelings of contentment might confound the situation because there is less desire to talk about what is happening to you than there is to be because the experience itself is so gratifying.

You will discover that your responsibilities actually increase and challenges become more complex now. Thank goodness your capabilities to handle them continue to mature.

Part III

Your Transformation

16

WHERE ARE YOU ON THE MAP TO WHOLENESS?

The transformation through which the inner journey takes the soul is not a change of her character, but a self-realization of true nature.

—A. H. ALAMAS

The Map to Wholeness offers a powerful way to view—and even experience—your life. The figure eight traces where you have been and where you are going. By recognizing your most recent transformational journey, you are able to understand what has occurred so far, what is happening inside and around you right now, and what is to come. Perceiving the meaning of your present location on the map can help you feel self-assured rather than uncertain, calm rather than distraught, and clear rather than confused.

This chapter provides tools to help you to discern your current location on the Map to Wholeness. If I were to interview you, as I have done with hundreds of people, I would ask you personally relevant questions. Here, I have adapted some of the exercises and instructions I give my interviewees so you can chart your transformation yourself.

Take an Online Quiz

If you have access to a computer and the Internet, you can take a quiz available on my website (www.suzyross.net) to establish the phase you are in now. It consists of about forty multiple-choice questions and takes between thirty and forty minutes to complete. If you are unaccustomed to examining your inner life, ask someone who knows you well to help you reflect on and respond to each question. The results include your likely phase, a few paragraphs describing the phase, and a video and poem for further illumination and support.

Chart Your Location on the Map

A more comprehensive and individualized way to determine where you are on the Map to Wholeness is to review your life in relation to the thirteen phases. Depending on the level of detail you wish to consider, you may spend a few hours or many days analyzing your personal history. When you see the events of your life plotted out, you can start to recognize the larger and smaller transformations you have undergone.

To plot your life's numerous transformational journeys, up to and including the one you are in now, follow these steps:

1. *Prepare a blank timeline.* On as many sheets of paper as necessary, print out the blank timeline table provided at the end of this chapter, or create a similar one, including the columns "Year," "Event," "Theme," and "Phase." Leave several lines of space for each year.

2. *List your major life events.* Reflect upon the major events of your life. Try to remember experiences that affected you physically, psychologically, or emotionally, and the years in which they occurred. Sample

events to consider include accomplishments, awards, graduations, big opportunities, extraordinary experiences, sizable purchases (such as buying a house, boat, or land), injuries, tragedies (yours or those of people very close to you), falling in love, breaking up, moving, sickness, embarrassment, travel, and home remodeling. Record your major highs, lows, and turning points next to their corresponding years. You might start with the three most significant experiences that come to mind and work from there. For each event, provide a word or two that describes it. For example, you might write, "June: Got married," next to "2010." (Pinpointing the month can give you more precision later, when you must identify phases that are very brief.) Keep pondering your past to recall and write down as many experiences as you can.

To help flesh out your timeline, you might consult the following sources:

- Family members and close friends, who can remind you of both major and minor events

- Emails, event calendars, and day planners, both at home and at work, for the occurrences and activities that consumed your time, thoughts, and feelings

- Personal journals, work diaries, and letters, which may remind you of important experiences you have forgotten

3. *Identify themes.* Go back over your timeline and attempt to identify periods, or "chapters," in your life. These episodes might last weeks, months, or years, and they can encompass one or more events. For example, you might recognize a time when you experienced a series of happy changes: you met a promising new love interest, received a long-deserved promotion, and remodeled your kitchen as you had dreamed of doing for years. Other examples of themes include recovering from a financial downturn, feeling overwhelmed, trying to establish yourself, healing from an illness, and looking for community. Indicate such themes on your chart, using lines and arrows to clearly mark where each period begins

and ends. If you are using a computer document, enter the theme in the cell to the right of each experience to which it applies. Don't worry about identifying a theme for every experience in your life. A handful of the major ones will suffice.

4. *Label phases.* With the Map to Wholeness diagram and brief phase descriptions nearby for reference (you can find these on suzyross.com or in the next chapter, "A Guide for Each Phase"), label the phases of transformation on your timeline by trying to match the themes you noted in the previous step with the thirteen phases. Begin with the biggest life-changing experience on your list, which likely represents phase 3. Then scan the events of the months and years that follow and precede it to establish the surrounding phases. Examine the qualities of the experiences. Finding Dismemberment tends to be easy, for instance, because this dark night of the soul, in which you feel out of control and helpless, is obvious. Work backward and forward from the themes and events that stand out to you, taking time to reflect on them in order to determine their positions within the transformational journey. You will eventually see multiple transformations that have occurred over your life.

Keep in mind the following idiosyncrasies about a few phases:

- The Seed and Departure phases can occur unconsciously, so you may have difficulty recalling your connection to transformation during these periods.

- The Displacement phase lasts only about two weeks.

- The Disorientation, Dismemberment, and Surrender and Healing phases can last several years each and are more painful than most other phases. It is surprisingly easy to feel like you have moved on to a less painful phase because your circumstances seem to be getting better when in fact you have not moved on. This is particularly easy to do if you tend to be optimistic, resilient, or hardened to pain and suffering. I am reminded of a situation that arose during a training I recently provided for grade school teachers, counselors, and administrators. An administrator named Charmaine described her current life circumstances with a long list of terrible losses and painful experiences. It was obvious to everyone around her that she was enduring Dismemberment, and yet she questioned whether or not she was actually in Dismemberment. I was surprised to hear of her confusion. When I looked more closely at her face, it seemed as if she wanted to say, "Things are bad, but not that bad." I turned to her friends and asked them, "How would you describe Charmaine's character, her ability to handle challenge and adversity?" They replied unanimously, "She is the strongest person I know—almost to her own detriment." I turned to Charmaine and asked her, "Is it possible that you are so used to surviving and are so good at making the best of your situation that you cannot see that you are living through the worst experience of your life?" She cracked a small smile and said, "Yes, you are right." When you focus on surviving it is not very easy to recognize the severity of your own plight.

It is also quite common for people to feel as if they have advanced to the Abundance and Creativity phase when in fact they are still in the Surrender and Healing phase. This probably occurs because daily life during Surrender and Healing is so much easier and more hopeful than in Dismemberment. You are so glad to be in an easier phase that it is common to mistakenly think, "Surely I have moved into the Abundance and Creativity phase." You might mislabel positive occurrences in your life as Abundance when they are probably essentially Healing. I have made this mistake more than once. I lovingly call this "transformation fatigue." The last time I experienced it, in an effort to cheer myself up and accept my present situation I began saying to myself, "Just a little bit longer." Somehow these words helped me get through each day until at last I found myself in the Birth phase. When you are going through a difficult aspect of transformation, it can feel like it will never end. Yet it does! All it takes is living through an entire transformation with awareness in order to appreciate it, and you will be able to begin to trust its predictability and that the joyful end does arrive. As you move toward Integration, you will be enveloped in joy and at peace with the struggles of the past.

Identifying the three moments of the Birth phase usually requires considerable time and effort. As a start, you may want to approximate when Birth happened as the point where Surrender and Healing seemed to transition into Abundance and Creativity. When you have some time to devote to this inquiry and maybe the help of a friend, you can revisit the mysterious details of your birth.

Here is a sample timeline:

YEAR	EVENT	THEME	PHASE
2011	May: Thought about looking for a new job.	Desire to be happier	Seed
	August: Began applying for jobs.	Taking action to be happier	Departure
	October: Marriage began to fail.	Everything started to crumble	Departure
2012	Jan.: Spouse moved out.	My world shattered	Transformative Experience
	Jan-April: Went to therapy.	In shock, not feeling normal	Return
	April: Realized our marriage might not make it.	In a daze, not feeling normal	Displacement

YEAR	EVENT	THEME	PHASE
2012-2013	March-January. Struggled in my ability to perform well at work.	In disbelief and sad that my spouse is not happy and might not ever return	Denial and Grief
2013	January: Spouse asks for divorce.	I think to myself, "What do I do now? Who am I now? This is not how my life is supposed to be."	Disorientation
2014	July: I am laid off from my job.	My world is shattered.	Dismemberment

Mapping transformation is a learned skill. If you want to become better at it, work on your ability to look within at your character, actions, and motives. Also, study the characteristics of each phase. With enough practice, you will even be able to assess where your partner, family members, friends, and colleagues are on the map. Once you determine your own location, you may enjoy the challenge of tracking your movement from phase to phase by paying attention to your feelings and experiences.

What to Do Now

After completing the online quiz or creating a timeline of your experiences and their corresponding phases, what is your current location on the Map to Wholeness? You might consider rereading the chapter in part II of this book that pertains to your present phase. Being reminded of those who have been where you are now can bolster your spirits, especially if you are going through a particularly difficult period. The details of their stories will likely resonate with you and help illuminate aspects of your own experience. Moreover, the chapter content may comfort you by reminding you that what you are experiencing is normal.

In addition, I highly recommend referring to the next chapter, which presents an overview of the thirteen phases on the Map to Wholeness.

My Timeline

Print this chart on as many sheets of paper as necessary to cover all the years of your life.

YEAR	EVENT	THEME	PHASE

17

YOUR GUIDE TO THE PHASES OF TRANSFORMATION

*Let yourself be silently drawn by the strange pull of
what you really love. It will not lead you astray.*

—RUMI

This chapter provides a guide to using the phases on the Map to Wholeness to gain a clearer perspective on your current phase or to familiarize yourself with the distinctive characteristics of all the phases. As you will see, each phase offers a gift and an opportunity, as well as a challenge. To get the most out of a phase, implement the suggestions for deepening your experience; to get in touch with the essence of the phase, repeat the affirmation provided. A tip to keep in mind for *all* phases is that it can be very reassuring to remind yourself that what you are going through is normal.

Phase 1: Seed

All life starts at inception—the beginning. The process of transformation, which births a new life, can be thought of as commencing from a seed. Like the little acorn that becomes a mighty oak, the seed of the transformational journey is a tiny idea that holds within it a new world. Representing your potential, the seed might be an insight about who you want to become, or it might remain unconscious. To be actualized, your potential requires two factors: inner readiness and the desire to be happier. This phase offers a glimpse of your wholeness, which will be realized through the transformational journey.

What You Need to Know

As you enter, experience, anticipate, or reflect on the Seed phase, keep the following information and advice in mind.

BEGINNING

The Seed phase begins when your unconscious readiness to become whole ignites a desire to grow. You may or may not be aware of this desire.

GIFT

The gift of the Seed phase is new life.

CHALLENGE

The challenge of the Seed phase is to recognize the impulse to grow.

OPPORTUNITY

The opportunity of the Seed phase is to pay attention to your longing.

DEEPENING YOUR EXPERIENCE

To enhance your encounter with the Seed phase, engage in activities that help you to listen to your body, mind, heart, or spirit with the intention of discovering what you really want to do or become. Examples of such activities include the following:

- Being in nature (sitting, walking, jogging, camping, etc.)
- Meditating
- Breathing practices
- Solitary activities (cleaning the house, making something with your hands, practicing your basketball shot, kayaking, etc.)
- Activities for getting in touch with yourself recommended by a trusted friend who knows you very well

Affirmation

Empower yourself during the Seed phase by repeating the following affirmation:

Somewhere in the depths of my being, I am ready to transform and to create myself anew.

Phase 2: Departure

The Departure phase marks the physical beginning of your journey. You leave what you know and what seems safe. You shift from the previous phase's thinking to this phase's doing—although you may or may not consciously be seeking change. If you are moving toward a peak experience in the next phase, you may encounter obstacles in this one. These barriers challenge you to ask yourself, "Do I really want this breakthrough?" If you are approaching a traumatic transformative experience, warning signs may confront you. These hints about what is to come may take the form of cautions from others or your own intuitions.

What You Need to Know

As you enter, experience, anticipate, or reflect on the Departure phase, keep the following information and advice in mind.

BEGINNING

The Departure phase begins the moment you take action to move yourself toward a new life or possibility for yourself.

GIFT

The gift of the Departure phase is leaving the past behind.

CHALLENGE

The challenge of the Departure phase is to be open to possibilities.

OPPORTUNITIES

The opportunities of the Departure phase are to tend to your feelings, perceive that your fears are erroneous, and recognize outdated ways of thinking and behaving.

DEEPENING YOUR EXPERIENCE

To enhance your progress through the Departure phase, ponder the following questions:

- How is my present situation helping me see and overcome my own limitations? How is it helping me recognize and move toward my potential?

- What about the present moment makes me feel alive?

- What makes me feel particularly free? How can I begin to incorporate this sense of freedom into my daily life?

- How do I create barriers to my own freedom?

AFFIRMATION

Empower yourself during the Departure phase by repeating the following affirmation:

> *I consciously leave behind the world I have known so I can become who I have always wanted to be.*

Phase 3: Transformative Experience

The transformative experience is ineffable, meaning it can't be described. There are two types of transformative events: peak experiences and traumas. Given enough time and effort, a transformative experience can change your entire life. In this phase, you go beyond your own boundaries to find your higher self or even the divine. The way in which you move into this altered state differs, however, depending on the kind of experience you have. A trauma tends to shatter the psyche, whereas a peak experience gives a sense of expansion. When you touch the light of the divine, something in you instantly dies—and something else is promptly conceived.

What You Need to Know

As you experience, anticipate, or reflect on your Transformative Experience, keep the following information and advice in mind.

BEGINNING

The Transformative Experience begins, and ends, with an uplifting or traumatic episode that removes you from everyday reality.

GIFT

The gift of the Transformative Experience is immersion in something larger than yourself.

CHALLENGE

The challenge of the Transformative Experience is to stay present with what is happening.

OPPORTUNITIES

The opportunities of the Transformative Experience are to absorb the experience and be fully present.

DEEPENING YOUR EXPERIENCE

The Transformative Experience, or life-changing event, captivates your body, mind, heart, and spirit. To become more aware of the experience while it is occurring, do the following:

- Consciously monitor your physical sensations, thoughts, and feelings.

- Focus on the activities going on around you and their importance or symbolism in your life.

- Watch your experience unfold from the perspective of a neutral observer. To do this, imagine you are floating at a distance from yourself, taking in the event with a video camera.

AFFIRMATION

Empower yourself during your Transformative Experience by repeating the following affirmation:

In the space between worlds, I am one with my limitlessness.

Phase 4: Return

The Return phase is essentially a contraction from the shattered or expanded state of the Transformative Experience. This period is never pleasant; you may feel doubt, hesitation, fear, disdain, ambivalence, or disbelief. You do not want to go back to normal life because you may have to explain what happened to you, do something you don't want to do, or face rejection by others. However, the thought of going home also promises solace, rest, and normalcy. Mythologist Joseph Campbell explains that during this time, you can get lost in a forest of melancholy; eventually, however, you must face the inevitability of your homecoming.

What You Need to Know

As you enter, experience, anticipate, or reflect on the Return phase, keep the following information and advice in mind.

BEGINNING

The Return phase begins when the immediate experience of the transformative event is over. You are still in an altered state, but the gripping episode has subsided or ceased.

GIFT

The gift of the Return phase is the many ways in which you can learn from your indescribable experience.

CHALLENGE

The challenge of the Return phase is to be subject to overwhelming emotions or shock.

OPPORTUNITY

The opportunity of the Return phase is to absorb the Transformative Experience.

DEEPENING YOUR EXPERIENCE

To make it through the Return phase gracefully, consider the following guidance:

- A life-changing event is immediately followed by feeling separated from everyone and everything. This sense of alienation happens because transformative incidents occur outside the realm of what you have known to be possible. When you return from the foreign territory of the life-changing experience, you try to make sense of this overwhelming event and incorporate it into your life. If you resist the fact that your understanding of yourself has been challenged by the transformative experience, you will feel distress. Try instead to accept that not feeling normal is normal at this stage of transformation.

- You may feel ambivalent about telling others the story of your transformative event. No one can really understand what you went through, yet you need to talk about it. Be advised that sharing what you experienced can have both favorable and unfavorable consequences, leaving you feeling relieved but intensely vulnerable. This means that it is important to control your impulse to talk about your transformative experience. Take many conscious breaths, maybe even sleep a night or two without sharing, and ask yourself, "Who are the people around me who can believe in what I have experienced?" Consider sharing a little bit of your story in order to see whether or not a person is interested in hearing what you have to say. If they appear open, compassionate, and interested, this might be a person with whom you can share more fully.

- Be gentle on yourself, and ask for the support you need, such as, "Would you be interested in looking at these photos of my travels?" or "Would you be willing to take a walk and hear about what happened to me?"

After a traumatic transformative experience, consider doing the following:

- Get to safety, if necessary.

- Seek support, help, comfort, and guidance. List the people who love and care about you, and reach out to them.

- Give yourself full permission to feel and react in whatever way comes naturally to you (e.g., proceed as though the event didn't happen, stop all activities, sob or scream uncontrollably, talk about the experience as much or little as you need to, etc.).

After a peak experience, consider doing the following:

- Take time to be alone, close your eyes, and re-live the experience many times.

- Each time you reminisce, notice as many details of the experience as possible. Here are some ways to make the most of the learning:

  - Sit in quiet stillness.

  - Breathe slowly.

  - Shut your eyes.

  - Pay attention to the sensations in your body and sink as deeply into the feeling as you can.

  - Let appreciation and your desire to learn guide your attention.

  - Ask yourself, "In what ways does my peak experience show me my true self?"

AFFIRMATION

Empower yourself during the Return phase by repeating the following affirmation:

I ventured beyond the world I knew into unknown territory. I can survive my return and recovery.

Phase 5: Displacement— Relief and Upheaval

Displacement occurs when you return home or experience the first semblance of normalcy after a transformative event. This brief phase lasts for the first few hours, days, or weeks after your return, which may be literal (you open your front door and go inside) or symbolic (the initial tumult related to your drama has passed). Displacement literally means that you are "out of place": You are not "here," because you are focused on the past, and you are not "there," because your transformative experience is over. As a result, you may feel disjointed, splintered, or detached.

There are two main elements of Displacement: relief and upheaval. You are relieved to be among the comforts of home, or you try to make yourself feel at home by surrounding yourself with familiar objects, people, and routines. Yet you also encounter upheaval, a disruption that ranges from inconvenient to intensely disturbing. It happens unexpectedly and tends to affect survival. The stress related to this event may be positive or negative.

What You Need to Know

As you enter, experience, anticipate, or reflect on the Displacement phase, keep the following information and advice in mind.

BEGINNING

The Displacement phase begins when you return home, to a place that makes you feel like "home," or to your routine. In the case of severe trauma, this phase begins when the physical shock wears off and you "return" to your body.

GIFT

The gift of the Displacement phase is appreciating home.

CHALLENGE

The challenge of the Displacement phase is to adapt to whatever upheaval you encounter.

OPPORTUNITY

The opportunity of the Displacement phase is to see positive aspects of home that you didn't appreciate before.

Deepening Your Experience

To move through the Displacement phase with self-assurance, approach it as follows:

- Recognize that a disruptive situation, either positive or negative, will arise and cause you stress.

- Shift your focus to the present moment if you find yourself fixated on the past, either because you wish you were back at a peak experience or you miss what you lost during a trauma.

- Identify what you need, separate from the expectations of others, so you can take care of yourself.

Affirmation

Empower yourself during Displacement by repeating the following affirmation, which pertains especially to the upheaval aspect of the phase:

My essence is not based on my possessions, food, shelter, money, others around me, or even my body. I can reorient to the truth that no person or event, even death, can take away my essential nature. I align with the purpose of my journey: to become whole.

Phase 6: Grief and Denial

Once the relief of having returned from the transformative experience wears off, you find yourself wanting to be somewhere else. You long to go back to the rapture of your peak experience or to life prior to your traumatic event. But the world you once knew no longer exists. A part of you has been left behind, creating a sense of loss. This loss arouses grief, which may permeate your existence in this phase. To escape from your grief and create a temporary feeling of stability, you engage in denial; for example, you might immerse yourself in work, family, or community.

What You Need to Know

As you enter, experience, anticipate, or reflect on the Grief and Denial phase, keep the following information and advice in mind.

BEGINNING

The Grief and Denial phase begins when the honeymoon of being home again is over.

GIFT

The gift of the Grief and Denial phase is regaining a temporary sense of balance by denying your grief.

CHALLENGE

The challenge of the Grief and Denial phase is to cope with heartache.

OPPORTUNITY

The opportunity of the Grief and Denial phase is to allow yourself to grieve, which is cleansing.

DEEPENING YOUR EXPERIENCE

The intensity of the Grief and Denial phase may make you wonder if you are really okay and not clinically depressed. To preserve your psychological equilibrium, give yourself permission and the mental and physical space to do the following:

- Feel your grief and remember that grief is a response to loss, which is integral to transformation. In other words, feeling sadness indicates that you are making progress toward wholeness!

- Engage in denial. Denial is a natural and healthy response to your circumstances. Creating a psychological buffer between you and your memories can help you feel more stable.

- Simply be alone, because in a real way, you are alone in your experience.

- Spend time in nature or with others who have had similar experiences.

Empower yourself during the Grief and Denial phase by repeating the following affirmation:

> I invite the waves of grief to wash over me and cleanse my heart of my losses. When I am brave in this way, I release the pains and burdens not only of the present time but also the grief of my past.

Phase 7: Disorientation

At a certain point, denial becomes impractical. You can no longer postpone life or give minimal attention to daily demands. In this phase, you fully reenter your life, although you feel totally different from how you felt before your transformative experience. The contrast between your inner and outer worlds may leave you feeling lost, with the sense that you no longer fit in. You may receive glimpses of a different life for yourself. Disorientation and despair stem from recognizing that overwhelming barriers seem to exist between you and the life you want. You must trust that you can reach your dream by progressing through the phases of transformation.

What You Need to Know

As you enter, experience, anticipate, or reflect on the Disorientation phase, keep the following information and advice in mind.

BEGINNING

The Disorientation phase begins when you are forced to take care of pressing responsibilities you have been putting off. You must start to deal with the implications of your life-changing experience.

GIFT

The gift of the Disorientation phase is self-exploration.

CHALLENGE

The challenge of the Disorientation phase is to be kind to yourself, even though you feel confused and seem to have failures as you attempt to change.

OPPORTUNITIES

The opportunities of the Disorientation phase are to be gentle and kind to yourself and to ask for help.

DEEPENING YOUR EXPERIENCE

The following tips can help you navigate the Disorientation phase:

- When you feel confused, focus on the hints your new self is giving you about the better life you truly desire. Think of yourself as a ballerina who fixes her gaze on a single location as she spins in order to enhance control and prevent dizziness.

- When achieving your dream seems impossible, realize the following: Transformation creates opportunities to achieve goals that you previously thought unattainable.

- If you experience setbacks in your attempts to implement healthier habits, be easy on yourself. Such missteps are a predictable part of the struggle between the old self (which has unhealthier habits) and the new, healthier self.

AFFIRMATION

Empower yourself during the Disorientation phase by repeating the following affirmation:

I am on a pathway to become healthier and happier. My inner struggle and my attempts to change are indications that my old self and my new self are wrestling to see which part of me stays and which part goes.

Phase 8: Dismemberment

Dismemberment is a dark night of the soul in which the "magic" of transformation occurs. This phase begins with an episode of being completely out of control and being challenged far beyond your capacity to cope. At the depths of Dismemberment, you may wonder if you will survive. You desire to be at home, alone and quiet; in fact, your body demands this type of solitude. During this intensely emotional and self-reflective phase, you release old patterns and beliefs, making space for your new identity. Dismemberment can occur over months or years.

What You Need to Know

As you enter, experience, anticipate, or reflect on the Dismemberment phase, keep the following information and advice in mind.

BEGINNING

The Dismemberment phase begins with an experience in which you feel you have no control over something very important to you.

GIFT

The gift of the Dismemberment phase is to sit and connect with the darkness and stillness and to pay attention to what you discover there.

CHALLENGE

The challenge of the Dismemberment phase is to stay with the feelings and feel them, as opposed to repressing them, and to spend time at home being still.

OPPORTUNITY

The opportunity of the Dismemberment phase is to view your own shadow, the unconscious part of your personality that you reject.

Deepening Your Experience

To ease the pain of the Dismemberment phase, try to do the following:

- Be present to your feelings.

- Spend as much time alone, at home, and in stillness as possible.

- Ask for support from select individuals (best friend, spouse, family member, therapist, etc.) whom you trust and who have the ability to assist you in your transformation.

- Engage in nurturing activities that allow you to be in solitude: getting a massage, taking a bath, listening to music, jogging, walking in nature, or writing music or poetry.

Affirmation

Empower yourself during the Dismemberment phase by repeating the following affirmation:

I sit so still and feel so deeply that between each breath, I touch the sublime beauty of the darkness. Show me the miracles that exist in the lair of what is unseen.

Phase 9: Surrender and Healing

The struggle of dismemberment leads to an episode in which you find you must surrender. In this situation, your traditional methods for staying safe and secure no longer work, and you are forced to depend upon others in a new way or to do something you have been dreading. In the process, you release an unhealthy, deeply ingrained pattern. Specifically, you let go of something you have been holding onto—a relationship, job, or belief—that is old and outdated. This surrender, or series of surrenders, opens the door to a period of healing that will eventually complete the purification begun during the Dismemberment phase.

What You Need to Know

As you enter, experience, anticipate, or reflect on the Surrender and Healing phase, keep the following information and advice in mind.

BEGINNING

The Surrender and Healing phase begins when a situation requires you to abandon a long-ingrained dysfunctional habit.

GIFT

The gift of the Surrender and Healing phase is the release of painful habits.

CHALLENGE

The challenge of the Surrender and Healing phase is to let go of unhealthy habits, thoughts, and relationships.

OPPORTUNITY

The opportunity of the Surrender and Healing phase is to feel lighter and happier by freeing yourself of unhealthy ways.

DEEPENING YOUR EXPERIENCE

To help yourself heal during the Surrender and Healing phase, you can do the following:

- Pay attention to the ways in which your life circumstances have shifted to become therapeutic for you: you have more time with your family, a fun project at work, extra breaks from employment or school, an opportunity for a healthful leisure activity, etc. Such conditions serve as important agents for healing.

- Seek out and participate in activities that help you be good to yourself: leisure pursuits, hobbies, therapy, vacation, time with loved ones, religious engagement, etc.

AFFIRMATION

Empower yourself during the Surrender and Healing phase by repeating the following affirmation:

> *Resting in the aftermath of the storm, I can breathe easier and be proud that I went into my inner darkness and returned. I can heal and become whole.*

Phase 10: Birth

In phase 3, during your transformative event, you conceived your new self; in this phase, you give birth to it. The Birth phase might occur over several hours, days, weeks, or months. It can be recognized by three distinct events, called Birth moments. In the first Birth moment, you are ready to come out into the world, and an opening occurs. In the second, you are seen by others. In the third, you are called by your new name, which reflects your new identity (such as artist, explorer, performer, teacher, etc.).

What You Need to Know

As you enter, experience, anticipate, or reflect on the Birth phase, keep the following information and advice in mind.

BEGINNING

The Birth phase begins with a situation that calls for your singular talents, and you meet the demands of the moment. You find yourself having the somewhat contradictory thoughts, "It's about time" and "Is this really happening?"

GIFT

The gift of the Birth phase is the satisfaction of finally being fully you.

CHALLENGE

The challenge of the Birth phase is to deal successfully with circumstances that require your unique skills.

OPPORTUNITY

The opportunity of the Birth phase is to step into the identity toward which you have been working.

DEEPENING YOUR EXPERIENCE

The Birth phase is elusive. Ideally, you will be aware of your three Birth moments as they occur. Here are two ways to increase your chances of being conscious of these subtle but profound instances in your transformation:

- Monitor your progress during the previous phase, Surrender and Healing, so you can anticipate your first Birth moment. The Surrender and Healing phase draws to a close when you seem to have reached a plateau in your healing, you feel significantly lighter, and your life starts to show signs of ease and abundance.

- Get to know the characteristics of each Birth moment so that when you have the opportunity to be seen for who you really are, you will recognize that as the first Birth moment. Then you will be poised to notice the second moment (being witnessed) and the third (hearing your name).

I have had the great fortune of consciously experiencing my own birth within the transformation process. I was paying such close attention to my circumstances that time seemed to slow down, and I watched what happened as if it were a movie. I paid the utmost attention to every word, sound, movement, feeling, and thought. Events unfolded just as predicted by the Map to Wholeness. As I perceived my new self coming out into the world, I coached myself to remain steady and not give in to fear. I reminded myself that I had been awaiting this magical, almost breathtaking, experience.

AFFIRMATION

Empower yourself during the Birth phase by repeating the following affirmation:

> *My entire life has culminated in this experience, which allows me to see my wholeness for the first time.*

Phase 11: Abundance and Creativity

After the new you is birthed, you enter a period of abundance and creativity. While you haven't finished healing, you are happier. You encounter opportunities, both anticipated and unexpected, in various arenas: relationships, career, home. Creative projects flourish. People in this phase report barely being able to keep up with the opportunities coming their way. Others who do not support or recognize your personal growth may not be pleased about your success. Their lack of backing can trigger your inner critic and old patterns of self-sabotage. These naysayers may even try to obstruct your progress, but they no longer have power over you.

What You Need to Know

As you enter, experience, anticipate, or reflect on the Abundance and Creativity phase, keep the following information and advice in mind.

BEGINNING

The Abundance and Creativity phase begins when your daily life becomes focused less on hardships and more on the opportunities, resources, and healthy relationships coming to you.

GIFT

The gift of the Abundance and Creativity phase is the joy of sharing and being who you are.

CHALLENGES

The challenges of the Abundance and Creativity phase are to graciously receive love, money, and recognition, and to act from your newly developed integrity.

OPPORTUNITIES

The opportunities of the Abundance and Creativity phase are to courageously act in ways that allow the gifts of the new self to be seen by others.

DEEPENING YOUR EXPERIENCE

Following are ways to get the most out of the Abundance phase:

- Explore the experience of accepting abundance. See how deeply you can feel the love, respect, and appreciation you are receiving.
- Identify and release underlying feelings of unworthiness, self-loathing, and pain accumulated through years of not receiving the love and support you have now.
- Relish the joy of doing what you love.
- Remain humble as you deliver your gifts.

AFFIRMATION

Empower yourself during the Abundance phase by repeating the following affirmation:

My strength has brought me to this place in my arduous journey, and I am having fun receiving the love, support, guidance, money, and opportunities I need in order to have a happier and healthier life.

Phase 12: Power

In the previous phase, you honed your ability to do what you love; in this phase, you become a master at it. You experience a growing sense of inner power. This power comes from your joy, which attracts others to you and commands respectful attention. You feel genuine, grounded pride in yourself. Your self-love deepens as a result of the humility and compassion you gained during your transformational journey. In the Power phase, your new identity is nearly established. Life slows down to a manageable pace. You settle into a routine and have time to relax. Your daily existence is comfortable and pleasant in all respects: finances, relationships, work, and play.

What You Need to Know

As you enter, experience, anticipate, or reflect on the Power phase, keep the following information and advice in mind.

BEGINNING

The Power phase begins when the opportunities of the previous phase slow down and you can be more at ease, enjoying the results of your creative activity.

GIFTS

The gifts of the Power phase are satisfaction, humility, and happiness.

CHALLENGE

The challenge of the Power phase is to let go of glorification of the self when you reflect upon your accomplishments by reminding yourself of humble lessons you endured during Dismemberment and to release the slightest desire to control through manipulation or dominance and instead exhibit mastery from your peaceful center.

OPPORTUNITIES

The opportunities of the Power phase are to remain open to favorable offers yet to accept only the best ones and to use your humility to check the ego's tendency to become inflated.

DEEPENING YOUR EXPERIENCE

To learn more about the nature and potential of the Power phase, ponder these questions, which may reveal your relationship to power:

- In what ways can I let go of control by asking a qualified person to take over a responsibility I have been overseeing?

- Is it necessary that I work so much? Is it time to go on a well-deserved vacation (or two)?

- How is my present experience of power different from in the past? What does the disparity suggest about my growth?

- In what ways has my transformational journey helped me achieve the humility necessary for true power?

AFFIRMATION

Empower yourself during the Power phase by repeating the following affirmation:

> I soak in and celebrate the love, support, and resources that I have that give me the freedom to enjoy life more fully than ever before, and I take joy in being a master at what I do best.

Phase 13: Integration

In this final phase of transformation, you achieve a state of completeness. You are unified, possessing everything that is essentially you. You acknowledge and accept all parts of yourself. Your existence is not perfect or free from challenges, but you can sincerely report experiencing increased balance and harmony. Because of the resilience, awareness, and compassion you developed by journeying into your own darkness, you are easily able to adapt to the constant fluctuations of life. As a result of your personal growth, you feel satisfied, vital, confident, and joyful. The Integration phase occurs over weeks or months.

What You Need to Know

As you enter, experience, anticipate, or reflect on the Integration phase, keep the following information and advice in mind.

BEGINNING

The Integration phase begins when nothing remains to be done. Your life is running itself, and you reside in deep satisfaction, joy, love, peace, and contentment.

GIFTS

The gifts of the Integration phase are inner and outer peace.

CHALLENGES

The challenges of the Integration phase are to be present, to enjoy your experiences and surroundings, and to appreciate yourself and all that you love.

OPPORTUNITY

The opportunity of the Integration phase is to be present to becoming whole in your body, mind, heart, and spirit.

DEEPENING YOUR EXPERIENCE

To maximize your experience of the Integration phase, do the following:

- Spend a little time each day concentrating on the present moment. Notice your thoughts and feelings.
- Enjoy what and who you have become.

- Appreciate your journey, with all its suffering and joy.

- Look within and note the polarities that coexist harmoniously inside of you, such as beautiful and ugly, feminine and masculine, flexible and rigid, disciplined and chaotic, fast and slow, passionate and tranquil, light and dark, small and vast.

- Resist the voice that says you must be doing something, starting something new, or accomplishing anything other than enjoying yourself.

- See how long you can stave off the impulse to initiate a new transformation.

AFFIRMATION

Empower yourself during the Integration phase by repeating the following affirmation:

I have earned the right to drink the nectar of the beautiful flower into which I have blossomed. May I savor it so thoroughly that it nourishes me for a lifetime.

✻ ✻ ✻

In this chapter, the "Deepening Your Experience" material was intended to help you make the most of each phase. The next chapter presents more general guidelines for enhancing your experience of transformation and reaching wholeness more swiftly.

18

THREE THINGS YOU CAN EXPECT DURING THIS PROCESS

Transformation involves integrating a transformative event into your life. During this process, you can count on experiencing grief, solitude, and changes in relationships. While these conditions may not sound very appealing, they allow you to let go of what is outdated about you and your life, thereby creating the "new you." I present these aspects of transformation here so you can better prepare yourself for what lies ahead or gain clarity regarding your current situation. Moreover, I hope this information helps you appreciate that you are not alone in what you are experiencing.

Grief

Grief is a constant companion during transformation, because transformation—and arguably all of life—always involves loss and the need to let go. Research has proven this fact, which can also be seen in nature. When a seedling sprouts, it sheds its shell; when a baby is born, it loses the placenta; when a being dies, its spirit gives up the body. Transformation is integrally and unavoidably connected to loss. To transform is to cast off your old identity, which has nourished you.

.   Grief is so consistently present in transformation that my co-researchers and I began to poke fun at it in order to provide some comic relief. Throughout the data-collection phase of the research upon which this book is based, my co-researchers and I found ourselves singing, "Follow the yellow brick grief!" Like Dorothy in *The Wizard of Oz*, we could find our way out of the labyrinth of integration only by continuing to follow—and feel—the grief. Something about grief helped us know we weren't lost. During our formal data analysis of our research, one woman reflected on the entire integration pattern:

> *Grief is forever. Grief is throughout the whole process, with moments of not having it. Well, I don't know about not having it; I think it's always there. In fact, even the grief transforms! There are different kinds of grief … grief changes form.*

This woman helped us look deeply at grief's role in transformation. We determined that grief tends to have different characteristics during each phase, changing along the journey. For example, grief might be related to letting go of a sense of innocence in one phase; connected to the loss of lifestyle, friends, or family in another phase; or composed of heavy sadness from unfinished heartache in yet a different phase.

I take a neutral view of grief's presence in transformation. Grief just is. Because grief is inevitable, understanding its purpose can be helpful and even comforting. I realized that as long as I was grieving over letting go of something, I was making room for what wanted to enter. Grief can let you to know if you are on the right track and are indeed transforming. Unless you have a previous diagnosis, you are probably not depressed. If you feel the waves of sadness as they occur, you can be confident you are making progress, and you will get to where you want to be sooner if you do not resist the grief. Allow the feeling of loss to help you recognize what needs to die ("What do I need to let go of?") and what wants to live ("What inside of me desires to be born?").

Solitude

Another experience integral to transformation is spending time alone. There are two reasons why solitude is essential. First, being alone gives you the space to spend considerable time focusing on your inner world—indwelling—and feeling your feelings deeply. Some people can pay attention to their ongoing feelings, thoughts, and sensations while interacting with others or going about their daily activities. This skill is great for life in general and particularly helpful for integrating a transformative experience. Yet solitude is necessary for the deep reflection and self-awareness that transformation demands.

The second reason why solitude is important is that no one can do your inner work for you. Hopefully you do enlist others—therapists, healers, bodyworkers, and competent friends or colleagues—to assist you, but ultimately you are the only one who can do the challenging internal work that integration requires. Transforming is your job, your opportunity. So while you may possess a strong desire to have someone or something fix you or make everything better, in the end you must decide to make time to be alone and feel your feelings, contemplate your experiences, and make meaning of your life.

This is much easier said than done. To sit down and do nothing except be with yourself is an extraordinarily difficult task for most. In general, Western culture does not support the development of capabilities for being; instead, many of us learn skills for doing. There are ways to ease into the discipline of being. You can engage in solitary, quiet activities that allow you to express yourself or explore your inner world while also engaging in some sort of movement: journaling, blogging, painting, drawing, walking outside, jogging, swimming, singing, writing poetry or songs, dancing, cooking, or gardening. If you are not accustomed to sitting and simply being with yourself, try one of these activities with the intention of exploring yourself, making meaning, and feeling your feelings.

If you are not used to solitude, the journey will make sure you get practice. Fortunately (or unfortunately), the Dismemberment phase will demand intensive, focused immersion in your interior alone, whether you want it or not. This focused time is like a candle's flame: it illuminates while burning up whatever is inside of you that needs to be released.

If you do not spend substantial time in solitude, immersed in your feelings and thoughts, you will most likely not transform. But don't worry if you typically would not choose to be alone. Eventually, the circumstances of transformation will lead you to *want* to spend time in solitary self-reflection.

Changes in Relationships

There is a theme among people who are transforming: out with the obsolete, in with the fresh and life-giving. This idea involves shedding aspects of yourself that are not in alignment with the new you, which, in turn, affects your relationships. There are numerous circumstances that prompt changes in relationships during the transformation process, including changes in who you are, the preexisting need for change, changes in leisure or lifestyle activities, and changes in personal priorities.

Changes in Who You Are

You may or may not enter the transformation process desiring changes in your relationships. Most people I talk to did not, at the outset of their transformation, intend to change or leave relationships. But as you transform, and as you increasingly believe in yourself, you will want to address outdated or unhealthy behaviors, and doing so may make you incompatible with some people who are currently in your life.

For instance, Larae began the transformation process feeling content with her relationships. But as she integrated, she slowly began to view her relationships in a different light. Larae had spent several years spiraling downward into a lifestyle of heavy drugs and laziness. That all ended when she "woke up" and saw herself reflected in the people around her, and she didn't like what she saw. One day she looked at her closest friend—a trusted yet drug-addicted man whom she loved and who had "mentored" her when the world seemed harsh and unloving—and *saw* him for the first time: "I just looked at him and said to myself, 'My God, I don't want to turn out like you.'"

As Larae started to care about herself more and more, she found the strength to stop doing drugs and let go of the drug lifestyle. Leaving the drugs meant leaving the people, and it was a relief to finally walk away from both.

Transforming alters who you are. The quality and characteristics of your relationships are directly related to who you are, what you think you deserve, and the kinds of interpersonal experiences you believe are possible for you. Because your relationships are directly connected to who you are, some of them will naturally change as you transform. For instance, if your transformation helps you recognize that your true essence is peaceful, you will develop friendships with people who are also more peaceful and will transition away from friends who tend to be dramatic, angry, or distracted. Or, if through transformation you accept yourself as beautiful just the way you are, you will attract someone into your life who regularly tells you that you are beautiful.

The Preexisting Need for Change

Some people enter into a transformation with the gut feeling that a relationship needs to change or end. Alternatively, the desire to change or end a relationship prompts the call to enter into a cycle of transformation. Ending a relationship is often very difficult, and the transformative journey can help facilitate it.

Elias who participated in a pilgrimage I led to Peru mentioned before we left that he was sensing his girlfriend might not be "the one." This thought was very disturbing for him. During the pilgrimage, Elias gained strength from his closeness to nature. He became clearer in his desire to be in relationships with people who were spiritual. After Elias returned, he and his girlfriend remained together but had persistent struggles. The changes Elias had experienced on the pilgrimage persisted, causing him to want to end the parties, shallow relationships, urban lifestyle, and meaningless conversations that characterized the life he shared with his girlfriend.

In an effort to honor his growing conviction that he needed to change his lifestyle, and specifically to be closer to nature, Elias asked his girl-friend to move nearer to the mountains. She reluctantly agreed, but as they began to take action, it became obvious to both of them that their relationship had run its course; it was time to part. Elias did move closer to what he loved (nature), and she moved closer to what she loved (her social life). Years later, toward the end of his complete transformation, Elias met the love of his life and became engaged, and he felt comfortable in his own body. For the first time in his life, not only did he love some-one else, he also loved himself. Transformation always has a direct impact on our ability to love more and feel more at ease with oneself physically, mentally, emotionally, socially, and spiritually.

Another one of my study-abroad students, Maggie, was engaged to be married. Though she knew she didn't want to wed, she couldn't find the courage to actually end the relationship. She felt tremendous pres-sure from her family and friends to stay with her fiancé. They would say, "What's wrong with you? He's the best thing that has ever happened to you." Maggie needed a "reason" to end the relationship and the strength to do it. That was when she jumped at the chance to go on a pilgrimage of personal and spiritual growth.

Throughout the pilgrimage, she thought a lot about herself: her life, limitations, insecurities, and fears. The journey involved backpacking the Inca Trail, which is physically grueling for most but nearly inconceivable for Maggie, who was not physically fit. She lagged so far behind that she would enter the camp at night three to four hours after the entire group had already arrived. For safety, one of the guides walked with her. "I was so embarrassed," she said. "It was one thing to have to deal with trying to hike over these huge mountains, but then it was another to deal with the humiliation of being so slow, coming in so late, and being alone." In a moment of utter despair, Maggie had a pivotal realization: "I am alone all the time anyway. Even when I am with someone, I am alone. So why am I so afraid of being alone?" In that moment, Maggie knew she could leave her fiancé. Within two weeks of her return, Maggie ended the rela-tionship and moved out of their apartment.

Changes in Leisure or Lifestyle Activities

As they transform, many people discover that an activity they have found slightly dissatisfying grows more and more unappealing—and eventually intolerable. For example, you may become disenchanted with social interactions that now feel meaningless, a religion you no longer believe in, or a job that doesn't suit you anymore. If you find the courage to remove yourself from these activities, you also leave behind the social connections integrally tied to them.

Maintaining relationships once you stop engaging in a particular leisure or lifestyle activity is difficult, because values and beliefs are fundamental to all such activities. For example, valuing a certain type of spirituality underlies going to a specific place of worship; valuing human potential underlies having meaningful conversations about personal growth; valuing nature underlies hiking; valuing independence and freedom underlies hot-air ballooning; and valuing cultural diversity underlies exposing yourself to different music, food, and worldviews. As we transform, our values and beliefs change, which stimulates us to engage in new leisure and lifestyle activities. Expressing what has become important to us feels good. New pursuits inevitably bring new relationships with people who care about and enjoy what we find worthwhile and pleasurable.

Changes in Personal Priorities

Transformation can shift something central to our lives—what we hold important—which, in turn, affects our relationships. For example, one man decided that what he really wanted to do was move closer to his aging parents, even though he would be far from his friends, many of whom might drift away.

As one woman's finances were falling apart, she realized she needed to pull herself together and put herself into "financial rehabilitation":

> My sister offered to let me move in with her to save money and get my life together. So I moved from Los Angeles to Santa Cruz and discovered that there is a twelve-step program for spending addiction. I never believed I would be a twelve-stepper.

Another woman named Andrea, whose life-changing experience at an ashram was described earlier, was born and raised in Germany during the Holocaust. She had a transformative experience as a teenager when it dawned on her that her religion was gender-biased and, in her view, treated women inhumanely. About a decade after this awakening, at age twenty-six, she left her mother and siblings in order to explore other belief systems. She left all the relationships she had ever known, aside from her boyfriend, to discover something she could believe in.

Worried about Change?

Before you panic that you are going to lose everyone in your life, remember that the magnitude of transformative experience reflects the types of changes that occur during your journey. You need not lose all your relationships. At the very least, the quality of some of your relationships will change. Some may become deeper or more authentic; others may weaken. The good news is that when you transform, you attract into your life new people who are aligned with the person you are becoming. This is one wonderful and predictable outcome of transformation.

19

MAKING THE MOST OF YOUR TRANSFORMATION

*Learn to get in touch with the silence within yourself
and know that everything in this life has a purpose,
there are no mistakes, no coincidences, all events are
blessings given to us to learn from.*

—ELISABETH KÜBLER-ROSS

A number of phases on the Map to Wholeness are difficult to go through. These phases are tests of endurance that can try the patience of many, including me. We question, "Is there any way to speed up this uncomfortable stage?" Ambitious types, on the other hand, might ask, "How can I take this opportunity to transform the *most*?" Fortunately, you can do things to both minimize distress and maximize change during your transformational journey.

Transformation is organic, so there are natural limits to the rate at which you can transform and the intensity with which you can do it. However, you can take actions to maintain a steady pace, make the journey more palatable or even enjoyable, and enhance your outcomes. Through the following efforts, you can get the most out of your transformation and accelerate the process:

1. Feel and release your feelings.

2. Seek and receive support.

3. Learn about yourself.

4. Engage in integrative activities.

5. Trust in a benevolent process.

In the next sections, I will review these five guidelines in detail and offer exercises for implementing them.

Feel and Release Your Feelings

As you transform, your inner world becomes a construction zone. Outdated aspects of yourself are dismantled, and your new identity is constructed. This internal activity is made possible by acknowledging and processing your feelings. For example, when you cry from grief, you move heaviness out of your body, mind, and heart. When you acknowledge and constructively express anger, you relieve yourself from anguish. When you talk about your fears, you release anxiety. Failing to process your feelings in this way creates stagnancy and hinders transformation.

Feeling your experiences as you have them or soon thereafter advances you through the figure eight at a healthy pace. At times, however, delving into your emotions may not be appropriate or wise. When you are at work or with your kids, for instance, you won't have the luxury of breaking down in tears or engaging in mad hysteria. But as soon as is practical, you can take some time alone or with your partner to feel what's inside and release it through talking, writing, meditation, or exercise.

To travel more quickly through transformation and heighten your change, seize every opportunity to feel your feelings—and get them out. Consider doing the following:

- *Provoke yourself to feel.* If you lack the ability to feel or simply need practice at it, put yourself in an environment that is particularly suited to arousing your emotions. You might play with children, watch a movie about the beauty or suffering of life, listen to soulful music, write poetry, visit an art gallery, volunteer at a homeless shelter, learn from an inspirational speaker, or go to church. Feeling your feelings cleans out aspects of yourself that you do not need or that are stuck inside. The deeper you go into your emotions, the more heartaches you remove from the dark corners of your past.

- *Dive into your feelings.* For a deep purge, overindulge in emotion. For example, if you are sad, allow yourself to become overcome with grief until you are limp. Indulge in your misery. Later, when the sadness returns, do it again. If you are afraid of something, yell out your fears to an empty space until you start to laugh. Or write down your fears and then burn the paper; repeat if you want to. If you are angry, vacuum the house with vigor, and shout out the details of what has upset you. Exercise until you are tired. Activities such as these facilitate the discharge of emotion.

To recap, feeling your emotions keeps you moving steadily toward wholeness, and feeling them *deeply* expedites the process of deconstructing and clearing out the old you. The more comprehensive your cleaning, the more balanced, peaceful, loving, capable, and wise you will be when your transformation is complete.

Seek and Receive Support

Everyone needs love, help, and guidance, but not everyone feels comfortable being close enough to another person to receive such support.

Relationships inherently cause emotional hurts. All wounds stem from a relationship, whether with a friend, family member, colleague, acquaintance, teacher, leader, or stranger. Therefore, opening up to others or expanding your support circle makes you vulnerable to getting injured—again. You might also be shy or introverted, or you may lack the skills or resources necessary to connect with others.

Fortunately, despite these barriers to relationships, we have an innate motivation to unite. We were born with a genuine need for others. It is your birthright to receive support from those you trust and to share your frustrations and joys with them. By initiating or deepening a relationship, you risk heartache; but you also gain the opportunity for insight, compassion, and closeness from another human being.

Relationships are very important in the journey of transformation because you can't get through the confusing, disturbing, and painful phases by yourself. As you transform, though, your friends will not necessarily have the capacity to understand what you are experiencing, much less help you. They might even abandon you because they can't handle your situation. As Magic Johnson has said, "When you face a crisis, you know who your true friends are."

The good news is that you really need just one trusted person who supports your dreams and your particular path to wholeness. This individual does not need to know *how* to assist you but must care about you and respect your choices. For instance, this type of friend would encourage you to drive five hundred miles to visit your grandmother's grave in another state in order to feel peace, if that was what you truly wanted to do.

Learn about Yourself

In the quote that opens this chapter, Elisabeth Kübler-Ross points out the importance of exploring your interior. For those who prefer to engage the mind rather than the emotions or the heart, this task may not be welcome. Learning about yourself requires self-reflection. A woman I interviewed illustrates this point. Hilda was an eighty-six-year-old widow, mother, and grandmother. Her house was a monument to the past, with porcelain figurines, old glassware, pictures of her children when they were young, and living room furniture that had been there for fifty years.

Hilda was intelligent and kind but not interested in self-analysis, much less personal growth. She had led a sheltered life as the daughter of overprotective parents and then the wife of a traditional young man straight out of high school. Although she put herself through college and even earned a master's degree, her responsibility was raising her children. She felt she had a fortunate existence.

When I began investigating wholeness, I doubted that transformation was possible for people like Hilda—individuals who were not inclined to explore or scrutinize themselves. Yet as I listened to the major events of her life, the phases of the Map to Wholeness unfolded perfectly. In all, she had experienced three complete transformations, each lasting about twenty years, with the third drawing to a close when we met.

Hilda helped me see that ordinary abilities to feel and self-reflect were sufficient to effect transformation. At each juncture of her life, she simply followed the course she thought was best for her and her family, whether it was marriage, education, having children, traveling, or moving. She pursued her curiosities, exposed herself to new things, and noticed what she liked and what she didn't.

I hope Hilda's story puts the work of transformation in perspective. Trust that you are naturally equipped with the basic skills necessary for transformation—and one of those skills is to learn about yourself so you can grow and heal.

Engage in Integrative Activities

Two-thirds of transformation involves integrating your transformative experience. Integration begins in phase 5, Displacement, after you have returned from the transformative event and have something to digest. The remainder of the figure eight involves physically, mentally, and emotionally absorbing the life-changing experience. Before the episode is completely incorporated, it seems separate from you. Once you have fully assimilated it, you feel settled, grounded, and empowered.

Integration entails both your conscious effort and the work of something beyond your control. You digest a meal in a similar way: after you go to the effort of chewing and swallowing, your body finishes the digestive process automatically.

I have found the following seven activities to be particularly useful in fostering integration.

1. *Act on what your body, mind, heart, and spirit need.* This activity might be taking a day off work to rest, soaking in a hot tub, reading a book, going on a date with someone you love, calling an old friend, or playing in the park with your family. Taking care of yourself in this way is particularly important during Dismemberment, even if others think something might be wrong with you. Assure them that you are fine but need time to yourself, with few phone calls or social engagements.

2. *Be kind and gentle with yourself.* During the transformational journey, you will make mistakes, experience painful emotions, and learn about your shortcomings. In these instances, try to limit negative self-talk ("What's wrong with me? This is not difficult!" "Why am I always screwing up?" "I am so mean!"). If you hear yourself being your own worst critic, say something nurturing and kind instead.

3. *Be still, literally.* During Dismemberment, your body will demand to stare into nothingness, sometimes for hours. Succumb to this impulse whenever possible; it is an integrative activity. Being physically still balances out the massive movement that is happening inside you. This rearranging is real. Many people can feel it, like an inner storm. You may also crave motionlessness and low stimulation in your environment, such as little or no noise, music, talking, or people walking around. Desires like these may make you feel strange or even unhealthy, but remember that Dismemberment will end.

4. *Create space for solitude.* Transformation is mostly private and inaccessible to others unless you share your experiences with them. Scheduling time alone to be with your thoughts and feelings and to process them is important. Doing so helps you integrate

your transformative experience. To create space away from others, you might take a drive, lie in the grass, work on your car, engage in a hobby or project, make a meal for yourself, spend time in nature, ride a bike in the park, exercise, nap, or soak in a hot bath. These types of activities are particularly helpful during phases 4 through 9, Return through Surrender and Healing. Once you pass through Birth, you will no longer require as much stillness or time by yourself.

5. *Release the old you.* Saying goodbye to your outdated self means letting go of unhealthier thoughts, behaviors, beliefs, and relationships. To become whole, you might even change the place where you live. Letting go is an ongoing activity. It is difficult, if not painful, at first; but the more you do it, the easier it becomes. As you release things that seem important to you, you better understand what you value most. For example, when a friend walks out of your life, you might ask yourself, "Is that the kind of friend I really want?" During my own transformation, I lost my beloved partner, two homes, and two cars, and my dog and cat died, among other misfortunes. To make a bad situation worse, about two years after the losses slowed down, my library of hundreds of books, which I had collected over a span of twenty years, was accidentally thrown away by the facilities staff at my university. I asked myself, "What do these books mean to me?" and "Why am I attached to them?" Over time, the practice of letting go teaches detachment. Losing most or all of what is precious to you leaves you with at least one thing that cannot be lost, stolen, or given away: yourself.

6. *Question the meaning of each moment.* The present moment can show you the condition of your life. For example, when the facilities staff at my university accidentally threw away twenty boxes of my books, as I just mentioned, I was very upset. But I also asked myself, "What is the purpose of losing my books, and why did it happen now?" The belief that everything occurs for a reason is very helpful because it assumes the universe is intelligent and does not make mistakes—a reassuring thought.

Regarding my lost books, I arrived at the truth that I no longer needed them to feel smart or capable in my career. As I became honest with myself, I could admit that I had always felt unworthy in my job. The books allowed me to feel potent and valuable. In a sense, books *are* the power symbol of my profession. Every interview of a professor I have ever seen has taken place in an office, in front of a beautiful wall of books. I lost my precious collection during the Surrender and Healing phase, which makes sense; this phase is about letting go of something you have been holding onto. I realized that my professional library was like a security blanket, and I wondered if the books were *inside* of me now and had become an internal source of strength. Remember that emotional experiences that have a significant impact on you always have something to show you, if you take the time to examine them.

7. *Ask for support.* To cope with difficult stages of your transformational journey, request help from others. This assistance might take the form of verbal encouragement, kind or comforting words, a thoughtful gesture, a hug, warm wishes, or a helping hand at work. Asking for support is one of the easiest ways to reduce stress, but many people hesitate to do so because they are worried about being a burden or do not want to appear weak. If you have this concern, think of your need for help as an opportunity for someone else to show they care about you. In fact, people probably care more about you than you know.

As an example, I used to teach a freshman class called "Creating a Meaningful Life." The course helped students across various majors examine their lives and consider how they might make choices in order to live more meaningfully. One year when we returned from spring break, we learned that a male student in the class had died in a motorcycle accident. Very saddened, I spent the hour of class time working with the students to process his tragic death and what it could teach us. His peers were shocked, and many were heartbroken. Although the deceased student had known just a few people in the class, everyone grieved, and some felt a personal connection to his passing. Several students who had never spoken to him remarked that he'd smiled warmly at them every day. Another said, "I forgot my pen one day, and he loaned me one."

I was amazed at how this young man had not forgotten this simple gesture. Had he not asked for help, he would never have received the gift of the kindness that was surprisingly memorable. This story illustrates the usefulness of asking for support. As you go about your days, those around you might be delighted to offer assistance, if only you dared to ask. There is only one way to find out.

Trust in a Benevolent Process

My main motivation for writing is to share why the most difficult periods in your life have an important meaning and purpose. The Map to Wholeness delineates the path by which people grow, heal, and eventually become whole. While the process always involves confusion, heartache, and loss, it also guarantees joyful surprise, fun, indulgence, deep satisfaction, overwhelming love, and peace. The overriding message of this book is that the rewards outweigh the pain, and your journey will end well. Once you traverse the entire figure eight totally aware of what is going on, knowing you will be okay becomes far easier.

If you follow the guidelines presented in this chapter, you will improve your outcomes and keep moving toward wholeness. To further intensify your personal growth and thereby deepen your healing, continue to the next chapter.

20

GOING DEEPER INTO PERSONAL GROWTH AND HEALING

It's only when we truly know and understand that
we have a limited time on earth—and that we have
no way of knowing when our time is up—that we will
begin to live each day to the fullest, as if it was the only
one we had.

—ELISABETH KÜBLER-ROSS

Although personal growth is inevitable, you can accelerate the process by bravely and proactively looking within and making changes for the better. This integrative activity is particularly useful during the Return, Displacement, Denial and Grief, Disorientation, Dismemberment, and Surrender and Healing phases.

Some people are especially interested in self-knowledge, psychology, spiritual development, and consciousness. If you are one of them, you probably regularly choose to look within and thereby facilitate or even slightly accelerate your own transformation. For example, if your aunt Naomi hasn't invited you to Thanksgiving dinner and if you don't say anything to her about it, you might question your silence. Going deeper, you might explore the fears, aspirations, resentments, and wounds surrounding your resistance to confront her. You might arrive at the conclusion, "What's the worst that would happen if I did say something?" This question helps to identify your unexamined fears. Repeat this questioning to unearth layers of fears until you arrive at your deepest fear. It is common to repeat the question as many as a dozen or more times in order to identify your deepest fear.

Intense self-examination requires maturity, courage, and a commitment to personal growth. If you are new to this degree of self-analysis, the following activities can help you begin:

- Read books about your problems and how to resolve them.

- Enlist the help of a trusted friend, family member, or professional. With the help of others we can more quickly arrive at better self-understanding, healing, and growth. You can ask them to help you to explore these types of questions.

Once you become more comfortable exploring your inner world, including your vulnerabilities, weaknesses, fears, frustrations, and heartaches, you can start to observe your life and use the information you find to make helpful changes.

Here are a few ways to take your self-exploration deeper.

- *Be open to seeing your faults—and embrace them.* Uncovering your own flaws and failings can improve your life tremendously. For instance, if you perceive and heal your fear of intimacy now, your future relationships will benefit. Consider the example of an oyster, which responds to the irritant of a grain of sand within its shell by covering it with layers of a mineral substance. The result is a pearl. You, too, can identify what is bothersome within and transform it into an asset.

- *Examine your own role in situations, especially arguments.* Quarrels and misunderstandings are sure indicators that there is something to learn, especially if you feel 100 percent correct or justified in your position. When you find yourself in a disagreement, ponder the following: "What can this circumstance teach me about my shortcomings?" "What am I not seeing about myself?" "How have I contributed to this situation?" "How have I acted similarly in the past?" The answers often take time to emerge.

A particularly provocative question to contemplate is, "In what way is there an element of truth to the other person's words or actions?" A related inquiry is, "How does this situation trigger my own unexamined fears?" Once you uncover the beliefs, truths, and fears underlying your part in an altercation, you can ask yourself, "Is this belief actually true for me today?" or "Is this fear helpful or is it hindering me?" Does it keep you from loving more fully or being more stress-free? How might you benefit by letting go of it?

You might even ask for feedback on your shortcomings from someone you trust and with whom you have argued. Instead of immediately yelling at the person or disregarding his or her criticism, seize the opportunity to see what you have not been able to see about yourself.

As you learn new information about yourself, you can take action to grow. For instance, you can decide to forgive a loved one instead of seeking revenge, help your spouse once you realize you have not been fair, take a risk to attend a dance class now that you recognize that you are uptight, or reduce your work hours to spend more time with your children. The action of positive change is an important part of transformation and becoming whole. When you choose to change your habits and grow, you begin to establish a new internal precedent, the foundation of a new you. Dismemberment disintegrates your identity almost like tearing your house down, and you rebuild through personal growth and adopting healthier beliefs and habits.

- *Let go of outdated dynamics that are controlling your life.* Another way to grow is by identifying people with whom you do not get along so you can resolve similar relationships from your childhood. According to traditional psychology, if someone in your life really irks you, he or she might be awakening memories of an old family connection. Explore how this annoying individual's behaviors, attitudes, words, or even mannerisms remind you of someone from your early years.

When you encounter such a person, you repeat the former dynamic, in which each party unconsciously plays a role. For example, your boss might remind you of your father. Soon, you are reacting to him as the "son" or "daughter," with the same feelings of inadequacy you experienced when you were young. Once you figure out who the individual in your present represents from your past, you can focus on healing your original wounds—the true source of your angst.

- *Learn about your shadow.* You can uncover concealed aspects of yourself by identifying people and situations that annoy you. For instance, a family member or friend might irritate you by always being late, never bringing food to share, monopolizing conversations, or looking down on you. You can either hold a grudge, or you can take the opportunity to ask, "Where in my life am I not being mindful of the needs of others?" or "In what circumstances do I judge others unfairly?" In other words, you may be perceiving in others your own negative characteristics of which you are unaware. Practice formulating questions that probe your dark side until you become skilled at this type of inquiry. Accept the challenge to discover and embrace rejected aspects of yourself.

- *Relax, if necessary.* If you are feeling overwhelmed by all the learning and growing involved in the journey to wholeness, give yourself permission to take a break. Nurturing yourself is a very important part of transformation. When you need some relief, be kind to yourself and stop worrying. Remember that transformation will take care of itself. The example of Hilda from the previous chapter shows that we do not need to be overly vigorous in our quest to be whole.

Whether you take an easygoing approach to transformation or actively pursue it, you can unconsciously undermine the process if you are not ready for radical change. The following chapter addresses temporary exits from the Map to Wholeness.

21

HOW YOU MIGHT UNDERMINE YOUR TRANSFORMATION

Lessen your fear, because if you let it grow, it is you who will become small.

—AMAZONIAN PROVERB

In this book, I have said that becoming whole is a natural process. It is organic because life is inherently engaged in the activity of transformation. The desire to evolve toward wholeness is innate to being human. But because we also have an unconscious mind that drives our choices, we can unknowingly sabotage our own transformation.

Transformation means radical change: the death of the old you and the birth of a new you. You may not be ready for this dramatic alteration of your identity. Being unprepared to transform doesn't mean you aren't good enough or are lacking in some way. Consider that in nature, an organism must be primed to grow. For example, if there is a drought or a cold spell, a seed will lie dormant in the soil until better conditions arise. Humans are no different. The conditions of your life need to be right in order for transformation to occur.

My research and the many stories of transformation I have encountered indicate that there is a specific point in the process of transformation at which people who are not ready to transform will exit the Map to Wholeness. To discover if you have left the figure eight, review your life for the following series of events.

Transformation begins just as has been described, with an impulse of life as the Seed phase and then Departure, when you leave what you have known. These two phases occur unconsciously for those who will later leave the transformational journey. Phase 3, the Transformative Experience, is either a crisis or a positive surprise that affects you profoundly, and you remain in an altered state for much of the fourth phase, called Return.

Like a leaf floating down from a tall tree via the force of gravity, you descend from the heights of your life-changing event through the Displacement, Denial and Grief, and Disorientation phases. You don't need to exert a lot of effort to integrate your life-changing experience during the phases. You must only live through your immediate experiences and do your best to take care of your basic needs. Even if you are not adept at feeling your feelings, a little effort in this regard will be sufficient to keep you moving toward wholeness.

During the Disorientation phase, the stress of feeling lost, unhappy, and unable to change your life is overwhelming. You are removed from your life-changing event, and you can no longer deny its impact (in the case of a trauma) or draw upon its positive energy (in the case of a peak experience). You lack the strength and clarity to make sense of your life or yourself.

You may or may not recognize where you are headed—toward the Dismemberment phase—but your unconscious knows. At this point, you either stay in the process or leave it. If, for whatever reason, you are not ready for the Dismemberment phase, your unconscious provides you with an exit plan. You have two options when you are not equipped to handle the dark night of the soul that characterizes Dismemberment.

The first option is to unknowingly cut yourself off from your emerging feelings. Most ways of disconnecting from your emotions involve engaging in some sort of addictive behavior. For example, you might take drugs, oversleep, work too much, or spend countless hours watching television, playing video games, or browsing the Internet. The activity is compelling enough to consume your attention and keep you from falling into the darkness of the Dismemberment phase.

The second way to exit the transformation process is to seek out a high, or a "false peak," that alleviates your suffering. You might search for a big distraction, such as going on a major vacation, making a huge purchase, becoming pregnant, or getting married. Travel allows you to be quickly captivated. If you're lucky, you might have days or even weeks of diversion. This time away gives you a break from the stress and discomfort you have been experiencing. But you desire more than to just feel good. You seek to transcend yourself and go beyond your problems. Even if the getaway isn't especially fun, it is usually therapeutic in the short run as you experience temporary relief from the burdens of daily life.

Upon returning from the false peak, you must again face reality and your responsibilities. If you truly went beyond yourself and felt expansive, you may go through the post-transformative phases of Displacement and of Denial and Grief again. In essence, you took yourself out of Disorientation and back to phase 3. It is possible to engage in this loop, from Disorientation to a Transformative Experience and back to Disorientation, over and over.

The more frequently you seize the high of the false peak, the shorter the duration between it and Disorientation. Many people in this cycle fantasize about or even plan their next false peak while still engaged in the current one. As soon as the high ends, you need relief again. Both daily distractions and additional false peak experiences are required in order to escape the inevitable low that follows the high.

If you recognize this cycle in your life, be gentle on yourself. For instance, if you have children or elderly parents to care for, or you are living on a very tight budget, you lack the time, energy, or space for Dismemberment. The Dismemberment phase demands an enormous amount of stamina and attention, and if others depend on you for survival, your unconscious might have you wait to go through it. In other words, your unconscious might guide you to avoid Dismemberment by saying, "I cannot afford to be a mess right now." Dismemberment asks you to endure heavy, consuming grief that will at times leave you staring blankly into space, falling apart in tears in the most unlikely of circumstances, and requiring stillness and quiet like you need water and air. Once in Dismemberment you cannot simply override the system with sheer willpower, and your unconscious knows this.

You may also discontinue your journey if you endured abuse or neglect during childhood. Dismemberment always brings up early issues and wounds. If you are not ready to address and heal what comes up in this regard, you will enter the holding pattern described here until you are ready. When you are poised for transformation, your unconscious takes over and helps you to enter Dismemberment so you can become freed of habits that no longer help you.

Although no one wants to experience Dismemberment, when you do finally enter into it you don't have to worry about any more delays to achieve Wholeness. The holding pattern is the only one in the process of transformation. Once you are in Dismemberment you need only allow your journey to naturally unfold. Keep in mind that the more you feel your feelings and seek to learn about yourself along the way, the more you gain.

Transformation may seem to be a wholly self-involved endeavor, relying heavily on your internal resources, but the new you is a *co-creation*.

Becoming whole is made possible by allowing yourself to be shaped by something beyond you—the new self that wants to become a part of you. The next chapter discusses how your participation in your personal journey is simultaneously helping the whole planet.

Part IV

Transforming on Purpose

22

THE GREAT WORK IS
TO BECOME WHOLE

*Extreme life challenges have the potential to transform
not just individuals, but also societies.*

—JEAN WALSTON

Whenever I teach groups of people about the Map to Wholeness, there is almost always someone in the audience who, after comprehending the entirety of the process, raises their hand with a horrified expression. I see this as a cue that a number of people in the group have jumped ahead to the quandary of "What next?" and they ask, "So, when I finish the process of transformation, will I enter into another one?" I nod and confirm their conclusion, and they look at me with dread. They clearly don't want to go into Dismemberment again! Even die-hard seekers of consciousness shy away when they learn about the inevitable dip into one's shadow.

Even though seeing this big picture is a sobering moment for many, it is actually a good sign when people make this realization. As thrilling, sexy, and adventurous as the hero's journey is, we now know that the upper transformative cycle is only half of the process. Without the lower integrative cycle, there is no triumph, no integration, no transformation, no wholeness. Although no one wants to experience adversity, the benefits outweigh the pain and suffering. For confirmation of this, ask any doctor who endured medical school, mountain climber on the day of their return to their hometown, or survivor of a natural disaster who rebuilt their farm.

This final section of this book is focused on important reasons why your commitment to transformation matters. If we had a room full of people pondering this thought, we could brainstorm dozens upon dozens of motivational possibilities. I will start us out by examining just four reasons why becoming whole is worthwhile not only for your health and happiness but for the well-being of all.

1. *You establish permanent access to the wholeness you achieved during Integration.*

I begin by inviting you to do a visualization. Close your eyes and imagine being in your favorite place in the whole world, whether it's the comfort of your favorite room, a gorgeous beach, your grandmother's porch, a distant wilderness vista, the end of a pier on a placid lake, or a festive village celebration. Allow yourself to reenter that experience and hear all of the familiar sounds, see the many details of your surroundings, smell the air and feel it pass across your skin, and sink into the emotions and sensations in your body. How does it feel to be you in this place? Now, remain connected to your sensations and visualize your surroundings slowly fading away so that you are simply residing with the essence of what it feels like to be you in your favorite place. When you do this you are in contact with yourself, the presence of your being, your wholeness. You can always access this reality.

Despite what is gong on externally, once you know the experience of wholeness, you can reenter your interior and access the ever-present peace, harmony, and integrity of Integration. No one can take away the wholeness you have achieved. You can always draw upon the strength of your hard-won internal coherence. Just like the wings a butterfly can flap after emerging from the chrysalis, the inner resources you gained are not simply fleeting positive feelings; they are assets you will forever possess.

In the future, when you go through the painful aspects of transformation, you can choose to face the challenges by residing in your center—the spacious presence that is your true nature. When you do, you will discover that it is also a window through which you can access new ideas, answers to your deepest questions, and information about the world and who you are. When you have access to insightful knowledge, you can make choices that improve your life.

2. *You can live more deliberately.*

Just as a road map can calm your anxiety when you are lost in a city you have never visited, so too does the Map to Wholeness provide great relief by explaining your location along your journey: "Oh, now I am in the Return phase. No wonder I feel this way." A road map helps you to interpret your environment. You can, for instance, understand why the air is so moist (because you are driving in the southeast U.S.), why there are giant cacti around you (because you are in Arizona), or why skyscrapers surround you (because you are in New York City).

Similarly, the Map to Wholeness helps you make sense of your inner and outer circumstances. Instead of helping you translate the weather, natural features, or man-made environments, the Map to Wholeness interprets the meaning of thoughts such as:

"No one is going to believe that I met the Dalai Lama" (I am in the Return).

"I just want to go back to Italy—it's where I belong" (I am in Denial and Grief).

"I am not in love with painting anymore" (I am in Dismemberment).

"I have spent thirty years delaying my desire to start a nonprofit, and now that I am really ready to do it, someone wants to give me money to start a nonprofit to reduce single-use plastics" (I am in Abundance and Creativity).

"It feels so great to be really good at what I do and that I am paid well to do it" (I am in Power).

Using the Map allows you to enter the experience consciously, with full awareness, rather than reacting unconsciously or feeling blind-sided or confused.

In addition to calming nerves, a road map also helps you to make informed choices. A road map gives you information about how to drive (because it might get icy in the mountains ahead), when to stop for the restrooms (because there will not be any for another fifty miles), or why you will need to allow more time to get to your destination (because there is a long stretch of scenic vistas, slow drivers, and historic sites you want to visit).

On your journey to wholeness you gain knowledge that also helps you to take informed action. For example, you can know how to navigate your reentry home from travel abroad (Displacement) by indulging in the joy of all that is familiar, and you know only to share your story when someone genuinely wants to hear it. You can be confident in this action because you know that the reason why genuine interest is important: your story is deeply important to you, and if it is not taken seriously, you are likely to feel hurt and alone. You can decide how and when you want to act or be in any given circumstance.

For instance, you can react to your coworker's snide remarks, your spouse's aloofness, your mother's medical issues, or your child's manipulative behaviors as either a problem or an opportunity to better understand and resolve your issues. You can choose how you want to act and be in ways that make you feel good about and reinforce your essential nature—who you are at your core.

When you reduce stress, plan ahead, and mitigate problems, your overall health improves and you live more intentionally. But if you limit yourself to only accessing more and better information in order to make smarter choices, you will never become free from fear and suffering. If you really want to become the grandest version of yourself, you must remember: *the more you help yourself to heal, change, and grow, the grander your wholeness will be.*

I will describe this using a story from my own journey. When I entered my deepest experience of darkness, I distinctly remember saying to myself, "If I am going to be in pain, I might as well make it worthwhile; I want feel the most pain that I can manage." While this might initially sound as though I enjoy suffering, this is not the meaning of my internal dialogue. What I meant by this statement is that if I am already in pain, I want to discover what I don't like about myself and accept that inadequacy; see what I am afraid of, discover why, and feel the original wounds; and inquire about the self-judgment I have that causes me to judge situations or others. In other words, I knew that my life circumstances were already causing me to see how I had made mistakes of which I was not proud (Dismemberment). I was already being humbled—why not take it a step further?

If the idea of allowing yourself to be in more pain sounds ludicrous, consider thinking about it in this way: Pretend that while hiking in a national park you tripped, fell, and fractured your leg (i.e., you are in a great deal of pain). If you are already in considerable pain, a mere flesh wound is but a nuisance. Your daily experiences always offer you the chance to live deliberately by becoming the director of your growth, cultivator of profound joy, and instigator of inner harmony. When you do, you place your suffering in service of your wholeness.

3. *You can trust that each moment is orchestrated to help you to transform.*

We know that there are several phases of transformation that look and feel as though you are stagnant, not progressing, or even slipping backward. When demands are high and you are just trying to survive or to make it to the weekend or to a deadline, how are you supposed to live joyfully and openheartedly? It is likely you won't. Instead, just below the surface of your interactions and activities of daily living will be an ever-present sensation of apprehension and fear.

When challenges naturally arise, it is easy to lose your center and forget that you are transforming and that as long as you feel some of your emotions you will always be moving toward wholeness. When you see how the people in your life and the challenges you are having right now are perfectly situated to help you change, you can soften the part of you that wants to protect or fight against something or someone you perceive as threatening and recognize that your circumstance (and the players in it) are essentially benevolent. You can relax and be at peace: you are evolving right now, even if you are doing "nothing."

Comprehending this single fact can cause a dramatic shift in the quality of your daily life. You need only change the way you think; the purpose of the present moment is your eventual blossoming.

You can start to adopt this perspective by exploring the opportunities I provided in chapter 17, "Your Guide to the Phases of Transformation," and seek out possibilities for personal growth. For example, a central element of the Disorientation phase is an identity crisis. When these feelings of internal conflict arise, you can use your knowledge of the Map to resist the impulse to see the crisis as a problem (something is wrong with me or something is against me) and instead choose to recognize it as a naturally occurring necessity to explore your outdated and emerging selves.

If you allow yourself to be a full participant in the journey, you might even find that you appreciate or even enjoy all aspects of it. Surprised to hear me say this? Think about how many millions of people, probably including you, who pay to witness the triumphs and tragedies of the transformative journey in movies. It's exciting to experience the pressure, intensity, and drama of what it takes to make a great contribution and become a grander human being. It's also considerably easier to pay to watch someone else live through it. If you can enjoy the movie, even the difficult parts—perhaps because you recognize the underlying sublime beauty—you can enjoy your process too.

4. *Your transformation is the Great Work—a contribution to all.*

Before the end of his honorable life, cultural historian Thomas Berry provided us, the next generation, with the clear wisdom gained from his arduous work. He explained that we have arrived at a time in which every being must co-create the "Great Work" of our age. This work is not to advance ourselves technologically or intellectually, culturally or materialistically. Rather, Berry stated that the healthy future of our planet and ourselves requires the Great Work of developing the capacity to become present in a way that is mutually enhancing and reciprocally healing—a difficult task that calls us to transform at our very core.

Author and visionary Eckhart Tolle has become an important trailblazer in the Great Work by significantly adding to Berry's message.

Through his writing and teaching he is helping millions of people learn about what he calls the "power of now" and the ways in which our ability to be present has a direct effect on the well-being of the Earth and the fate of humanity itself.

Both of these visionaries show us that a select few gifted individuals cannot accomplish the Great Work of our time, because the solution does not require an external conquest. Instead, they make it very clear: if we truly want to have a better world where people are kinder, gentler, and happier, we must become present—and you will be present when you are whole.

You might feel compelled to run out and force yourself to change and to adopt new behaviors. Though this is a noble activity, you need not panic. You do not yet have the capacities that will be required of you in the future, and it is easy to get overwhelmed and even frozen if you fixate anywhere other than now.

In an effort to help yourself, you can learn meditative exercises to calm your mind or set an alarm to remind you to become present in the now, and know this: the direct path to having the capacity to be fully present comes when we dare to transform into iterations of progressively greater wholeness until our very presence is all that is needed to change the world. When you are emanating peace and love, action is secondary.

We know that millions upon millions of people who practice various religions and spirituality might not describe their goal as "being fully present." However, we can look at their leaders, the most holy and enlightened people who have walked the earth, and recognize that each of these sages achieved wholeness. When we consider just a few of the many hallowed leaders—Jesus of Nazareth, Siddhartha Gautama Buddha, Saint Teresa of Avila, Confucius, Tenzin Gyatso (the fourteenth Dalai Lama), Abū al-Qāsim Muhammad, Hildegard of Bingen, Joseph Smith, George Gurdjieff, Sri Aurobindo, Thich Nhat Hanh, Nelson Mandela, Mother Teresa, Martin Luther King Jr., or Bede Griffiths—we can see that their greatest gift was and still remains their embodied integrity, wisdom, compassion, and strength—that is, *their enormous wholeness.*

If you doubt that you can achieve this state, remember the inherent simplicity of the Map to Wholeness. Being present to each unfolding moment of your life is a state of being that requires that you transform, and transformation is achieved by making the most of your daily life by feeling your feelings, asking for and receiving support from a select few individuals, and choosing to learn, grow, and heal. Oddly, this pathway consists of simple, utterly human, and slightly mundane moment-to-moment activities. All too often the mind wants to make the journey complex, but in actuality, it is only these commonplace actions that caused inspirational forerunners to manifest their inherent greatness.

Beethoven, for example, slowly lost his hearing and became suicidal until he finally had a realization: "It seemed to me impossible to leave the world until I had brought forth all that I felt was within me. So I endured this wretched existence…. Patience, they say, is what I must now choose for my guide, and I have done so. Perhaps I shall get better, perhaps not; I am ready" (Cope 2012, 191).

As Beethoven implies, we cannot teleport, fly, buy, or wish our way to our goal. Rather, as you live naturally through the process of transformation, you will develop enormous patience, committed action, and deep humility. You always have what it takes to advance to the next step, so refrain from getting stuck in the trap of looking too far ahead. As the characters in the *Wonderful Wizard of Oz* say, "Follow the yellow brick road!" We need only focus on the step that lies before us and take focused action, placing one foot in front of the other, which means feel your feelings, ask for support, and regularly learn, grow, and heal.

As you do this you will join the multitudes of people moving forward on the Map. When you do, you will reach for liberation or even union with the ultimate mysteries of the universe; touch something beyond yourself; return home to confront grief, denial, and disorientation; dissolve into the void and heal; and rise like a phoenix from the ashes. Gloriously you will experience yourself as utterly magnificent and entirely average, a unified, whole, and radiant human being, and in so doing, play your part in co-creating a new world.

REFERENCES

Brinton Perera, Sylvia. 1981. *Descent to the Goddess: A Way of Initiation for Women.* Toronto, Canada: Inner City Books.

Campbell, Joseph. 1968. *The Hero with a Thousand Faces* (2nd ed.). Princeton, NJ: Princeton UP.

Cope, Stephen. 2012. *The Great Work of Your Life: A Guide for the Journey to Your True Calling.* New York: Bantam.

Deikman, Aurthur. 1966. "De-automatization and the Mystic Experience." *Psychiatry: Interpersonal and Biological Processes* 29, no. 4: 324–38.

Gressler, Julian. 2013. *Piloting through Chaos: The Explorer's Mind.* Los Angeles: Bridge 21.

Grof, Stanislav, and Christina Grof. 1989. *Spiritual Emergency: When Personal Transformation Becomes a Crisis.* New York: Putnam.

Hannan, Hollie Jeanne. 2005. *Initiation through Trauma: A Comparative Study of the Descents of Inanna and Persephone.* Santa Barbara, CA: Pacifica Graduate University.

James, William. 1902. *The Varieties of Religious Experience: A Study in Human Nature.* New York: Modern Library.

Lorde, Audre. 1980. *The Cancer Journals.* San Francisco: Aunt Lute Books.

Lutyens, Mary. 1997. *Krishnamurti: The Years of Awakening.* Boulder, CO: Shambhala.

Ross, S.L. (2019). Finding Our Way to the Precious Knowledge, Together: One Study's Use of Cooperative Inquiry. *International Journal of Transpersonal Studies.*

Ross, S. L. (2019). Temple Stay as Transformative Travel: An Experience of the Buddhist Temple Stay Program in Korea. *Journal of Tourism Insights.*

Ross, S. L. (2017). The Making of Everyday Heroes: Women's Experiences of Transformation and Integration. *Journal of Humanistic Psychology*. 1–23. https://doi.org/10.1177/0022167817705773.

Ross, S. L. (2018). Who Put the Super in Superhero? A Treatise on Transformation and Heroism as Evolutionary. *Frontiers in Psychology*, https://doi.org/10.3389/fpsyg.2018.02514.

Turner, Victor. 1969. *The Ritual Process: Structure and Anti-structure*. Ithaca, NY: Cornell University Press.

————. 1982. *From Ritual to Theatre: The Human Seriousness of Play*. New York: Performing Arts Journal Publications.

Underhill, Evelyn. 1974. *Mysticism*. New York: New American Library.

van Gennep, Arnold. 1960. *The Rites of Passage: A Classic Study of Cultural Celebrations*. Translated by M. B. Visedom and G. L. Caffee. Chicago: University of Chicago Press.

Wilkenson, Tanya. 1996. *Persephone Returns: Victims, Heroes and the Journey from the Underworld*. Berkeley, CA: Page Mill.

INDEX

T

ABOUT THE AUTHOR

SUZY ROSS, PHD, is an assistant professor and coordinator of recreation therapy and complementary and alternative medicine at San José State University in California. She is known as a trusted, compassionate thought leader in the areas of personal growth, transformation, and play as medicine. *The Map to Wholeness* is her first book.

About North Atlantic Books

North Atlantic Books (NAB) is an independent, nonprofit publisher committed to a bold exploration of the relationships between mind, body, spirit, and nature. Founded in 1974, NAB aims to nurture a holistic view of the arts, sciences, humanities, and healing. To make a donation or to learn more about our books, authors, events, and newsletter, please visit www.northatlanticbooks.com.

North Atlantic Books is the publishing arm of the Society for the Study of Native Arts and Sciences, a 501(c)(3) nonprofit educational organization that promotes cross-cultural perspectives linking scientific, social, and artistic fields. To learn how you can support us, please visit our website.